BLACK DRAGON

BLACK PERFORMANCE AND CULTURAL CRITICISM
E. Patrick Johnson, Series Editor

BLACK DRAGON

AFRO ASIAN PERFORMANCE AND THE MARTIAL ARTS IMAGINATION

Zachary F. Price

THE OHIO STATE UNIVERSITY PRESS
COLUMBUS

Copyright © 2022 by Zachary F. Price.
All rights reserved.
Published by The Ohio State University Press.

Library of Congress Cataloging-in-Publication Data
Names: Price, Zachary, author.
Title: Black Dragon : Afro Asian performance and the martial arts imagination / Zachary F. Price.
Other titles: Black performance and cultural criticism.
Description: Columbus : The Ohio State University Press, [2021] | Series: Black performance and cultural criticism | Includes bibliographical references and index. | Summary: "Deploys martial arts as a lens to analyze performance, power, and identity within the evolving fusion of Black and Asian American cultures in history and media, including case studies such as Kareem Abdul-Jabbar's appearance in Bruce Lee's film *Game of Death*, Ron van Clief and the Black Panther Party for Self-Defense, the Wu-Tang Clan, and Chinese American saxophonist Fred Ho"—Provided by publisher.
Identifiers: LCCN 2021029417 | ISBN 9780814214602 (cloth) | ISBN 0814214606 (cloth) | ISBN 9780814281703 (ebook) | ISBN 0814281702 (ebook)
Subjects: LCSH: Martial arts—Social aspects. | African Americans—Relations with Asian Americans. | Blacks—Race identity. | Blacks in the performing arts.
Classification: LCC E185.615 .P76 2021 | DDC 305.896/073—dc23
LC record available at https://lccn.loc.gov/2021029417

Cover design by Angela Moody
Text composition by Stuart Rodriguez
Type set in Minion Pro

*For my father, Edwin Curmie Price Jr., (1940–2021),
a fearless dragon in his own right*

CONTENTS

List of Illustrations		ix
Preface	Performing Gender in a Broken City	xi
Acknowledgments		xvii
INTRODUCTION	The Crisis of Black Masculinity	1
CHAPTER 1	Enter the Black Dragons	27
CHAPTER 2	Black Panther Martial Art	71
CHAPTER 3	How Do You Like My Wu-Tang Style?	104
CHAPTER 4	The Sound of a Dragon: Fred Ho's Afro Asian Jazz Martial Arts	137
CHAPTER 5	Here Be Dragons: The Odyssey Toward Liberation	175
POST	A Virtual Kinesthesia	194
Bibliography		199
Index		207

ILLUSTRATIONS

FIGURE 0.1	Christopher Gray teaches aikido while Jim Klar takes *ukemi* (the art of being thrown) at the Cleveland Aikikai circa late 1990s	xiv
FIGURE 0.2	Ronald Duncan circa 1968	2
FIGURE 1.1	Moses Powell is seated in za zen	38
FIGURE 1.2	The closed yellow fist with black, green, and red markings is an example of one of the BKF patches	63
FIGURE 1.3	*BKF Kenpo: History* and *Advanced Strategic Principles* (2002) book cover	64
FIGURE 1.4	*Championship Kenpo* (1983) book cover	64
FIGURE 2.1	Steve McCutchen with martial arts students	72
FIGURE 2.2	Steve McCutchen leads students from the OCS	81
FIGURE 2.3	An advertisement from the *Black Panther Party* newspaper for the martial arts program	86
FIGURE 2.4	McCutchen teaches at the OCS/OCLC	93
FIGURE 2.5	Members of the OCS/OCLC team perform in demonstration at the OCS/OCLC auditorium	100

FIGURE 2.6	Steve McCutchen throws a right cross, knocking his opponent backward	101
FIGURE 3.1	Williams and a nameless karate instructor portrayed by Steve Sanders in the dojo	110
FIGURE 3.2	Han and Roper gaze onto Williams's dead body, which hangs like strange fruit	113
FIGURE 4.1	The character of Chen Jak, stage left, battles with a soldier loyal to Gar Man Jang	146
FIGURE 4.2	The character of Ng Mui emasculates her opponent	148
FIGURE 4.3	Aaron Armstrong, stage right, as Colonel U. S. A. Armageddon, and Yoshi Amao, stage left, as Rogue Assassin	153
FIGURE 4.4	Having taken his six shooter, Rogue Assassin shoots Colonel U. S. A.	153
FIGURE 4.5	Toni Renee Johnson, in a modernist looking dress, looks back at the audience, bringing her first solo to a close	167
FIGURE 4.6	Johnson, dressed in a *khimar*, appears alongside Ho in her second solo	167
FIGURE 4.7	Roderick Callaway stands with fist raised high after having knocked out the others who are on the ground	169
FIGURE 4.8	The ensemble has transitioned into suits resembling the style of the Nation of Islam	172
FIGURE 5.1	A member of the ensemble in the role of Odysseus holds the fans that he used to defeat the Suitors	176

PREFACE

Performing Gender in a Broken City

Cleveland, Ohio, was a site of violence, devastation, and stagnation when I was growing up in the '90s. Like many Black families who had left the Jim Crow South for the industrialized North during the 1950s, mine had been led by my grandmother who, along with her two sons, moved from Arkansas to Flint, Michigan, and eventually into Cleveland's Glenville neighborhood. With the 1954 Supreme Court ruling to desegregate and the subsequent Civil Rights legislation of the 1960s, more Black people moved into what had been white neighborhoods, such as Glenview and Hough. Incensed by the idea of having to live with Black neighbors, whites fled to the suburbs and so did the economic infrastructure and tax franchise. In 1966, frustrated by the lack of jobs, access to capital, educational opportunities, and persistent police violence, Hough's Black residents clashed with the all-white Cleveland Police Department in a series of armed battles that unfolded over several days. Ohio's Governor Jim Rhodes called in the National Guard to exercise martial law, literally turning Cleveland into an occupied war zone. A subsequent steady divestment from skilled manufacturing further deindustrialized Cleveland's economic landscape and stoked the ire of working-class and middle-class whites who blamed "the minorities for taking their jobs away." The city remained stagnant and financially "broke" for the next fifty years.

My parents provided a stable, suburban home in Shaker Heights, but somehow that was not enough. I grew up in a burnt-out Cold War relic of a left-behind city that overshadowed even the suburbs and trapped its youth, especially Black youth, in a cycle of poverty, drugs, and psychic dislocation for Black men, no less Black boys. I was racially marked, but something more—ineffectual, marginal, especially since I could not rap. Even talking could get you killed. In his discussion on Black male intersectionality, John O. Calmore writes, "The black man is the paradigmatic representation of unwanted traffic. As the term unwanted traffic suggests, the negative representation flows with black males through time and across space, from youth to older years and from predominately black settings to predominantly white or mixed settings. Because of the high degree of residential segregation, most black men are perceived as unwanted traffic within the very neighborhoods that should represent support home places."[1] Hence, the threshold for police violence and extrajudicial violence directed at Black people (Black men in particular) is always far lower than any other ethnic or racial group. It seemed as if Rodney King was especially beaten down by Los Angeles police officers in 1992 because he resisted, and stood up for himself, as a man. The police beat him down into a relic of male non-subjectivity and then were acquitted. The discursive message of that beating reverberated through Cleveland and me: don't stand up to anyone or they will murder you. Then, of course, there was the slow murder that American culture handed out to you in Cleveland. I remember seeing my father pace the room in frustration, anger, and despair when he saw the Rodney King video and subsequent LA uprisings. But what could he do? What could anyone of us marked Negroes do but take it, submit, and be submissive, if you wanted to live? I did not want to be trapped in that feeling of lack and powerlessness that seemed to grip all the male survivors of American racism. I needed something that would make me move and get out of the trap of immobility, the stasis, the paralysis of what it meant to be discarded in the dump heaps of urban '90s America.

For a reason I cannot remember, I went to a *dojo* (place where the way is trained) around this time and saw a tall Black man named Christopher Gray performing aikido. He seemed to be doing more than performing martial arts—he was choreographing manhood. The dojo was reminiscent of the underground that the protagonist in *The Invisible Man* inhabits—a catacomb under a business establishment, the Cedar Lee Movie Theater that screened independent films like *The Rocky Horror Picture Show* and martial arts films such as *Game of Death* (1978). The latter film featured the late martial artist Bruce Lee and basketball legend Kareem Abdul-Jabbar. After watching Chris-

---

1. Calmore, "Reasonable and Unreasonable Suspects: The Cultural Construction of the Anonymous Black Man in Public Space (Here Be Dragons)," 138.

topher and *Game of Death,* something clicked. I realized that the six-foot-six-inch Christopher Gray was a Cleveland version of Abdul-Jabbar, who had also studied aikido before he became a student of Bruce Lee.[2] But Christopher was there, right before me, showing me the way. He wore a crisply woven white *gi* (uniform) with what looked like a skirt or long wide bellbottom pants called *hakama* (part of a Japanese kimono). I watched how Christopher moved and the effect it created. As he approached the side of the mat, silence came over the students. They assembled in a straight line and focused their attention to the front of the dojo's mat space referred to as the *shomen*. The shomen was decorated with a delicate adornment of flowers, a vertically written *shodo* (Japanese calligraphy) of 合気道 (aikido), and a black and white photo of O'Sensei. Christopher took a moment to look at me and smiled. He bowed toward the shomen, stepped onto the mat, and made his way to the center where he sat down facing the shomen with his feet folded straight back underneath. His hands rested on his knees and he closed his eyes. Christopher epitomized something I had only imagined before—that one could be calm, controlled, and powerful despite the chaos raging outside—and inside me.

Christopher performed a sequence of rituals that undergird the tenets of aikido. From the seated position known as *seiza*, Christopher opened his eyes, bowed toward the shomen, clapped his hands twice together with the rest of the students, bowed again to the shomen, and then turned and bowed to the students, who bowed back in response, and collectively they uttered the Japanese courtesy of "*onegaishimausu*" (please). Chistopher moved gracefully across the mat, almost like a dancer, as he performed the role of *sensei* (teacher) and redirected the energy of the students that attacked him, in turn tossing them in the air. They floated, landing softly on the canvas mat, only to attack again. The students then practiced the techniques that Christopher demonstrated (as seen in Figure 0.1), as if attempting to restore the behavior that they had observed during Christopher's instruction. Later that week, I joined the Cleveland Aikikai and began training.

The dojo became my second home. A new sense of identity emerged from performing martial arts that was also a kinetics of racial survival. The dojo was a place to face one's fears, to learn and grow in a multiracial community of female and male instructors and practitioners. Though an underground, the dojo was also a transcendental space that eluded the hardened racial divisions of the city. Skin came in contact with skin, bodies bumped and clashed with other bodies, but found some choreographic harmony despite how different they were. Or were they?

---

2. Abdul-Jabbar, *Becoming Kareem: Growing Up on and off the Court*, 246.

FIGURE 0.1. Christopher Gray teaches aikido while Jim Klar takes *ukemi* (the art of being thrown)

Something in my exposure to aikido, Japanese language, teachers, and cultural practices through Christopher resonated with my imagination of what Black Power could look and feel like if it inhabited its own country. There seemed to be an unstated connection between the colonized subject in Black Cleveland and the post–World War II Japan that righted itself. I realized I had to get to Japan. And I did. From 2005 to 2008, I lived and worked in a rural fishing town located in Hyogo, Japan, and managed to even start a small aikido dojo that continues to this day. I joined in fashioning a new identity for myself out of the practice of aikido and the experience of interculturality that is performed. Additionally, I trained in *shitoryu* karate in Japan and intensively trained in judo in Los Angeles. Needless to say, I have noticed similarities and have been humbled by the stark differences.

But I never forgot Christopher. As a graduate of Williams College and the Cleveland-Marshall College of Law, he was a cultural guide who challenged and defied dominant stereotypes of Black masculinity in the US. He didn't simply teach aikido. He taught how to negotiate racism both on and off the mat. It was not until standing in the hallway of my high school at Saint Ignatius that I realized that Christopher was also an alumnus of the same school when I noticed a photo of him amongst the hundreds of Euro-American (predominantly Irish, Italian, Czech, and Polish) faces from the class of 1982.

Christopher passed away in 2012 after a six-year battle with cancer. I miss him deeply, for he exemplified hope and faith in oneself, but also the wisdom that to maintain hope and faith, one has to *practice* it. He taught me that the essence of that practice was movement, a choreographic agency I call racial kinesthesia that came up from that basement in Cleveland, out of a highly racialized community, and transformed the dojo into a site of rejuvenation. *Black Dragon: Afro Asian Performance and the Martial Arts Imagination* is my homage to an underground history that has escaped the attention of identity politics studies because it crosses so many of the usual lines, boundaries, borders, and demarcations that, ironically, reproduce some of the boundaries and borders I experienced growing up. This book suggests that the racial kinesthesia I learned from Christopher embodies what Fred Moten asks of us—that we "consent not to be a single being." And like Christopher Gray, do it with grace.

ACKNOWLEDGMENTS

The act of writing a monograph is a communal experience, and there are many people to thank for the development and fruition of *Black Dragon*. I am indebted to my doctoral committee—Suk-Young Kim, Leo Cabranes-Grant, Gaye Johnson, and Judith Green—for their investment in my scholarly training and continued support. As my graduate advisor, Suk-Young, you have continually supported me and taught me so much more than I could have ever asked.

I owe an incredible debt to Jeffrey C. Stewart, who has been a source of support for me at every turn. Jeffrey, you are an amazing historian, scholar, teacher, writer, and an invaluable friend who always puts a healthy chuckle in my heart. Additionally, I would like to thank all of the faculty members (and graduate student peers) at the University of California, Santa Barbara in the Departments of Theater and Dance, Black Studies, Asian American Studies, and East Asian Languages and Cultures, who supported and enabled the emergence of *Black Dragon*'s transdisciplinary journey.

Michael Morgan, thank you for *seeing* me and inviting me to be part of The Odyssey Project from the start! I have learned so much from your passion and commitment to theater and social justice. In the same breath, I must acknowledge the many undergraduate and graduate students and independent artists who have contributed to the continual development of The Odyssey Project. Most importantly, all of the YOUTH and the many families who have been involved with The Odyssey Project; you are Dragons and your stories are the dreams of the future.

I am truly appreciative of The Ohio State University Press for all of their support and guidance. Thank you to the series editors for Black Performance and Cultural Criticism, E. Patrick Johnson and Valerie Lee, for taking on *Black Dragon*. I am most grateful for the support of the anonymous readers and their supportive feedback. A special thank you to the editorial staff at The OSU Press, and I cannot express enough appreciation for Ana Maria Jimenez-Moreno for her constant guidance.

At the University of California, Los Angeles, I was fortunate enough to find a mentor in Darnell Hunt at the Bunche Center for African American Studies and subsequently as a mentor for the President's Postdoctoral Fellowship Program, which supported research for the development of this book. Thank you to the University of California Office of the President and the cohort of fellows who helped sharpen this project. I would especially like to acknowledge Kimberly Adkinson and Mark Lawson for all that they do. A heartfelt thank you to Douglas Haynes for his continued mentoring and leadership. The Department of African American Studies at UCLA was an intellectual hub and provided manuscript workshops. A special thank you to Cheryl Harris, Tiffany Willoughby-Herrard, Marcus Hunter, and Robin D. G. Kelley for reading drafts of the manuscript. Thank you, Eboni Shaw, for your administrative discipline.

Early research for this project was also supported by the Fred Ho Fellowship at the University of Connecticut's Asian and Asian American Studies Institute. The late and "great," Fred Ho's archives are housed in the Special Collections of the Thomas J. Dodd Research Center. A special thank you to Cathy Schlund-Vials, Roger Buckley, Kristin Eshelman, and Fe Delos-Santos.

Many thanks to colleagues at Texas A&M University in the Department of Performance Studies and the Department of Health and Kinesiology for supporting practice-based research and the undergraduate and graduate students who took the unique journey to explore Performance in Movement: *Aiki Way*. Thank you to colleagues in the Department of Drama at the University of California, Irvine and the Department of Theatre and Dance at the University of California, San Diego.

Colleagues across several fields have provided insights and inspiration at numerous talks, conferences, and over conversations: Maryam Aziz, James Ball, Dominique Steavu-Balint, Stephen Barker, Julie Burelle, Leonardo Cardoso, Broderick Chow, David Donkor, Donnalee Dox, John Eason, Brett Esaki, Diane Fujino, D. J. Hopkins, Yasmine Jahanmir, Chris "Buddy" Jones, Kim Kattari, Ketu Katrak, Anthony Kubiak, Eero Laine, Daphne Lei, Sean

Metzger, Matthew Mewhinney, Christopher McCauley, Bill Mullen, Jade Power-Sotomayor, Rumya Putcha, Martin Regan, Andy Rice, Tara Rodman, Rael Jero Salley, Jean Scheper (for her timely intervention), Richard Schechner (who read numerous pages on Fred Ho), Angenette Spalink, Shannon Steen, Sherod Thaxton, Shane Vogel, Frank Wilderson III, David Wilborn, and Harvey Young (who read multiple drafts).

To the artists, martial arts practitioners, and community members who helped form connections as well as those from whom I learned so much: Yoshi Amao, Zahalea Anderson, Stephan Berwick, Marina Celander, Kevin Choate, Christopher Gray, Jose Figueroa, Flores Forbes, Etsuji Horii, Hiroshi Ikeda, Christine Jordan, Paul Kang, Sonoko Kawahara, Bill King, Steve McCutchen, Urban Muhammad, Kenji Osugi, Christopher Royal, Mitsugi Saotome, Robert Temple, Ron Van Clief, and Christine Wong. And to the many more with whom I have trained with and collaborated, thank you!

I am fortunate to have a sagacious older brother who has always been there for me, and to the Long Beach Prices, thank you for your continued support. Thank you to my extended Price and Okura family from Chicago, Atlanta, Houston, Cleveland, and Nara; to my parents, Edwin and Peggie, who have given everything, and to my partner, Junka, who makes it all fit together; to Sumire and Gakuichi, who have been my greatest teachers of all, your every breath is a blessing.

INTRODUCTION

The Crisis of Black Masculinity

In August 1969, a group of local Japanese martial arts masters in New York invited Ronald Duncan, a burgeoning Black[1] American practitioner of the Japanese martial art of *ninjutsu,* commonly translated as the "art of stealth," to exhibit his techniques as part of the second International Convention of Martial Arts hosted by *Black Belt* magazine at the Waldorf Astoria Hotel.[2] Eager to test and display their skills through competitions and demonstrations, practitioners from the US and Asia participated in the three-day event, which primarily consisted of Chinese, Korean, and Japanese martial arts. Duncan's performance surprised and impressed his audience. His virtuosity in the use of joint locks, kicks, strikes, and throwing techniques of ninjutsu was outstanding. But, it was Duncan's performative aesthetic use of ninjutsu daggers, blow darts, and *shuriken* (metal stars meant to be thrown at a person, as seen in Figure 0.2) that wowed the spectators in attendance, many of

---

1. I capitalize the "B" in Black when referring to people of the African diaspora in part because the focus of this project is on Black people and their lived experiences, but also to call attention to the fundamental problem in the lexicon that we use to talk about and describe the experiences of Afro-diasporic people, especially Black people in the Americas who are recursively relegated to a state of nonbeing or of a nonperson. Certainly this is not the case when we refer to other ethno-racial groups such as Asian, Latina/o, Euro-American, Caucasian, Filipino, Japanese, Korean, Polish, Irish, Italian, and so forth. In this project I use the terms Black, Black American, and African American interchangeably.

2. *Black Belt,* September 1969, 21–24.

FIGURE 0.2. Ronald Duncan circa 1968 with an array of tools and weaponry

whom were martial arts practitioners of one capacity or another. Duncan's most impressive and signature demonstration technique was grabbing an arrow out of midair that was fired at him from a bow at close range. The technical and spectacular display of weaponry demonstrated Duncan's mastery not only of the objects that he used and the bodies of the performers that he demonstrated on but also of the secret knowledge of the unconventional and guerilla warfare of Japanese ninjutsu. Born in Panama in 1937, Duncan was a former US Marine who had trained in Marine Judo at Camp Lejeune, North Carolina. Duncan subsequently relocated to New York and was introduced to koga-ryu ninjutsu, vis-à-vis a confluence of US and Asian teachers. Duncan learned boxing in Panama as a child, and his practice in judo at Lejeune gave him a solid foundation in throwing techniques as well as *ne waza* (the art of ground fighting). Duncan was small in stature and easily under six feet. Yet, with his quick movements, darting in and around his opponents as they tried to attack him, Duncan's demeanor commanded respect. Everything about him was martial, drawing on what could be defined as *budo seishin* (martial spirit).

While Duncan had been building a reputation as a master of ninjutsu, he was also pioneering a unique African American form of martial arts unsanctioned by the Japanese and Japanese American community, some of whom saw themselves as the gatekeepers of Japanese cultural practice. Duncan's performance angered some in the audience, most importantly the Hawaiian-born Japanese American promoter and organizer of the event, Mitoshi Uyehara, who was the founder and chief executive officer of *Black Belt*. Having founded the publication a decade earlier, Uyehara used the publication to present himself as an authority on martial arts both in the US and internationally. Aside from creating *Black Belt*, a periodical that also helped popularize Asian martial arts in America and helped propel the careers of individuals such as the revered Bruce Lee, Uyehara was also a practitioner of aikido.[3] While Uyehara had introduced Kareem Abdul-Jabbar to Bruce Lee, who was developing his own style of martial arts called *Jeet Kune Do* (way of the intercepting fist), Duncan's appearance in full ninjutsu regalia symbolizing his "way of the winds" school confounded Uyehara, who questioned the authenticity of a Black man demonstrating and claiming the knowledge of a Japanese cultural artefact.

Uyehara confronted Duncan after his performance, demanding to know how an African American acquired the knowledge he displayed that day. According to Duncan, "Mito says to me, 'Duncan, who taught you ninjustu? You're not Japanese. . . . Who taught you all of the weapons, the darts, the blowguns, and all of this?" Duncan refused to give up his sources, in part because the way of ninjustu is a secret knowledge. Duncan responded, "Who authorized you to ask me?" Enraged at Duncan's refusal to give up his source, Uyehara yelled, "You're nothing but bullshit! You're Mickey Mouse. You're not Japanese. What gives you the right to do this anyway?" Desperate to find out how a Black American had accessed what he considered to be Asian cultural property, Uyehara sought to bribe Duncan by giving him "carte blanche for ninjutsu" in *Black Belt* if Duncan complied.

While performing in exhibitions such as the ICMA afforded martial arts teachers the opportunity to reach local audiences and broaden markets, the circulation and proliferation of martial arts–dedicated media provided a global audience through which to secure a practitioner's position as a prominent teacher and entrepreneur. To be placed on the cover of a publication

---

3. The traditional Japanese martial art founded by Ueshiba Morihei at the beginning of the twentieth century. Like Ueshiba, who popularized his new martial art that he called aikido through *embukai* (public exhibitions), including a trip to Hawaii in 1961 that we can reasonably assume Uyehara attended, embukai also helped proselytize the martial arts across the country during the 1960s and well into the latter half of the twentieth century.

such as *Black Belt* was a legitimatization of skill and mastery within the martial arts world. It offered practitioners their street credibility and provided an international audience through which to promote their school and hence to secure their livelihood. But Duncan refused and as a result never appeared on the cover of the periodical or in its pages except for advertisements for his ninjutsu training videos. Through his performance and his refusal to give up his secrets to the most powerful martial arts authority in popular media, Duncan adhered to the "code of secrecy" that gave ninjutsu its foundation as well as its mysticism and, to an extent, criticism and skepticism. In so doing, Duncan also disrupted the notion that only Asian bodies, and in particular Asian men, were capable of such practices and were due deference by those who were not Asian.

Duncan's practice of ninjutsu was representative of the way in which African American men practiced Asian martial arts beginning in the mid-twentieth century as a theater of Afro Asian performance that not only served to refigure their own subjectivity but also functioned as a contested form of racialized and gendered struggle, the remnants of which would impact theatrical and popular culture well into the twenty-first century. As I discussed in the preface, my experiences in the dojo in Cleveland and the martial art of aikido served as a form of rejuvenation for members of the community who were confronted with the social economic crisis of stagnation and blight of racism. While the conflict between Duncan and Uyehara at the ICMA in 1969 far preceded my encounter with Christopher Gray at the Cleveland Aikikai in the early '90s, both were emblematic of how the movements of aikido or ninjutsu provided a response to the stymying effects of what Cedric Robinson referred to as racial regimes.[4] From the cargo holds of slave ships, to the plantation, the US military occupation of Asia, to the prison cell of modern day mass incarceration, a core principle of racial oppression has been the confinement of bodies and social economic opportunity immobilization. The response has been to take on new forms of movement practices to create social economic mobility and opportunity. Soyica Diggs defines *Black movements* as "embodied actions (a change in position, place, posture, or orientation) that draw from the imagination and the past to advance political projects." We can think of these movements as varying pathways toward self-liberation such as the Underground Railroad, Black Power and Civil Rights movements, and the Black exodus out of the agricultural South to the industrial North that my grandmother took when she left West Helena, Arkansas, for Cleveland, Ohio. Contemporaneously, Duncan, who self-identified as African American,

---

4. Robinson, *Forgeries of Memory and Meaning: Blacks and the Regimes of Race in American Theatre and Film Before World War II*, xii.

migrated from Panama to the continental US, and as I will discuss, Uyehara's life was informed by movement from ancestral Japan, to Hawaii, and to the US mainland.

However, Black migration brought new possibilities of labor, style, and art such as blues, jazz, hip-hop, and of course martial arts. These movement practices provided a feeling of hope for marginalized people who were denied ownership of their identity and flesh, and reminded them that one's body could be claimed as their own.[5] Duncan and the Black martial artists like him changed their position and their posture, and engaged in a form of recuperative self-fashioning designed to repair the loss of "personhood," a la John Locke, and, in their eyes, manhood, by exercising control of their bodies and other bodies through martial arts. This was no easy matter, for these mid-twentieth century Black bodies were haunted by a heritage and practice of bodily death and dismemberment, lynching and castration, quite fresh in US collective memory.[6] Martial arts afforded an opportunity to (re)claim possession over one's body (and hence, representation), and develop a "repertoire, *style*" that exercised agency and challenged master narratives. As Stuart Hall noted, Black people "have used the body—as if it were, and it often was, the only cultural capital we had. We have worked on ourselves as the canvases of representation."[7] Black people achieved this new cultural capital through "mastery" of acts, gestures, and routines that were a part of Asian martial performative traditions, through what I refer to as "racial kinesthesia." The feeling of the invincible warrior is the body of imagination (a body of fantasy)—that becomes actualized through kinetics and corporeal discipline. The title of this book, *Black Dragon*, draws upon the auspicious and even untamable qualities of the dragon found in Asian mythology whose amorphous imagery proliferates throughout folklore and martial arts practice.

Racial Kinesthesia

While the term *kinesiology* may refer to the study of the anatomy, physiology, and mechanics of body movement as well as the evaluation and treatment

---

5. Colbert, *Black Movements: Performance and Cultural Politics*, 5.
6. Young, *Embodying Black Experience: Stillness, Critical Memory, and the Black Body*, 168. As Harvey Young notes in his discussion on the spectacle of lynching, there were "more than three thousand black men, women, and children who were lynched across the United States between 1880 and 1930," and it would not be an overstatement to say that tens of thousands more African Americans suffered extra judicial violence during the period of de jure Jim Crow or de facto racism that continues into the present.
7. Hall, "What Is This 'Black' in Black Popular Culture?," 109.

of muscular imbalance and derangement, the empiricism of kinesiology falls short in locating the intersection of the discursive and somatic. Proprioception emphasizes the neurological ability to locate the different parts of the body in space without consciously having to think about it,[8] but the cognitive turn in theater studies does not fully account for the political and economic conditions under which bodies of color live, move, and survive.[9]

Rather, kinesthesia continues to be an interlocutor through which to interrogate the politics of the body and its signification. Echoing Judith Butler's assertion that "the body is a historical situation,"[10] dance scholar Susan Leigh Foster posits that movement practices such as "dancing also foregrounded the production of kinesthetic experience, making it an important source for how the body and its movement are experienced in a given historical moment."[11] Racial kinesthesia can be a useful tool for understanding not only how a body such as Duncan's experienced the world in a given moment but also how his proprioceptive entrainment challenged the assumptions that others had made about his identity. As Foster has observed, kinesthetics is "a designated way of experiencing physicality and movement, that, in turn, summons other bodies into a specific way of feeling about it."[12] Kinesthesia has the power to choreograph and to summon bodies into enabling valences of racialized performance, including everyday performance, film, print media, and theater. Racial kinesthesia is a way of thinking about how the aesthetics of sartorial presentation prepares and suggests the potential for a particular kind of movement. As was the case with Duncan dressed in a kimono and hakama with a display of buki (weapons) in front of him reminds his spectators that the "body is a set of possibilities" that signifies "that its appearance in the world, for perception, is not predetermined by some manner of interior essence."[13] To see a person in a martial arts uniform already primes the practitioner for a particular form of movement, and it telegraphs to the observer that the other is prepared to move in a particular manner. Racial kinesthesia calls attention to the way that adorning the body with clothing, patches, emblems, and weapons/tools is not apolitical. Rather it is a politically charged semiotics in which ornamentation was a process of creating an Afro Asian performative aesthetic whose goal

---

8. Gallagher, *How the Body Shapes the Mind*.
9. See McConachie, *Performance and Cognition: Theatre Studies and the Cognitive Turn*.
10. Butler, "Performative Acts and Gender Constitution: An Essay in Phenomenology and Feminist Theory," 521.
11. Foster, *Choreographing Empathy: Kinesthesia in Performance*, 9.
12. Foster, *Choreographing Empathy: Kinesthesia in Performance*, 2.
13. Butler, "Performative Acts and Gender Constitution: An Essay in Phenomenology and Feminist Theory," 521.

may not have had a specific political objective other than to survive the very conditions with which it was confronted.

My use of the term kinesthesia is a way of thinking of movement and hence "mobility as produced within social, cultural and, most importantly, geographical contexts,"[14] and elucidates how people respond to racial oppression through kinesthesia as a method of self-rejuvenation, as a form of cultural production, a system of knowledge production, and a method of interpretation. Martial arts and the vernacular performance practices addressed in *Black Dragon* reveal an awareness among self-trained organic intellectuals such as Duncan who were not only performers of martial arts but also interpreters capable of articulating the meaning of their style of movement. Yet, Duncan's interpretation chafed with Uyehara's expectations of who should control and represent the cultural property of ninjutsu. Carrie Noland has suggested that "kinesthesia is a sixth sense, a source of sensations of which the subject is more or less aware," and that such sensorial experience is highly indebted to gesture and the performative in order to have an "intimacy with the other that is sustained by an intimacy with the self."[15] However, I take Nolan's understanding of such "intimacy" to also be implicated in those performative acts, gestures, and routines that structure what Marcel Mauss referred to as the "techniques of the body,"[16] that hence lead to moments of rupture and contestation. Racial kinesthesia allows us then to understand how one's particular movement, presentation, and ornamentation of the self functions as a kind of sign system. Again, Duncan attempted to use the technology of martial arts movement to position himself as a ninjutsu master and perhaps even an authority of a particular philosophy of embodied knowledge and cultural practice that was not commonly associated with Black bodies. Certainly, we can argue that he felt like an authority in terms of his own sensory organs (proprioceptors) in the muscles and joints, but he was also emotionally connected and committed to the art of ninjutsu. Yet, despite his skill and acumen when discussing his practice, he was still considered suspect because of the way that his body was racially perceived.

The exchange between Duncan and Uyehara revealed a confluence of anxiety, tension, and struggle over who owns cultural property and how barriers to cultural appropriation are erected and transgressed. Charged with racial

---

14. Cresswell, "'You Cannot Shake that Shimmie Here': Producing Mobility on the Dance Floor."
15. Noland, *Agency and Embodiment: Performing Gestures/Producing Culture*, 14.
16. Noland draws from Marcel Mauss's essay "Techniques of the Body" or "Les Techniques Du Corps," *Sociologie Et Anthropologie*, 4th edition (1960): 363–386, and Merleau-Ponty's *Phenomenology of Perception*.

ambivalence, anticipation, and misunderstanding, their confrontation was a gendered conflict of competing masculinities. Uyehara not only challenged Duncan's racialized identity but also "checked" his authority to claim the title of "master" that had historically been reserved for Japanese men within Asia. Given that this maneuver was delivered to a Black practitioner, it is hard not to see it as suggesting a pecking order in which the Japanese man is closer to the privileged white position of "master" than a Black man. The encounter suggests that even in spaces that ostensibly are removed from the discourse of whiteness, like a martial arts competition, discourses of white masculinity continue to permeate in the exchanges between "minorities." By calling into question Duncan's authority to perform the role of a ninjutsu master, Uyehara sought to metaphorically emasculate Duncan and "put him in his place," whilst simultaneously securing his own subjectivity. In turn, Uyehara aligned himself with the discourse of ownership of a cultural property at the very moment, ironically, when it was clear that he no longer had sole possession of it—largely because of the world domination of the United States. Uyehara acknowledged, unwittingly, his own decenteredness for losing control of his "cultural property."

In that sense, Uyehara acknowledged his own fractured masculinity in attacking Duncan's "mastery" of a Japanese cultural formation. For if it is true, as the philosopher John Locke asserted, that "every man has a 'property' in his own 'person,'"[17] and thus property included not only external objects and people's relationships to them but also all of those human rights, liberties, powers, and immunities that are important for human well-being, then a Japanese-identified man like Uyehara no longer had complete control of his person, that is, what Japanese culture had produced as extensions of Japanese bodies. Martial arts were and are appendages of the body, technologies of resistance to enslavement of one's body by another that are performed in space.

Racial Formation and the Kinesthetic Response

As Omi and Winant argued, "racial formation" is "the process by which social, economic and political forces determine the content and importance of racial categories, and by which they are in turn are shaped by racial meanings."[18] As a Hawaiian-born Japanese American, Uyehara grew up in an interlocking system of gendered and racialized relationships that defined Japanese Americans

---

17. Locke and Filmer, *Two Treaties on Civil Government*, 204.
18. Omi and Winant, *Racial Formation in the United States: From the 1960s to the 1990s*, 55.

as inferior to white Americans. This inferiority was structured by powerful economic trading relationships that utilized the Hawaiian Islands as outposts of commercial American capitalism. Thus, Uyehara's racialized and gendered putdown of Duncan was, in some respects, an attempt to recover his own displaced mastery in a system that called his ancestors, no less than the enslaved ancestors of Duncan, "docile." Unfortunately, neither man connected simply through the performance of a *kata*; instead, their connection came through discourses of colonialism and gendered racism. Part of the anger and violence of Uyehara's attack is a recognition that Asians have no "self-evident" ownership of anything in America or its territories. The attack on Duncan suggests what Asians got in return for their support of a cruel system of racial hierarchy: the "privilege" of being viewed as a "model minority" that would never call into question or attack the entire system because of their benighted position within it.

While Scott Kurashige contends that "model minority" ideology has its origins in the Exclusion Acts of the nineteenth century and Japanese American mass incarceration of 1942,[19] for our purposes, sociologist William Peterson's use of the term in his 1966 *New York Times Magazine* article titled "Success Story: Japanese-American Style" matters most. According to Peterson: "By any criterion of good citizenship that we choose, the Japanese Americans are better than any other group in our society, including native-born white."[20] Handing over temporary superiority around whiteness was part of the particular strategy of model minority mythology to further the work of racial regimes. Framing Asian Americans as model minorities assisted in eliding the history of Asian American oppression at the moment when the Civil Rights and Third World Liberation movements threatened to enlist Asian subjectivities in a collective challenge to white global hegemony. In order to thwart the possibility of coalitional solidarity between African Americans and Asian Americans, the ideology of model minority positioned Black Americans, especially the Black working class, as the polar opposite of Asian Americans. Chong Chon-Smith has described the polarities of race as a form of "racial magnetism," in which Black and Asian masculinity was in turn situated along "binary axes that defined a system of social meanings in symmetrical contrast to each other—brain/body, hardworking/lazy, nerd/criminal, culture/genetics, acceptability/monstrosity, submissive/aggressive, self-reliant/government dependent, student/convict, feminization/hypermasculinization, technocrat/

---

19. Kurashige, *Shifting Grounds of Race: Black and Japanese Americans in the Making of Multiethnic Los Angeles*, 186, 187.
20. Peterson, "Success Story: Japanese-American Style," 22.

athlete, and solution/problem."[21] The friction between Duncan and Uyehara reified what Claire Jean Kim has referred to as "racial triangulation,"[22] wherein interlinking chains of relative valorization position Asians as superior/outsider, Blacks as inferior/insider, and whites as the constant dominant superior/insider. As editor of *Black Belt* and organizer of the event, Uyehara not only attempted to redress Japanese American masculinity under the rubric of American racism, but he also sought to position himself as the authority and owner of cultural property who could sanction the right to perform "Japanese maleness" and determine who was an insider and who was an outsider within a subset of the American cultural schematic.

Martial arts are contested cultural terrain in what Antonio Gramsci referred to as a "war of position." Schools, organizations, demonstrations, media, and performances of Far Eastern disciplines are sites, as Gramsci would put it, that could lead to a "war of maneuver," except, of course, that with model minorities and Blacks performing like model minorities, the victory of the war of maneuver is always just out of reach. In the resultant trench warfare, cultural production carries out struggles of power, often violently, within Western society. Duncan and Uyehara navigated, disrupted, and at times reified the hegemony of racial regimes even when they tried to negate them. While neither the practice nor the consumption of the representation of martial arts can make one invincible, martial arts can provide a feeling of invincibility or what theorists of affect theory argue is an "affective bodily" capacity or efficacy "beyond the body's organic-physiological constraints" imposed by racism and gender regimes.[23] As affective labor, martial arts create a cultural imagination of the invincible warrior capable of taking on any challenge no matter how daunting. Sometimes this means cultivating techniques used for civilian self-defense or training combat warriors: guerillas, soldiers of a state entity or militia such as an army, police, or private security. Martial arts performance is thus a form of imagination that entertains and releases the oppressed through spectacle, as in the ICMA where Duncan and Uyehara met. The lines separating the authentic and inauthentic actor and practitioner collapsed when the imagined invincible subject encountered the reality of intersubjectivity.[24]

---

21. Chon-Smith, *East Meets Black: Asian and Black Masculinities in the Post-Civil Rights Era*, 3, 4.
22. Kim, "Racial Triangulation of Asian Americans."
23. Clough and Halley, *Affective Turn: Theorizing the Social*, 2.
24. Recently the lines between spectacular performance and competition and reality entertainment have completely converged through the production, consumption, and global popularization of Mixed Martial Arts (MMA). While a thorough discussion of MMA is outside of the scope of this project, it should be noted that MMA is a cesspool rife with the most explicit forms of intersectional identity that reveals much about the US cultural landscape and invest-

Racial kinesthesia is not only about mastering the repertoire of another cultural template; it also elucidates the incongruence and anticipates the misunderstandings that emerge when performance does not meet preconceived assumptions about racialized and gendered identity. Much like dance, training the body through repetition is a key component to the discipline of martial arts practice. Echoing Richard Schechner's assertion that performance is rooted in "twice-behaved behavior,"[25] the science of repetition has been the essence of the practice of katas (in the Japanese context) or form training found in many martial arts. Practice in the forms existed as an approach to proprioceptive entrainment through which to transmit knowledge from master to disciple or build a community of practitioners who supported the perpetuation of a particular style or philosophy through the rehearsal of a specific repertoire. It was also the obligation of the student to develop one's own interpretation of the form and the philosophy embedded in the form that moved beyond mere repetition, but rather pushed the form into a new iteration of the self, a restored behavior for a new identity. In a striking example of the effects of racial kinesthesia, Uyehara did not understand the repertoire, the form, and the innovation of the discipline embodied in the Black flesh of Duncan.

Signifyin'(g) *Budo*[26] in the Diaspora

Martial arts became a popular form of cultural production during the late '60s and '70s, and along with it came the powerful notion that anyone could be a *sifu* (kung fu master) or sensei (in the Japanese context). The transformative potential of rehearsing one's self into a powerful body capable of self-defense from an onslaught of interpersonal violence or the violence of structural racism became the basis for the turn of many working-class youth to the martial arts. In US cities, dojo, taekwondo dojang, and kung fu daochang (all terms for schools) opened to eager students.[27] These practitioners and organizations, while overwhelmingly male dominated, resulted in diverse cultural formation. In some cases, Black martial artists were members of the Nation of Islam or members of the Black Panther Party for Self-Defense. Many were also exposed

---

ment in expression of corporeal power. However, the explosion of MMA is also the child of a form of cultural production that grew in popularity during the 1970s' fascination with Hong Kong kung fu cinema, the apex of which was Bruce Lee's *Enter the Dragon* (1973).

25. Schechner and Turner, *Between Theater and Anthropology*, 36.
26. *Budo* is a somewhat esoteric term in Japanese that connotes the martial way, way of martial arts, or the way of war.
27. Prashad, *Everybody Was Kung Fu Fighting: Afro-Asian Connections and the Myth of Cultural Purity*, 133.

to martial arts through the US armed forces and continued their practice while working for local police agencies. For an individual such as Duncan, the exposure to martial arts vis-à-vis the US military placed him in a position to support himself as a teacher and cultural entrepreneur. It also provided a business that he would pass on to his son, Gregory Duncan, upon his death in 2012.[28]

Articulated in an interview with Martial Arts World, Duncan provided a particular historical understanding of ninjutsu that he referred to as "the art of endurance."[29] Gesturing to the political nature of martial arts, Duncan stated, "Those people who evolved as ninjas during ancient times in Japan were forced out of political necessity to endure, and by learning how to endure they were able to be victorious and survive."[30] Duncan's emphasis on the political aspect of martial arts was a recurring theme when giving seminars and interviews. In the Japanese context, the functions of stealth meant the infiltration into hostile environments, performance of various acts of sabotage or assassination, and management of a successful escape once a mission had been accomplished.[31] The ninjas could be hired as spies, assassins, arsonists, and terrorists by great and small lords or by the Tokugawa clan of feudal Japan. The reproduction of the mythology of the ninja was shrouded in secrecy and yet filled with stories of covert operations in which the ninja would scale vertical walls, drop in behind enemy lines, blend in with the local culture, use poison or hypnosis upon their enemies, causing them to lose their senses, or assassinate them and then disappear into thin air! Unlike Uyehara, who focused on an authenticity of lineage, Duncan maintained that the transnational nature of martial arts meant that it was constantly being reconstituted out of necessity for survival based on particular political historical conditions. His approach was a collection of many different styles of combat, and was implicated in political proj-

---

28. Ironically, I had an interview scheduled with Duncan in late October that never occurred. Thinking that there had been a miscommunication, I continued to try to contact him only to discover that he'd passed on November 19 at the age of seventy-seven. His obituary can be found here: http://obits.dignitymemorial.com/dignity-memorial/obituary-print.aspx?n=Ronald-Duncan&lc=1182&pid=161149046&mid=5311196. Duncan is an interesting study. He trained his son in the form of ninjutsu in which he was proficient and was one of the early practitioners to demonstrate during the martial arts exhibitions organized by Aaron Banks at New York's Madison Square Garden during the 1970s. His son currently runs a school in Jersey City, NJ: http://duncanmartialarts.com.

29. See the 1989 interview with George Strickland in Martial Arts World, a program that aired on local public access television from the late 1970s to the early 2000s and featured Ronald Duncan and his students.

30. See the 1989 interview with George Strickland in Martial Arts World, which also featured Ronald Duncan and his students.

31. Ratti and Westbrook, *Secrets of the Samurai: The Martial Arts of Feudal Japan*, 324–25.

ects of "stealth, spiritual training, psychological combat, physical combat, and intelligence gathering."[32] This esoteric approach demonstrates the fungibility of ninjutsu in service of enduring and surviving the experiences of modernity.

Much of the mythology of ninjutsu would make its way into the US popular imagination through a deluge of Hong Kong- and Japanese-based ninja films during the 1970s. These films featured Japanese male actors who further personified the mystique of the ninja. During the 1980s, US film studios further popularized the ninja through a series of American ninja films that featured Caucasian male actors who had "mastered" the way of ninjutsu, oftentimes through the help of an "old and wise Asian master." The training sequences of these films presented a performative movement Joseph Roach refers to as "substitution" and "surrogation"[33] in which the white actor served as an avatar of Asianness. In contrast, Duncan resisted Uyehara's insistence that someone must have trained him, which meant that Duncan was the master. Duncan's resistance further cloaked ninjutsu in a secrecy that made the ninja so elusive and fascinating. Duncan knew that he could not adhere to an orthodoxy of a Japanese martial art that relied upon a recursive citationality exclusive to ethnic and national origins. In other words, Duncan could never be Japanese no matter how well he played the part and performed the role of the ninja. It was not only Duncan's Blackness that troubled Uyehara's "field of vision"[34]; it was also the manner in which Duncan improvised and created his own identity and field of study.

Duncan's philosophical interpretation of martial arts was not only an essential element of being able to defend oneself from any position, perhaps often a position of seeming weakness. It was also a strategy for reconciling the way in which modernity shatters the self. For Duncan, "modern day man" was "forced to live nine different existences because in our day to day living we come in contact with people who pay us wages, we come in contact with the elders, we come in contact with ourselves,"[35] and hence the self is imposed upon by a hierarchical knowledge and regimes of power that must be reconciled through the application of subsystems meant to discipline the self through the art of ninjutsu. The meaning of *nin* in ninjutsu signifies "nothingness" or "emptiness" and in turn could be *everything* and *nothing*. That is to say that the ninja was stealthy and capable of being camouflaged even by a Black body on the urban streets of the US. The ninja was also a trickster figure, always there, but never here. "It's a mystique. . . . In Japan, for a long time

32. Ratti and Westbrook, *Secrets of the Samurai: The Martial Arts of Feudal Japan*, 324–25.
33. Roach, *Cities of the Dead: Circum-Atlantic Performance*, 2.
34. Fleetwood, *Troubling Vision: Performance, Visuality, and Blackness*, 6.
35. Duncan, *Way of the Winds System: Koga-Ryu Ninjitsu*, 1987.

the ninja was part of Japan's folklore. He was sort of a mythical person, really not taken seriously by the vast majority of Japan's population. . . . You have to realize that the ninja of old was a trickster. He was a conman. He utilized illusions and he played upon superstitions of the times to get across effectively."[36] Tricksterism is prevalent throughout Japanese mythology embodied in figures such as *tengu* (trickster demons of the mountains) or *tanuki* (a magical shape-shifting amalgamation of a fox and raccoon). The ninja was liminal and could blend into and out of various communities. They were tricksters that could learn different dialects and hypnotize.

As Henry Lewis Gates suggests "signifyin(g)" through orality, music, and corporeal stylistics in dance was a way of acknowledging and coping with the traumatic rupture of the Middle Passage and the subsequent experience of slavery in the New World.[37] Black martial artists signified by producing their own repertoire style often integrating West African concepts, clothing, and language into the Asian martial arts systems that they were interpreting and developing. However, signifying was also a way of "putting someone in check" through a verbal or corporeal exchange in which one could skillfully demonstrate a greater control over a lexicon of speech or movement against a challenger. At the ICMA in 1969, Duncan engaged in two forms of signifying. First, by dawning the sartorial markers and kinetics of the ninja, Duncan demonstrated his acuity to borrow from the cultural mythology of the ninja in a manner consistent with that of a master. Second, Duncan demonstrated that by checking Uyehara in their exchange after the demonstration that he was in fact his own master and not beholden to Uyehara or any form of racial hierarchy. In fact, by performing an agile and generative corrective response to Uyehara's challenge, Duncan reconnected to and made visible the mythology of the circum-Pacific through his Afro-Panamanian ancestry of the circum-Atlantic. This chronotropic overlap rendered a stealthy simultaneity of reinvention through training in the martial arts that did not start or end with Duncan. Rather Duncan was part of a constellation of cultural workers who engaged in racial kinesthesia that resulted in what could be summed up as Afro Asian performance.

---

36. Duncan's 1986 interview.

37. For further discussion on "signifiyin(g)," see Gates, *The Signifying Monkey: A Theory of African-American Literary Criticism*.

Afro Asian Performance and the Martial Arts Imagination

"The problem of the twentieth century is the problem of the color-line,"[38] wrote W. E. B. Du Bois in 1903. The Afro Asian disjuncture between Uyehara and Duncan in 1969 was part of a longer historical trajectory that did not stand outside of the broader rubric of the racialized and gendered Cold War geopolitical economy that Du Bois had anticipated a half-century earlier. Racial triangulation identified Black and Asian polarization, and *Black Dragon* wrestles with the tension of racial triangulation that emerged in the conflict between Duncan and Uyehara and the mediated narratives of the Los Angeles rebellions of 1992 that emphasized a Black and Asian (specifically Korean) conflict. However, scholars of comparative ethnic studies, cultural theory, and performance studies have also articulated the way in which Afro Asian connections have elicited coalitional politics that emerged out of the Bandung Conference of 1955 that brought together twenty-nine countries from Africa and Asia to define the direction of recently liberated aligned and nonaligned territories. Furthermore, it is important to embrace the generative possibilities of coalitional politics that were performed within what Naoko Shimazu has defined as a "theater of diplomacy"[39] of the Bandung Conference or what T. Carlis Roberts identified as a "(re)sounding Afro Asia"[40] that brings different racial groups into harmony through musical production.

In search of what he framed as a "new skin,"[41] as a counterdiscourse to neoliberal multiculturalism, cultural theorist Vijay Prashad worked through the complexity and contradictions of multiple diasporic trajectories of struggle that have formed the basis for an antiracist imperative embodied in both popular culture and vernacular interactions. The work on Afro Asian coalitional politics has been a rejoinder to Du Bois's interests with the uncertain rise of political and economic power in Japan and then in China during the first half of the twentieth century. As Bill Mullen has demonstrated, Du Bois's practices and theories on Asia and the crossings of the world color line, enlightened by his international solidarities with leaders such as Mao Tse-Tung, anticipated the activism and radical interventions by scholars of the latter half of the twentieth and the beginnings of the twenty-first century. Writing on Japan, China, India, and the South Pacific, "Du Bois perceived globalization, national

---

38. Du Bois, *Souls of Black Folks*, 10.
39. Shimazu, "'Diplomacy as Theatre': Recasting the Bandung Conference of 1955 as Cultural History," 2–19.
40. Roberts, *Resounding Afro Asia: Interracial Music and the Politics of Collaboration*, 1.
41. Prashad, *Everybody Was Kung Fu Fighting: Afro-Asian Connections and the Myth of Cultural Purity*, ix–xii.

interdependence, and multiple ethnic diasporas as ineluctable elements of the modern world."[42] Mullen and Fred Ho further expanded the possibilities of Afro Asia as a political movement in a compendium of essays on the revolutionary political and cultural connections between African Americans and Asian Americans[43] that furthered the concept of coalitional politics as well as Afro Asian disjuncture in cultural production. Furthermore, Asian American Studies scholars such as Diane Fujino have engaged in extensive ethnographic work that has historicized the coalitional politics of "Yuri Kochiyama, arguably the most influential Asian American activist to emerge in the 1960s,"[44] and examined the ways in which the Black liberation movements triggered the development of a radical consciousness amongst Japanese Americans. In addition, Bill Maeda contends that the performative aesthetics of the Black Panther Party had a profound impact on Asian American organizations such as the Red Guards who "adopted the Black Panthers' language and style—two key elements of the Panther mystique—as a political statement that underlined their espousal of the Panthers' racial politics."[45] Maeda's critique indicates how Asian American movements have also engaged in a form of racial kinesthesia through the appropriations of Black performance in which Asian bodies are organized into, again, what Foster has referred to as "choreographies of protest."[46] As I demonstrate in my discussion of Fred Ho's Afro Asian jazz martial arts performances, the organization of movement and sound offered a "generative force of a venerable phonic propulsion"[47] for transfiguration that centered around a form of performative resistance that Diana Taylor has described as "cultural memory"[48] in which "performances, gestures, orality, movement, dance, singing—in short, all those acts usually thought of as

---

42. Mullen, *W. E. B. Du Bois on Asia: Crossing the World Color Line*, xiii. See also Mullen, *Afro-Orientalism*.

43. Ho and Mullen, *Afro Asia: Revolutionary Political & Cultural Connections between African Americans & Asian Americans*, 1–19.

44. Fujino, "The Black Liberation Movement and Japanese American Activism: The Radical Activism of Richard Aoki and Yuri Kochiyama,"164–65. See also Fujino, *Heartbeat of Struggle: The Revolutionary Life of Yuri Kochiyama*. See also that while Seth Rosenfeld's book *Subversives* brings to light inconclusive evidence that Aoki was possibly an FBI informant from 1967 to 1977, Aoki's relationship to the Black Panther Party as well as the Asian American Political Alliance is solid. Furthermore, as an interned Japanese American during World War II who was also honorably discharged from the US Army, Aoki's shifting identity and conflicting loyalties at once evoke an Asian American form of double-consciousness under the gaze of US hegemony.

45. Maeda, "Black Panther, Red Guards, and Chinamen: Constructing Asian American Identity through Performing Blackness, 1969–1972," 1103.

46. Foster, "Choreographies of Protest."

47. Moten, *In the Break: The Aesthetics of the Black Radical Tradition*, 12.

48. Taylor, *Archive and the Repertoire: Performing Cultural Memory in the Americas*, 20.

ephemeral, nonreproducible knowledge"[49] are summoned forth in order to allow for the emergence of an alternative epistemology.

Performance studies scholars such as Shannon Steen, Heike Raphael-Hernandez, and T. Carlis Roberts have furthered the terrain of Afro Asia as a performance of race that disturbs traditional racialized binaries through varying modes of cultural production such as music, theater, and literature.[50] The compendium *AfroAsian Encounters: Culture, History, Politics*, edited by Steen and Raphael-Hernandez, sought to drop the hyphen between "Afro-Asia" and interrogated the negotiation of race in Afro Asian buddy films such as *Rush Hour* (1998), *Rush Hour 2* (2001), and *Romeo Must Die* (2000) while also digging into the complicated cultural links between oppressed peoples across a variety of national, racial, and political contexts as seen in the work by artist-citizen Paul Robeson, who forged connections through performances such as the Chinese national anthem, Chi'lai (March of the Volunteers) in Harlem during the 1950s. Steen further developed a theory of "racial geometry"[51] through the interrogation of figures such as Robeson, Mei Lanfang, and Anna May Wong alongside international performances such as Gilbert and Sullivan's *The Mikado* and Chinese productions of *Uncle Tom's Cabin*. Racial geometry helps explain how Afro Asian performance impacted America's relationship to Asia in terms of immigration and the maintenance of domestic racial categories between the World Wars and the subsequent politics of the Pacific theater of World War II.[52] Lastly, T. Carlis Roberts's most recent work focuses on the interminority politics of music and interrogates how contemporary Afro Asian performance ensembles create "physical and/or sonic spaces in which blackness and Asianness coincide within a juxtaposition of musical traditions, visual representations, and the identities of the artists that perform them."[53] Similar to Roberts's concept of the "sono-racial," the process through which music becomes raced within a pre-existing taxonomy of racialized bodies, I propose not only that racial kinesthesia is a way of understanding a history of martial arts as Afro Asian performance but that the cultural memory of Afro Asian coalitional politics and disjuncture is a kinesthetic process—a choreography of bodily politics that binds together practices such as the martial arts, theater, film, and dance to an otherwise hidden struggle.

---

49. Taylor, *Archive and the Repertoire: Performing Cultural Memory in the Americas*, 20.
50. Raphael-Hernandez and Steen, introduction to *AfroAsian Encounters: Culture, History, Politics*," 1–16.
51. Steen, *Racial Geometries of the Black Atlantic, Asian Pacific and American Theatre*, 5.
52. Steen, *Racial Geometries of the Black Atlantic, Asian Pacific and American Theatre*, 5.
53. Roberts, *Resounding Afro Asia: Interracial Music and the Politics of Collaboration*, 3–4.

The individuals and organizations explored in this book are part of an interrogation of how martial arts were used as a performative strategy in response to US racism and neocolonialism. In the case of the martial arts practitioners themselves, the identity that they inscribed into the world becomes legible through their movement as they developed their own particular form of racial kinesthesia. Such is also the case in the mediated movements of the martial arts cinema, print media, and performative sounds of the Wu-Tang Clan and Chinese American baritone saxophonist, Fred Ho. However, because this project is also concerned with how to respond to racial violence and racial capitalism, it is important to ask: what are the mechanisms for producing violence and normalizing systemic racism?

Thus, this project also takes under consideration the way in which martial arts has been deployed as a recuperative process for those who have been incarcerated. Specifically, it examines the possibilities that emerge when youth who have been incarcerated engage in martial arts. Referred to as The Odyssey Project, this prison intervention tool for incarcerated youth incorporates martial arts in conjunction with theater exercises for dramatic storytelling purposes. All of the incarcerated youth who are participants in The Odyssey Project are males who, like Duncan, Uyehara, RZA, and the other characters in this project, are confronting their masculinity while also negotiating the impingements of neocolonialism.

Categories of Kinesthesia

Though I offer kinesthesia as a broader concept for the study of performance through movement, I also categorize different forms of kinesthesia in order to differentiate how movement, race, and gender function within specific performance modalities. Aside from the practice of martial arts described in this book, kinesthesia is also understood as the discursive and mundane everyday movements (acts, gestures, and routines), clothing, and language that form the social-somatic contested identities that I probe throughout. Each chapter of this book examines a variation on kinesthesia through case studies that consider the specific social political conditions under which Afro Asian performance unfolds. I distinguish between the type of racial kinesthesia of live performance events such as every day practice in a dojo relative to the racial kinesthesia that emerges in martial arts filmography and choreography, and is hence mediated by the camera lens as well as the screen. Furthermore, I distinguish the everyday practices of martial arts and their itinerate constituents from the live theatrical Afro Asian jazz martial arts performances of Fred Ho.

Collectively, the chapters provide a panoramic for working through racial kinesthesia as a form of agency as well as the implied contradictions. Unsurprisingly, many of the examples of the people, groups, and locations that I identify and discuss reside in multiple categories simultaneously.

Transcultural Kinesthesia

In this chapter I develop an ethnographic intervention that rehearses a politics of what I call transcultural kinesthesia, a process wherein Black men engaged in a form of what Jacqui Alexander refers to as "crossbordering pedagogies"[54] by grounding each other through the practice of Asian martial arts. As Alexander suggests, "colonization has produced fragmentation and dismemberment at both the material and psychic levels," and the desire for decolonization is a deep yearning for wholeness that is "both material and existential, both psychic and physical, and which, when satisfied, can subvert and ultimately displace the pain of dismemberment."[55] Transgressing cultural borders signaled a form of decolonization and an attempt to reassemble, a *rasanblaj*, that is, what were previously dismembered subjectivities. However, transcultural kinesthesia did not happen in isolation, but rather through communal practice that was created by sharing information and knowledge during practice. This meant that Black men and women (as well as Asian men and women) engaged in a form of what Walter Rodney describes as "grounding together"[56] through the practice of Asian martial art that was a form of discipline, study, and conversation. By crossbordering and grounding in the cultural template of an Asian cultural property, Black people attempted to refine the kinetics of what were non-Western and non-Eurocentric based artforms to address the dismemberment of their bodies as well as the political and economic conditions under which they lived in the US. While the goal may have been liberation from the dismembering effects of colonialism, as this chapter concedes, many of the practitioners and individuals who participated in the crossbordering and grounding practice of martial arts kinesthetics were also implicated in and inculcated into US military and domestic policing agencies, especially the Vietnam War.

---

54. Alexander, "Groundings on *Rasanblaj* with M. Jacqui Alexander."
55. Alexander, "Groundings on *Rasanblaj* with M. Jacqui Alexander."
56. Rodney, *Groundings with My Brothers*, 64. In his book, Rodney discusses moving from the confines of the university and into the common spaces wherein he could work with Black masses in Jamaica in preparation for revolutionary change.

Transcultural kinesthesia also suggests the way in which crossbordering pedagogies cut across boundaries, or as Dwight Conquergood suggested, a "world crisscrossed by transnational narratives, diaspora affiliations, and, especially, the movement and multiple migrations of people, sometimes voluntary, but often economically propelled and politically coerced."[57] The transcultural also takes into account the crossing of borders such as the Mason-Dixon line through migrations out of the agricultural South, migrations from Asia across the Pacific to US territories, the movements of Black and Asian bodies who entered into the military and were transported into war and back, and simply cutting across a city's borders to enter into new spaces and types of martial arts practice. Transcultural kinesthesia also applies to the daily habituated movements of the body, or what performance and theater theorist Eugenio Barbara referred to as "extra-daily techniques"[58] that comprise the repertoire of a particular martial art practice used as a way to transmit knowledge from one live body to another.

Chapter 1, Enter the Black Dragons, focuses on the way in which Black people encountered and mixed with Asian cultural practices such as the martial arts especially during the 1960s through the practice of *randori* (sparring), *kata* (forms), tournaments and exhibitions, and as everyday performance. This chapter takes up the lived experiences of four African Americans, including Ron Van Clief, who began his training as a child in the mid-1950s in the working-class neighborhood of Bedford-Stuyvesant in Brooklyn where he was born and raised. Van Clief was a student of the aforementioned Ronald Duncan as well as Moses Powell, who developed his own interpretation of jujitsu called Sanuces Ryu that became a training regimen for the protectorate services within the Nation of Islam. Contemporaneously, the Black Karate Federation (BKF) emerged as another fraternal martial arts community during the 1960s and early 1970s that grew in popularity through the karate/kickboxing circuit in Southern California. Founded by Steve Muhammad (formerly Steve Sanders) and Donnie Williams, the BKF was a response to what Muhammad and other Black karate competitors perceived as discrimination within racially mixed or predominantly white organizations and tournaments.

---

57. Conquergood, "Performance Studies: Interventions and Radical Research."
58. Barba and Savarese, *A Dictionary of Theatre Anthropology: The Secret Art of the Performer*, 8.

Communal Kinesthesia

Communal kinesthesia suggests the way in which communities mobilize and organize themselves around political movements and parties through movement practices. Chapter 2, Black Panther Martial Art, pays particular attention to the process through which the Black Panther Party used martial arts a pedagogical platform to organize and mobilize within the Oakland Community School (OCS) during the 1970s. Run by Party member Steve McCutchen, the martial arts program at the OCS and Oakland Community Learning Center (OCLC) existed from 1974 to early 1979 and was one of the Party's community service programs. Like the BKF, the martial arts program at the OCLC grew in membership due to their performance at various California martial arts tournaments as well as demonstrations presented in local community events. However, the philosophical underpinning of the OCS/OCLC was Huey P. Newton's conceptualization of revolutionary intercommunalism, an ideology that sought to imagine and build a decolonized space beyond the ideological concept of the nation-state. Intercommunalism also drew on the philosophy of Mao Tse-Tung and Kim Il Sun's ideology of *juche,* "self-reliance," which influenced McCutchen's practice of martial arts. Entering into the Black Panther Party at age seventeen, McCutchen later utilized taekwondo as a way of educating, organizing, and mobilizing the Black working-class communities of Oakland.

Mediated Kinesthesia

I use the term mediated kinesthesia to examine the relationship between performance, power, identity, and movement in martial arts cinema and popular culture. In *Black Dragon,* mediated kinesthesia is not simply about the choreographed movements of martial artists and actors; mediated kinesthesia also identifies the ways in which the ideas around martial arts become animated and mobile through what Gilles Deleuze referred to as the "movement-image."[59] As martial arts cinema proliferated and became accessible to mass audiences and fans, it created an affective economy that inspired and to an extent empowered working-class Black men to imagine and create a new identity and intellectual terrain based on the mediated movements of Asian martial arts. Chapter 3, How Do You Like My Wu-Tang Style? interrogates how Black masculinity becomes legible as a form of Afro Asian performa-

---

59. Deleuz, *Cinema: The Movement Image,* 2.

tivity through mediated kinesthesia. The film *Enter the Dragon* (1973) set a trajectory that morphed into an array of representations of Black masculinity. The framing of the Black martial artist in Jim Kelly in *Enter the Dragon* reveals how Black masculinity was tamed and contained when Black activism and agitation was perceived as a threat. *The Last Dragon* (1985), featuring the comedic hero Bruce LeRoy, was portrayed by a racially mixed martial arts practitioner Taimak Guarriello, who was part of the New York martial arts scene and student of Ron Van Clief. From *The Last Dragon* to the *Karate Kid* (2010) reboot featuring Jaden Smith, Black martial arts filmography has produced varying forms of Black masculinity that oscillate between hypermasculinity to a form of global queerness, simultaneously managing and leveraging forms of black-yellowface and yellow-blackface performance that become legible through mediated acts, gestures, and routines.[60]

Martial arts cinema also impacted musicians, dancers, and MCs. Originally from Staten Island, the hip-hop group Wu-Tang Clan was formed during the early 1990s and rose to become one of the preeminent hip-hop groups that has influenced the genre throughout the world. Comprised of a nine-member crew, Wu-Tang Clan was inspired by the 1970s Hong Kong martial arts cinema, which they then used as the framework through which to construct an imagined identity and tell stories of survival within the deindustrialized landscape of New York City while simultaneously offering a critique of the global markets that the group chafed against in their battle for control over cultural production. Wu-Tang's lyrics and narrative structures appropriated stories of mystical lands and battles amongst clans like that of the Tokugawa who were the dominant clan during the Edo era in Japan and of the monks of the Shaolin Temple in China. One of Wu-Tang's founders, RZA (born Robert F. Diggs), was inspired by the kung fu films that he went to see on 42nd Street in Times Square. Not only did Wu-Tang take their name from the movie *Shaolin and Wu-Tang* (1983), but RZA became a student of kung fu and a disciple of Shi Yan-Ming, a contemporary Shaolin Monk who both teaches kung fu in Manhattan and has also choreographed many martial arts films, including RZA's recent directorial debuts. While Wu-Tang is an example of the Afro Asian fantasy of resisting and reinventing, one cannot ignore what have been highly normative constructions of masculinity played out in the interstices of rhizomatic flows and of cultural traffic.

---

60. Whaley, "Black Bodies/Yellow Masks: The Orientalist Aesthetic in Hip-Hop and Black Visual Culture," 188–203.

Sonic Kinesthesia

In Chapter 4, I use the concept of sonic kinesthesia to describe how movement becomes embodied through sound and music to imagine new possibilities of identity and power within theatrical performance. I suggest that music is a kinesthetic process that is an organizing platform through which martial arts emerges as a live artistic process. Specifically, the sounds of the music of the Black-blues musical tradition embodied in the jazz aesthetic offered a platform through which the Chinese American saxophonist Fred Ho formulated his own radical Asian American consciousness in conjunction with the martial arts. Chapter 4, The Sound of a Dragon: Fred Ho's Afro Asian Jazz Martial Arts, engages Ho's Afro Asian jazz martial arts performances as yet another example of Black masculinity—albeit embodied in the life of the Chinese American radical artist saxophonist cultural worker. As the late Fred Ho suggested, Bruce Lee served as a figure through which to stage Asian masculinity as virile, autonomous, and capable of "kickin' the white man's ass."[61] Like Van Clief, Ho also suffered from domestic violence, racist abjection from whites, and was dishonorably discharged from the US Marine Corps due to a racist physical altercation. In order to recuperate, Ho developed an avant-garde counternarrative form by using jazz in conjunction with martial arts in order to announce an Asian American political consciousness, offer a critique of imperialism, and to form a strategic political alignment with Third World Liberation movements of the twentieth and twenty-first centuries.

Aside from appropriating from the jazz tradition, Ho's work borrowed from various Asian folk traditions in conjunction with US and Asian popular culture to express an Asian American consciousness and to critique elements of the Asian American community whom he believes betrayed leftist movements such as the League of Revolutionary Struggle (LRS). *Voice of the Dragon* (2004) was a critique of Asian Americans who have settled for model minority mythology in order to gain access into the social privileges of whiteness through an assimilationist campaign, simultaneously taking advantage of the work of Asian American activists who continued to see their struggle in line with other radicals of color. Ho created this kind of work as "something that also would convey a Chinese American consciousness and aesthetic—something that conveys who I am through music and performing arts."[62] However, Ho's work also attempted to trouble gendered normativity and transnational politics, and involved the reimagining of Japanese Samurai mythology through

---

61. Ho, "Kickin' the White Man's Ass," 296.
62. Ho and Mullen, Interview for MartialArchiveTV (1997).

the lens of a female protagonist in *Deadly She-Wolf Assassin at Armageddon* (2006). The piece drew upon the martial arts cinema such as the Japanese epic *Lone Wolf and Cub*, which depicted a fictional folk martial arts hero embodied as a master-less and disgraced samurai. However, Ho's version employed a female heroin, embodied as the deadly She-Wolf. The piece complicates the dominant historical narratives of colonialism and both Eastern and Western conceptions of patriarchy. *Sweet Science Suite: A Scientific Soul Session Honoring Muhammad Ali* (2012) was another dialectic between the repertoire of boxing and jazz as expressions of Ali's polemics. The collaboration between Ho and choreographer Christal Brown turned Brown into a filter for staging Black masculinity, which at once troubles and disturbs presumptions of ethnic and gendered authenticity.

Restorative Kinesthesia

The prison, like the cargo hold of slave ships, is a site of racialized and gendered immobilization, and has been used as a technique through which to further social economic injustice. While not a panacea, I use restorative kinesthesia to describe the way in which movement arts have been employed to hail and organize incarcerated youth and university students into restorative justice performance projects. Not unlike Ho's performance pieces, Chapter 5, Here Be Dragons: The Odyssey Toward Liberation, is concerned with the convergence of martial arts, dance, and hip-hop theater as pedagogy through a prison intervention program called The Odyssey Project. I riff on James Baldwin's essay *Here Be Dragons* in order to construct a template for a class offered through the Department of Theater and Dance at the University of California, Santa Barbara. The Odyssey Project partners university students with wards of the court (young men ages thirteen to seventeen) from the Santa Barbara Department of Youth Probation's Los Prietos Boys Camp (LPBC). Homer's epic poem *The Odyssey* serves as a template through which these young men narrate their own journey over the six-week class/rehearsal process, during which the ensemble learn acting, writing and spoken word exercises, mask making, choreography, and martial arts.

It is my contention that as Baldwin suggested in his essay, the Black and Brown dragons who participate in The Odyssey Project (third world youth) are in fact the vanguard of change "breathing fire" and "belching smoke" through their poetry and through movement and choreography as they dance with antiquity and restore Homer's poetry with their own words and rhythms in order to challenge the "mores, morals, and morality of this particular and peculiar time and place."[63] Martial arts concepts are introduced as a vocabulary for performance movement and an interlocutory process for building confidence and interrogating conflict within their own lives and the narrative of the story. Their collaborative work culminates in a final public performance that, like Ho's work, calls forth members of the community to witness the testimony of the performers as well as serve as co-performers during extensive post-show discussion. Through learning martial arts, the young men from the LPBC are provided a forum through which to exercise a corporeal discipline over their own bodies and are hopefully empowered to explore the possibilities of creative expression and develop critical strategies toward understanding and negotiating their own intersectionality.

Black Dragon works through the possibilities and limitations of racial kinesthesia by exploring a constellation of narratives in the struggle over the politics of vernacular cultural expression. Martial artists, like musicians and choreographers, are cultural workers who have been engaged in sculpting the political economy of cultural landscapes through movement, gesture, and repertoire, and who have inscribed their identity into the world through a myriad of performative acts. As with the aforementioned ninjas of premodern Japan who endured under the weight of a ruling lord or vassal, concealing one's identity was necessary to preserve one's life. While hired as assassins or reconnaissance agents, the ninjas, much like the guerilla warriors, moved under the cover of night and in the "shadow of leaves." The ninja, like the guerilla, utilized the art of stealth to surreptitiously operate within the presence of an enemy or targeted asset, or to escape into the middle of the night when under the assault of the state or someone in the "hood." The ninja became a mythic symbol for those invested in the tactics of secrecy and resistance regardless of the political agenda. For Black martial artists like Duncan, who contended for legitimacy within the martial arts world, adherence to the code of stealth made him more elusive and validated his knowledge of the practice. Duncan was both visible and invisible in plain sight. He could teach young Black people the "warrior's way" because he'd studied the way of the ancient warrior as well as the way of contemporary military arts and translated these assets and skills into the struggles of young Black men (as well as non-Blacks) in need of communal self-defense. In other words, performing the identity of the ninja and curating and cultivating its "ancient ways" within professional martial arts venues and settings enabled Duncan to create a Blackness that was not just a phenotype (yes, he was still a Black man) but a third skin in which to shroud his body. In classic paradoxical Du Boisian form, it was double-consciousness

---

63. Baldwin, "Here Be Dragons."

with its "two warring ideals in one dark body whose dogged strength"[64] kept it from being torn asunder and provided the third parallax through which to envision the world anew. Hence *Black Dragon* aims to acknowledge the particular historical, political, economic conditions under which racial kinesthesia emerged and enabled people to develop a more nuanced and elastic understanding of identity formation and knowledge production within the maelstrom of violence that has come to be understood as modernity.

---

64. Du Bois, *Souls of Black Folk*, 3.

CHAPTER 1

Enter the Black Dragons

> Some folks say it was really around World War II that a lot of American G. I.'s who were in Japan and Korea, Japan in particular, who were exposed to traditional Japanese martial arts and a lot of those guys brought this back here. As far as Black men, Latino men, it wasn't really until you started getting into the 50s possibly the 60s—Korean War time—Vietnam War—where there were much greater numbers of men of color who spent time in Asia and got to see a lot of those things for themselves.
>
> —Stephan Berwick, *Urban Dragons: Black and Latino Masters of Chinese Martial Arts*[1]

Dragons Arising in the East

As the above quote by Stephan Berwick suggests, during the mid-twentieth century, after World War II and what I referred to in the introduction as a theater of Afro Asian performance, African American working-class men in particular began to take up the practice of Asian martial arts. Engaging and mastering the repeated acts, gestures, and routines of Asian martial arts not only served to refigure African American working-class subjectivity but also functioned as a contested site of racialized and gendered struggle, the remnants of which would impact theatrical and popular culture well into the twenty-first century. This "taking up" and self-fashioning of African American masculinity through Asian martial arts could be relegated by critics to the realm of appropriation and orientalism. However, I argue, as was the case with the exchange between the Black ninjitsu practitioner Ronald Duncan and *Black Belt* magazine owner and Japanese American, Mitoshi Uyehara,

---

1. This quote is from a forty-five-minute documentary titled *Urban Dragons*, which is unavailable to the general public. It was provided to me by Jose Manuel Figueroa, who is a Chen Taijiquan practitioner and filmmaker/producer. I initially interviewed Figueroa for my chapter on Fred Ho as Figueroa was one of the first choreographers that Fred Ho worked with when conceptualizing the early iterations of his Afro Asian jazz martial arts operettas.

the appropriative process in this case was not one in which the historically dominant white normative hegemonic gaze dictated the exploitation of the racialized other. Still, the negotiation between Duncan and Uyehara occurred under the broader rubric of colonialism and US imperialism. Just as much as Duncan was stealing back a kinetic energy that had been stolen, he and Uyehara were Third World people, Black American and Japanese American, each trying to work out Third World positioning and survival within the larger colonial, imperial, and capitalist metastructure that had fundamentally relied on the subordination and subjection of the Third World. Perhaps, then, they were doomed to fail from the start; but the question remains, how then do we account for this contested chafing of Third World people who attempted to stake a claim for themselves in a world that rendered them invisible, nameless, and even nonhuman?

In order to address this question, this chapter develops an ethnographic intervention that rehearses a politics of what I call *transcultural kinesthesia*, a process wherein Black men engage in a form of what Jacqui Alexander refers to as "crossbordering pedagogies"[2]—in this instance, by engaging in a form of what Walter Rodney describes as "grounding together"[3] through the practice of Asian martial arts. Alexander's intervention on grounding and crossbordering pedagogies emerged from a "transnational feminist imperative"[4] for the preservation of ancestral knowledge and indigenous spiritual traditions that were essential for the survival of Caribbean ecology and climate. My use of crossbordering and grounding through study, practice, and reflection also locates a form of knowledge production and identity formation for steps toward self-preservation and decolonization. As Alexander suggests, "Colonization has produced fragmentation and dismemberment at both the material and psychic levels," and the desire for decolonization therefore is a deep yearning for wholeness that is "both material and existential, both psychic and physical, and which, when satisfied, can subvert and ultimately displace the pain of dismemberment."[5] Transgressing cultural borders thus can potentially signal a form of decolonization and an attempt to reassemble, a *rasanblaj*, what were previously dismembered subjectivities. However, transcultural kinesthesia did not happen in isolation, but rather through communal practices that were created by sharing information and knowledge during practice. This meant that Black men and women (as well as Asian men and women) engaged

---

2. Alexander, "Groundings on *Rasanblaj* with M. Jacqui Alexander."
3. Rodney, *Groundings with My Brothers*, 64.
4. Rodney, *Groundings with My Brothers*, 64.
5. Rodney, *Groundings with My Brothers*, 64.

in this form of "grounding together"⁶ through the practice of Asian martial art that was a form of discipline, study, and conversation.

By crossbordering and grounding in the cultural template of an Asian cultural property Black people attempted to refine the kinetics of what were non-Western and non-Eurocentric based artforms to address the dismemberment of their bodies as well as the political and economic conditions under which they lived in the US. While the goal may have been liberation from the dismembering effects of colonialism, as this chapter concedes, many of the practitioners and individuals who participated in the crossbordering and grounding practice of martial arts kinesthetics were also implicated in and inculcated into US military and domestic policing agencies, especially the Vietnam War.

The ethnographic intervention made in this chapter focuses on the lives of several Black martial artists and organizations, such as Ron Van Clief who started the Chinese Goju system, Moses Powell who created Sanuces Ryu Jujitsu, and Steve Muhammad and Donny Williams who formed the Black Karate Federation (BKF). Their emergence as cultural workers was marked by a particular epoch of radical shifts that saw a flourishing of movements for liberation and decolonization that demanded self-determination and were articulated as Black Power. While they were not organized under one umbrella or organization, they nonetheless organized themselves into lineages, federations, happenings, and events that rendered them as hybridic subjectivities with a greater sense of agency than they would have otherwise had.

In her discussion on the intersections between martial arts and African American expressive culture in the compendium, *Afro Asia: Revolutionary Political and Cultural Connections between African Americans and Asian Americans,* Kim Hewitt contends that there were three distinct points in common between African American cultural aesthetics and martial arts philosophy. She posits that "martial arts training values self-expression within a defined structure; martial arts strives to promote internal strength and self-respect as well as physical skill; and martial arts schools encourage the student to ground his or her achievement within the martial arts tradition and to create a strong sense of mutual respect between the individual and the martial arts community."⁷ To augment Hewitt's claim, doing this kind of practice first necessitated crossing cultural borders and picking up the language systems of martial arts and then, importantly, practicing with each other and for each other in order to cultivate self and community. Through this process of both

---

6. Rodney, *Groundings with My Brothers,* 64.

7. Hewitt, "Martial Arts Is Nothing if Not Cool: Speculations on the Intersections Between Martial Arts and African American Expressive Culture," 266.

appropriation for liberation and interpretation for innovation, Black communities grounded together through study and practice. The descriptions of the figures in this chapter are not exhaustive of the performance of Afro Asian martial arts but rather aim, as Hewitt's work suggests, to present the grounding that took place through the techniques that were passed from one body to the next during the corporeal practices that ensued.

Afro Asian performance is a crossborder pedagogy, by which the knowledges learned by dismembered victims of Western slavery and hegemony borrow movement systems to suture back together the body in pieces they have been left with by systems of domination. Part of the transcultural means doing crossbordering that cuts across boundaries and fosters, as Conquergood suggests, a "world crisscrossed by transnational narratives, diaspora affiliations, and, especially, the movement and multiple migrations of people, sometimes voluntary, but often economically propelled and politically coerced."[8] My use of the term "transcultural" in this chapter also refers to the crossing of borders such as the Mason-Dixon line through migrations out of the agricultural South, migrations from Asia across the Pacific to US territories, the movements of Black and Asian bodies who were transported into war and back, and the cutting up of borders into new spaces and types of cultural practice within urban cartographies. In that sense, transcultural kinesthesia means giving oneself permission to see the entire non-Western world as an archive to dip into and raid its fugitive knowledges for the purpose of resistance to hegemonic norms of who and what is human. A primary way this raiding takes place is by performing martial arts as cultural workers who interpreted cultural collisions through and on their bodies.

Frustratingly, for too long practices and discussions around "interculturalism" or intercultural theater and performance have focused on the struggle over new forms of cultural identity in which Westernism mined Asian, African, and Indigenous practices, communities, and individuals. As Jacqueline Lo and Helen Gilbert noted in their discussion on cross-cultural theater praxis, "Western fascination with non-Western performing arts has a long history, beginning in the early part of the 20th century and intensifying over the past three decades."[9] Much of the scholarship around intercultural theater revolved around European actors and directors such as Bertolt Brecht (though Brecht did have a particular political agenda), Peter Brook, Robert Wilson, Jerzy Grotwoski, Eugenio Barba, and even to an extent, Richard Schechner.[10] Intercultural praxis mediated through the Western lens often apoliticized direc-

---

8. Conquergood, "Performance Studies: Interventions and Radical Research."
9. Lo and Gilbert, "Toward a Topography of Cross-Cultural Theatre Praxis," 33.
10. Lo and Gilbert, "Toward a Topography of Cross-Cultural Theatre Praxis," 36.

torial choices and conventions in order to universalize. While Schechner's position has shifted significantly over time, and "his critical work shows less of a tendency to idealize cross-cultural exchange, and a keener awareness of power relations,"[11] such power relations still mean everything. Hence Schechner's greatest contribution might be his radical impulse during his work in the early 1960s with John O'Neal and the Free Southern Theatre.[12]

To the colonized person who demands a voice, demands a body (discursive and somatic), apolitical and ahistorical fantasies of intercultural encounter and performance are dangerous. They mask the exploitation of labor and resources, human recourses in particular, that are the foundation of modernity, modernism, and the postmodern intellectual and artistic enterprise. In his critique of modernism and postmodernism, specifically surrealism, Robin D. G. Kelley contends, "Surrealism may have originated in the West, but it is rooted in a conspiracy against Western civilization. Surrealists frequently looked outside Europe for ideas and inspiration turning most notably to the 'primitives' under the heel of European colonialism."[13] The "primitives" were those same Third World people who first provided Picasso ideas and inspiration for cubism. Third World people would demand decolonialization as both revolutionary philosophy and practice through Third World happenings such as the Africa Asia Conference in Bandung, Indonesia, in 1955 and through quotidian spaces of Afro Asian Black martial arts performances.

While it is essential to take into account Kelley's critique of Western appropriation of non-Western strategies of survival, my intention here is to explore something unexplored in Kelley's and others' critiques of cultural borrowing as theft and appropriation—the idea of what I call brother-to-brother borrowing. Brother-to-brother borrowing goes on in Afro Asian performance, specifically when a racialized and domestically colonized people, African American men in the post–World War II period, borrow the kinesthetics of another racialized other such as the Japanese. Yet, this transcultural Third World borrowing is complicated by the fact that in the case of Japanese martial arts such as judo, karate, and jujitsu, and aikido were bound up in both local folk practices as well as Japanese and nationalist and colonialist projects. Japan had never been formally colonized, but was nonetheless influenced by Eurocentric

---

11. Lo and Gilbert, "Toward a Topography of Cross-Cultural Theatre Praxis," 39.
12. Moses et al., "Dialogue: The Free Southern Theatre," 63. Also see Fleming Jr., "Transforming Geographies of Black Time: How the Free Southern Theater Used the Plantation for Civil Rights Activism," and lastly Dent et al., *Free Southern Theater by the Free Southern Theater: A Documentary of the South's Radical Black Theater, with Journals, Letters, Poetry, Essays, and a Play Written by Those Who Built It.*
13. Kelley, *Freedom Dreams: The Black Radical Imagination*, 159.

imperialist ideology, and Japan's post-Meiji period's nationalist identity was predicated on Japanese colonization of Asia. However, what should not be lost is that many of Japan's martial arts were also common folk practices that predated the emergence of *tenno* (heavenly emperor ideology) used by militarist regimes. The effort to restore a Black subjectivity then occurs in the midst of a white American hegemonic grab for world dominance, i.e., the Vietnam War and other Asian incursions by the United States government, including General McArthur's formal occupation of Japan and subsequent move onto the Korean peninsula. In other words, what I am after is the idea that the potential that technologies of thriving from one cultural formation can be useful to people in another formation to dismantle the workings of dehumanization used by a race-obsessed America to dismiss the humanity of Black men. Though Kelley's intervention is critical of Westernism and Eurocentrism, he also suggests surrealism is part of a larger constellation of "freedom dreams" animated by anti-capitalist and anti-imperialist impulses.[14] African American practitioners of martial arts are like the surrealists in seeking the unseen power behind the visual/performative and attempting to cultivate a new epistemology of the self in order to repair Black subjectivity—itself a Western formation, after three centuries of existence in America—and launch a New Negro subjectivity. Rather than a simply "white" or a simply "Black" self, Afro Asian performance is a *third vision,* transcultural hybridic subjectivity that seeks to destroy the binary of Black and Asian by converting the doubleness of living into a complex and amalgamated form of identity that is as destabilizing to Blacks and Asians who see those subjectivities as necessarily separate and pure. This is why the encounter between Duncan and Uyehara discussed in the introduction is not just racial chafing, but a disruption of the taken-for-granted relations by which the West keeps separate those formations it has dominated and reformulated, so that no transcultural dances of resistance can threaten Western hegemony. And these binaries are taught to those who are the victims of these binaries. Once we begin to notice these disruptions of taken-for-granted binaries, they begin to appear almost everywhere.

Consider one of the most significant interviews in the documentary film *The Black Kung Fu Experience* (2013), which is set in a martial arts studio with a wall of mirrors in the background. An array of martial arts training equipment can be seen in the reflection, including a punching bag and training weapons. A gi hangs from the ceiling and numerous certificates plaster the side walls. Bald-headed and clean-shaven, a seventy-two-year-old Ron Van Clief is dressed in an all-black gi cut off at the shoulders with a green and red

---

14. Kelley, *Freedom Dreams: The Black Radical* Imagination, 160.

circular patch symbolizing his Chinese Goju Ryu system. The seventy-two-year old ex-Marine introduces himself in a soft voice. "I'm Ron Van Clief, five-time world champion, fifteen-time all American, The Black Dragon."[15] While Van Clief suggests that he received his nickname from the legendary Bruce Lee when Lee saw him compete at Madison Square Garden in 1970, Van Clief's martial arts journey began in in the early 1950s in Brooklyn, New York, where he initially learned martial arts from the esteemed ninjutsu practitioner Ronald Duncan and another gentleman named Moses Powell.[16] As Van Clief states, "My teacher Moses Powell was a really superior teacher to practitioner. I mean he really was superior. He was the first Black man to teach the FBI. He was Malcolm X's bodyguard, I mean he was somebody, you know? When I met him, I was fifteen. I was, you know, wholly!"[17] Powell was in fact a member of the Nation of Islam (NOI), follower of the late Elijah Muhammad, and by all accounts, his Sanuces Ryu Jujitsu system has been one of the primary training repertoire used to cultivate the protectorate services for the NOI, commonly referred to as the Fruit of Islam (FOI). Powell trained legions of African Americans, as well as non-Black students, who would perpetuate his lineage through the repertoire style that he created and referred to as Sanuces.[18] Upon his return from Vietnam, Van Clief continued to train with Powell and met Malcolm X when Powell was teaching the FOI in a mosque in Harlem that was referred to as the Moses Powell Harlem Dojo.

Like the aforementioned Ronald Duncan, Van Clief sought experiences indicative of the way in which going to an Asian country, Vietnam, punctuates—signals—that something more than simply learning how to fight is taking place in this documentary. Afro Asian performance prepared these Black men not only to serve in America's colonizing armed services but also to participate in the creation of anti-colonial Black Americans in the United States, who will become a subject of constant investigation by the FBI, whose "troops" Powell had also trained. While Lo and Gilbert locate the transcultural as a subcategory of cross-cultural theater that slips in and out of essentialist and problematic understandings of cultural production, it is my belief that transcultural kinesthesia also marks a particular conjunction in which Black

---

15. Burr and Chen, *Black Kung Fu Experience* (2013).

16. Toward the end of his life, Powell spent more time in the Caribbean teaching and conducting workshops. He passed away in 2007 from respiratory failure and did not leave formal archives, which is often a component of racial kinesthesia; it must be found in the repertoire passed from student to student and captured in the trade magazines and training videos in which Powell and other martial arts practitioners appeared. At times the ephemeral and temporal nature of transcultural kinesthesia is difficult to trace.

17. Burr and Chen, *Black Kung Fu Experience* (2013).

18. Muhammad, "Legacy Continues in the Movement," *Final Call,* May 17, 2007.

men such as Van Clief and Powell created new spaces in which there are no clear insides or outsides, no clear place of implicated Blackness. And they navigate this complex terrain of the "martial"—with both meanings: armed and also military—performance, through daily habituated stylized acts, routines, and gestures, or what Barbara referred to as "extra-daily techniques"[19] that are infused with the daily lived experiences of Black, African Latinx, and Asian men in a new presentation of self both in and out of the dojo. The dojo becomes a third space, not simply Black, or American, or Asian, but a "third world," where Black men get to become something far more complex than is communicated by the word *nigger* in spaces such as the plantation, prison, bank, country club, or school, for that matter.

Conquergood's refrain on De Certeau's "practice of everyday life" only begins to capture the complexity of negotiation of multiple identities in what is otherwise understood in the dojo as "an indication of stability." Rather, the dojo is a space of radical destabilization and disruption, which is mastered through *practice*. Sites such as Powell's Harlem dojo, or any dojo for that matter, exist because of "vectors of direction, velocities, and time variables"[20] actuated by an ensemble of movements that deploy bodies that come to exist because of movement. The dojo space, like the Waldorf, which was transformed into a competition space where Duncan and Uyehara battled over the cultural property of ninjutsu, "occurs as the effect produced by the operations that orient it, situate it, temporalize it, and make it function in a polyvalent unity of conflictual programs or contractual proximities."[21] The dojo and martial arts practice sites (a storefront, a community center, or a mosque) are constituted by the relations of vectors and the grounding that give the space its symbolic meaning—a contested practice of placelessness.[22]

While Powell remained within the NOI and Sanuces Ryu, Van Clief trained in multiple forms and engaged in transnational performances within the theater of war in Vietnam and also launched careers in cinema, theater, and discotheques, where he ran security operations. Contemporaneously the BKF emerged as another fraternal martial arts community during the 1960s and early 1970s that grew in popularity through the karate/kickboxing circuit in Southern California. Founded by Steve Muhammad (formerly Steve Sanders) and Donnie Williams, the BKF was a response to what Muhammad and other Black karate competitors perceived as discrimination within racially

---

19. Barba and Savarese, *Dictionary of Theatre Anthropology: The Secret Art of the Performer*, 6.
20. Certeau, *Practice of Everyday Life*, 117.
21. Certeau, *Practice of Everyday Life*, 117.
22. Certeau, *Practice of Everyday Life*, 117.

mixed or predominantly white organizations and tournaments. In fact, the BKF were determined to create another space, a third space, and hence a kind of Third World *kenpo* karate distinct from the Ed Parker's organization, which was predominantly white. The chapter concludes with a discussion on transcultural kinesthesia with the BKF as a kind of rejoinder to Powell in order to demonstrate how transcultural kinesthesia places into conversation similarly positioned figures who were not necessarily in direct contact, but nonetheless crossed borders and grounded together in order to make a third space of Afro Asian performance rasanblaj.

Moses Powell and the Sanuces Formation

During the twentieth century, urban landscapes such as New York City were transformed by families such as Moses Powell's who left Norfolk, Virginia, and relocated to the enclaves of East Brooklyn. Black migrants formed new communities that provided the labor that drove the industriousness of the US economy in factories, ports, civil service institutions, construction, and, of course, military and police agencies. As these communities formed, they reassembled themselves into new ways of understanding and being through vernacular cultural practices such as martial arts that were beyond the confines of the factory or the police station. Powell, who was born in 1941, embodied a conjunction of two cultural practices that were embraced by Black Americans as he came of age in the 1950s—Asian martial arts and Islam. At the age of thirteen, Powell began training with the Filipino American teacher, Florendo M. Visitacion, commonly referred to as Professor Vee. As Powell stated, "The martial arts just caught my eye. I got into this karate thing and jujitsu when I saw that. I had learned about judo from books and movies. And friends of the family told me about this karate thing and I just had to see it and I found a school. I found many schools, but I only found one true instructor, Mr. Florendo M. Visitacion, which I have been with ever since."[23] Born in 1910 on the island of Ilocos Norte in the Philippines, Visitacion's parents were sharecropper peasants who migrated first to Hawaii to cut sugar cane and then to Stockton, California, where his family worked as grape pickers. He enlisted in the US Army during the outset of World War II and subsequently relocated to New York where he would become part of the martial arts wave of the late '50s and '60s.[24] Popularly known as Professor Vee within the martial arts com-

23. Abbott, *San Nukas* (1969).
24. Kaufman, "Florendo M. Visitacion, 88, Martial Artist Master, Is Dead," *New York Times,* January 10, 1999.

munity, Visitacion is remembered as the founder of Vee Jujitsu, and Powell was one of Professor Vee's many students. The relationship between Powell and Vee was an Afro Asian juncture brought about through varying diasporas coming into contact through transcultural kinesthesia within the nexus of martial arts practice.

However, Powell's Afro Asian performance was embodied in his transformation from Moses Powell into Musa Muhammad through his conversion to Islam and indoctrination into the Nation of Islam. This process of taking on the aesthetics of Asian spiritual-cultural practice of Islam was a crossbordering that appealed to Black working-class people, men in particular, because it provided a feeling of being part of a Black communal experience that fostered a sense of discipline and control of their bodies while simultaneously claiming connection to a past that was not rooted in Eurocentrism. Most importantly, the NOI's performative codes attempted to reconcile the violence of chattel slavery and reassemble a dismembered people by providing a template through which brothers could ground with brothers. Furthermore, the founder of the NOI, Elijah Muhammad, engaged in a kind of performative speech act when he declared in *Message to the Black Man in America* (1965) that the Black man was in fact the descendant of on an Afro Asian group known as the "Tribe of Shabazz," which had supposedly left Asia and migrated into the African continent.

> It is knowledge of self that the so-called Negroes lack which keeps them from enjoying freedom, justice and equality. This belongs to them divinely as much as it does to other nations of the earth. It is Allah's (God's) will and purpose that we shall know ourselves. Therefore he came Himself to teach us the knowledge of self. Who is better knowing of who we are than God. Himself? He has declared that we are descendants of the Asian black nation and of the tribe of Shabazz.[25]

As tenuous as it was, claiming lineage to the fictitious lost tribe of Shabazz allowed for a reconceptualization of Black identity that was not beholden to the ills of slavery. One could dispense with their "slave name" and become their own master; Elijah Poole became "the messenger" Elijah Muhammad, Cassius Clay became Muhammad Ali, Malcolm Little became El-Hajj Malik El-Shabazz or Malcolm X, as he was and is still commonly known. Again, Malcolm X's conversion to Islam was in fact a form of crossbordering in which

---

25. Muhammad, *Message to the Black Man in America,* see the section titled "Original Man: Know Thy Self," 32. The text was originally printed in Muhammad's *Temple* No. 2 in 1965.

he picked up on the Asian philosophy through the practice of being a Muslim, but he also grounded with the brothers in the prison, Mosque, pool hall, street corner, and cafes in order to galvanize Black people to the mission of the NOI.

Similar to the indoctrination of the martial arts student, the Islamification of the Black body and the indoctrination into the NOI was a form crossbordering that relied upon repeated acts, routines, and gestures, a transcultural kinesthesia, comprised of ritual practices in order to reassemble a disassembled person. The repeated behaviors were rehearsals for how to perform the identity of the NOI in public and moved one from the secular outsider to the position of insider/practitioner and hence member of the community. Once they were part of the community, they could ground with each other and share in the development of new technologies both borrowed and remade. These ritual practices included taking on a new name, new diets, donning NOI clothing for men (signature bow tie and suit), and training in martial arts. Together they were in fact scripted responsibilities required to carry out the duties within the mosque and in the Nation. The rituals of the Nation and the dojo were intended to convert the Black body into an idealized state of sustainability capable of surviving and even flourishing. As Eric E. Curtis argues in his discussion on Islamizing the Black body,

> Members of the NOI adopted many turn-of-the century black middle-class "uplift" themes like thrift, sexual propriety, industriousness, and temperance by recasting them in an Islamic mold; this use of Islam, in turn, allowed members to reject what they viewed as the ideological burdens of African American Christianity, which had functioned as the religious source or container of these norms. These new African American Islamic rituals focused on the reformation of the black body, which was depicted as a main battleground for the souls of black folk. The black body was constructed as a gendered vessel, a symbol for the fate of the black race, where black folk could be saved from white Christian violation, poison, and in the case of emasculation.[26]

The performed cultural identity of the Black Muslim was one of a discipline that overlapped with that of the Black martial arts practitioner such as Moses Powell.

Take for example a photo of Powell seated in seiza with eyes closed as if in meditation as seen in Figure 1.1. It is a posture most commonly associated with

---

26. Curtis, "Islamizing the Black Body: Ritual and Power in Elijah Muhammad's Nation of Islam."

FIGURE 1.1. Moses Powell is seated in za zen with Professor Vee's image immediately behind him

Japanese za zen meditation, which may be practiced before or after a martial arts class such as karate, judo, jujitsu, and aikido. An image of Professor Vee appears behind Powell, and the image almost seems to float in the clouds of Powell's mind, suggesting an awakening consciousness. Powell is in a posture associated not only with martial arts, but also with Islam during prayer, in which the feet are folded back and one sits on their knees as Malcolm X did in the mosque when he made his infamous pilgrimage to Mecca. Even in the stillness of Powell's posture there is a kinesthesia, a summoning and organizing of his own body into the same meditative posture as Vee's image directly behind Powell. The image creates an Afro Asian dialogue between teacher and student. While the Afro Asian image was temporal, it was still rooted in the repertoire that Powell learned, took up, and made his own through the kinesthesia of teaching to the next generation of students.

Powell could have never become Musa Muhammad and an established martial arts instructor and entrepreneur who went on to teach the FBI without first crossbordering and grounding with Professor Vee for fifteen years.

By 1969 Powell had established himself as a leader within communities in Brooklyn and in Harlem and had created his own dojo in Harlem where he became a fixture in the local uptown Manhattan community, as seen in the short ethnographic film by Randy Abbott titled San Nukas.[27] The Moses Powell Harlem dojo served as a site of grounding as well as a transcultural liminal zone where the way of Sanuces was taught and trained. Many students were also Black Muslims and like Powell, followers of the NOI; the dojo was blocks away from the infamous Harlem mosque known as Mosque Number 7, which Malcolm X had led when he became a minister within the NOI. Powell taught the classes to predominantly African American women, men, and children who practiced on a mat used for tumbling that substituted for a tatami mat often used in judo, aikido, and jujitsu. The non-African American students and participants included Professor Visitacion, who observed Powell's instruction, as well as several Asian female students.

The Harlem dojo was a community space for brothers to ground with brothers and whomever else was dedicated to the pedagogy of rasanblaj through the kinesthesia of Asian martial arts. In order to teach values of self-expression within a defined structure, the classes consisted of an ensemble of repeated, acts, routines, and gestures such as striking, kicking, and joint locks, that often ended with a throw followed by a pin in which the attacker was immobilized. Powell's techniques focused on controlling the whole body of an attacker from various positions. Sometimes this consisted of joint manipulation such as using the wrist of *uke* (the attacker). Uke turned their body to get into a better position only to find that the *nage* (the person receiving the attack) had found another appendage to manipulate such as a finger, elbow, or the neck. Often these techniques were predicated not only upon applying force to a joint in a direction in which the joint does not naturally bend, but also elongating the joint while simultaneously creating torque by turning and rotating the hips in the direction of the projection of the technique. A student attacked Powell with a hook punch directed at his head and in response received a strike to the face with the fist and then a reverse elbow back to the

---

27. The description that I provide of Moses Powell teaching class at the Moses Powell Harlem Dojo is based on an ethnographic film titled *San Nukas* directed by Randy Abbott in 1969. The film is credited as having been produced by Black Horizon Films, and the film's credits also state that the film was produced with assistance of a grant from the Urban Center of Columbia University. The film is in black and white and is eighteen minutes and twenty seconds long. Powell's voice-over is the only voice heard in the film. In my analysis I take what Powell says about his practice and the students at face value, as there does not appear to be any embellishment or sensationalism. Whether or not all of the students featured in the film are full-time students of the Moses Powell Harlem Dojo or if the students are an amalgamation of various practitioners from other schools is uncertain.

jaw. The two quick but feint blows from Powell were not intended to end the technique by knocking the attacker out, but rather were a method through which to disrupt the student's balance, momentarily knocking the uke back onto their heels and hence creating a pocket of space and an opening for the nage to then enter and turn, generating a centrifugal force that could be used to whirl uke through the air. As the nage, Powell then moved his body to the other side of the attacker and grabbed the attacker's opposite arm. From this position, Powell rotated his hips forward with the uke's arm immobilized, forcing him to execute a forward roll in order to prevent his head from slamming into the mat.

The techniques were predicated on the cultural aesthetics and philosophical principles common to judo and aikido that enabled a smaller and diminutive individual to potentially take away an attacker's balance. Such off balancing concepts are referred to as *kuzushi* (breaking balance) and *atemi* (striking to the center). Most importantly, the concepts such as kuzushi and atemi were a method through which to teach confidence in the notion that Black people in America could claim their bodies and their communities as well as defend themselves. In a combative sport such as judo, which is also a derivative of jujitsu, judoka (the judo player) utilizes some kind of a feint, in the form of a push to entice their opponent to move in one direction. This is a stealthy movement because when the opponent or attacker tries to recover their balance, it creates an opportunity to execute a sharp and explosive pull in a different direction in order to topple their foe. The toppling often includes placing an obstacle such as the hip or the foot in front of the opponent's hip, foot, or knee so that the opponent cannot take an additional step to recover their balance. I am laboring on these details here because one of the most important elements of martial arts was that by mastering the repertoire of a particular skillset a smaller individual could defeat or defend themselves against a larger and more aggressive person. Translated into the American conditions, the kinesthesia of what Powell taught, provided an opportunity for Black people to consider defending themselves and preserving the sanctity of their lives.

Grounding together therefore created a pedagogical experience in which Black students could take with them the knowledge that was gained in the dojo and continue to further train on their own. Powell articulated his own philosophical approach to dealing with martial arts as a wholistic practice. "What I'm teaching my students is self-defense which is survival because me myself as a person I believe in simplicity and the school is named Sanuces which means survival. And you couldn't just say karate or something alone is the strongest. So, I have a mixture which I call self-defense complete which my students are learning."[28] The total self-defense system that Powell aimed to develop included conditioning exercises such as free squats and knuckle push-ups, which aimed to preserve the health of a community that needed nurturing and repair.

In the process of reassembling a dismembered community (through the discipline of remembering individual bodies), Powell demonstrated techniques and practiced with the students as he also engaged them in dialogue. Powell sought to both sustain and form a new community through the kinetics of every new student that entered the dojo.

> When I first get a new student in the martial arts, I usually pull them to the side or take a little time with them. In due time I tell them that the martial arts are great part of your life. And I'm giving you a life insurance that's not on paper. I'm teaching you how to keep yourself alive if you listen and learn. I feel that the first thing that I teach them is how to think. As far as meditation because if you couldn't think you couldn't pick up all of the techniques that I teach, the punching, the kicks, the throws and so forth. So I think the first part that's physical and mental, is to think and condition the body and one's mind.[29]

The exercises that Powell provided for the students relied on individual effort to build a collective group identity that was cultivated through kinesthesia. Paradoxically, the sustainability of the Sanuces Ryu communities were always as fragile as the bodies that participated in them. Such exercises fell into the category of calisthenics, but with modifications such as pushups done on the knuckles to help develop the strength in the forearms to deliver a bareknuckle punch. Each exercise develops a specific function in its application. Without repetition, a practitioner does not learn proper form, and can easily break the wrist or forearm if they punch something solid or uneven. Furthermore, doing horse squats develops stamina in the legs, lower back, and abdomen or what we refer to commonly as core muscles. Most importantly, holding the squat position when the heart rate is elevated from the previous exercises, as was the case with students in Powell's class, develops breath control so that the exercises when done together become a meditative practice through which to discipline and focus the mind and the body together. To again echo Hewitt's assertion, Powell's training regimen strove to promote internal strength and self-respect as well as physical skill that encouraged the students to ground

---

28. Abbott, *San Nukas* (1969).
29. Abbott, *San Nukas* (1969).

their achievement within the martial arts tradition and cultivate mutual respect between the individual and the martial arts community.

While the majority of students at the Harlem dojo were male, Powell notably also taught female students and broke with the more traditional patriarchal practices of not integrating female practitioners. "I feel that . . . you see more women taking the martial arts because it's better for them because very seldom a woman attacks a woman. It's always a man."[30] A young Black female student practiced a variation of the *tai otoshi* (body drop) technique, only she added an upward spiraling wrist lock on to her male opponent's wrist before reverse elbowing him in the ribs and then throwing him forward. Unlike organized combat sport such as karate or judo, Sanuces's emphasis on survival necessitated that female and male students practice together. One could argue that the role-playing exercises (between uke and nage) were not only opportunities for female practitioners to practice techniques for future situations in which they needed to defend themselves, but the actual execution of the technique in the dojo provided an emotional resonance and sense of achievement for women who could take that feeling of confidence outside the dojo when dealing with male aggression in any situation.

Powell also taught the art of ukemi (how to fall down safely) by teaching students how to roll forward and slap the mat with their hands to dissipate their energy. These practices provided confidence in one's ability to survive and encouraged the student to ground his or her achievement within the efforts that they were putting into the rehearsal. Once Powell demonstrated the techniques, principles, and the art of ukemi, he bowed to his more senior-ranking adult student who led the group in practicing the technique that was demonstrated and the appropriate ukemi for the technique. Powell then supervised as he watched the senior student lead and instruct the younger students. This meant that the community of students were becoming self-reliant and learning to teach one another through the prescribed behavioral codes associated with martial arts. The students formed a line at the edge of the mat and performed roll after roll as other students worked out in another section of the dojo searching for the exact angle for how to turn the wrist for a wristlock or how to manipulate the elbow. The students conversed with each other as they helped one another develop their techniques. This was often the case in many martial arts schools, especially those that attempted to build a lineage between teacher, student, and a subsequent generation. In the Moses Powell Harlem Dojo, kinesthesia was a system of knowledge production wherein stu-

---

30. Abbott, *San Nukas* (1969).

dents and practitioners became interpreters and keepers/transmitters of the martial arts.

As Powell observed the students, he offered corrections and suggestions on their locks and on their ukemi, which is a significant component of the knowledge exchange in the martial arts because it is difficult, if not impossible to explain to someone how to move their body. Rather, technique and movement have to be taught and learned through the process of practicing the art, by executing the techniques, and listening with the entire body to what your partner or opponent is doing. To that end, martial arts is a form of immersive theater and participatory anthropology. To develop this kind of competency, the body must first be conditioned to move, which requires learning the art of falling (ukemi) without injuring oneself. In martial arts such as judo, aikido, and jujitsu, one learns by being thrown. If a wrist lock is executed with power and speed, and the novice student or nonpractitioner is thrown to the ground, it can result in severe injury, sometimes with the student's humerus popping out of the socket of the shoulder joint. Hence, to lead a class of children and adults requires focus, discipline, and concentration in order to ensure that a severity of training is maintained without causing wanton injury. As Powell suggested, learning to fall in the dojo is, of course, a literal and metaphorical lesson for falling in life. "Falling is very important because you might slip in the snow and if you're not relaxed you'll break yourself up. With the knowledge of the martial arts you might slip in the snow and you might scrape your arm, but you won't break it. You won't get hurt as bad by not having the knowledge of falling. That's why we hit the mat hard and do pushups on the palms of their hands to strengthen the hands. It's a way of getting people to do the things they say they can't do. It's all based on technique and the art in the particular thing that they're doing."[31]

The practices at the Harlem dojo encouraged the student to ground his or her achievement within the martial arts tradition and to create a strong sense of intergenerational respect between the individual and the martial arts community. These crossbordering practices enabled a senior adult student to practice with a child who had a white belt. The black belt bowed to the white belt. The senior adult then chambered his fist and delivered a reverse punch to the child student who in turn stepped off the line of the attack of the punch and slid toward the attacker's center and opposite arm which was chambered. The child simultaneously delivered a block to the attacker's armpit, threw a reverse punch to the attacker's center, and then quickly pivoted on one foot while placing the other foot in front of the attacker's foot so that he could not

---

31. Abbott, *San Nukas* (1969).

take another step forward. While this movement was indicative of the technique in judo known as tai otoshi, as the student quickly brought both hands to the elbow of the attacker's arm, the student simultaneously dropped to his knees and turned the technique into a sacrifice throw and forced the attacker to fall, which he of course did using the ukemi and performed a forward roll, slapping the mat accordingly. The pair executed the same technique repeatedly. Each time, they improvised and added slight variations by either using a different attack or different entry and changing the response pattern while still maintaining the essence of the initial technique that Powell had demonstrated at the beginning of the class.

> Take for instance the young people from five, six, seven, eight on up to twelve, they should start [at] an early age because this teaches them a certain amount of dignity and pride because they're doing something that's [*sic*] . . . a lot of energy is being used especially the mental part of the body too and it gears them toward wanting to be something . . . more and more, better and better. And it teaches them how not to fight with other kids because they know that they are stronger because they know a little bit more about fighting.[32]

Transcultural kinesthesia fostered an environment through which to engage in intergenerational grounding. Both students smiled in mutual appreciation for having completed the exercise together. Smiles came across the face of all of the students; they appreciated both the difference in size and strength between a preadolescent, and an adult and the mutual benefit and cooperation that went into the dynamism of the technique. The adult student picked up the child and gave him a hug. Upon placing him back down on the ground, the child grabbed both arms of the adult student and executed another judo technique known as *tomoe nage* (circle throw). The exchange between the two students was serious and playful, as the younger student seemed to have surprised the adult student with the unexpected move.

An adult student with a white belt who watched from the side seemed impressed and yet uncertain of his own ability to execute the tai otoshi technique. The novice, who was in his late forties or early fifties, attempted to perform the same technique that the young boy and the senior student had executed. However, he struggled to keep his balance and lacked the coordination and suppleness to extend his leg in order to block uke's foot from moving forward. As a result, when he threw the uke, their body didn't quite

---

32. Abbott, *San Nukas* (1969).

elevate and uke flopped to the floor without their balance being fully compromised. Noticing the student's frustration and disappointment in himself, Powell intervened and provided more examples for the struggling student as he stood next to him and used his own body as a model. Encouraged by the instruction, the student attempted the tai otoshi technique again with greater confidence. Powell also recognized the psychological strategy that went into teaching—that the student had to internalize the movement as their own and not something that Powell or anyone else could force them to do, or do for them.

> Sometimes you have a student and you know he has a certain thing in him and he won't bring it up because he's afraid. So, I constantly work with him and work with him and I give him a lot of attention and all of a sudden I just make him think "ahh he's never going to be able to do it." Then I start playing his game and he becomes more real and then all the sudden he starts doing it. And I don't take any thanks for it. I just walk away and I smile and he knows what he's doing then. Because there's no such thing "as I can't do." A man needs self-confidence.[33]

Powell chuckled as the student smiled at his own accomplishment. Through the small feat of his student, Powell could also feel confident in his vision of developing Sanuces as a strategy for survival for the individual as well as the broader community. This was a concept that, like Walter Rodney's cultivation of relationships with the brothers who were in Jamaica, the NOI also sought in order to reform those most marginalized in society who had been incarcerated or were struggling with addiction. The NOI, through their emphasis on discipline and self-care, sought to repair and reassemble, much like what happened to Malcolm X. But most importantly, the execution of the tai otoshi technique gave the struggling adult student confidence in himself and confidence in the fact that martial arts training provided a structure for developing an internal strength and self-respect as well as physical acumen that grounded the student in his achievement within the martial arts tradition that Powell sought to foster.

By grounding with the people in the dojo through the kinesthetics of martial arts, Powell was able to summon in people a feeling of a sustainable community.

---

33. Abbott, *San Nukas* (1969).

> The martial arts self-defense, karate, jujutsu what have you, it all gives you a sense of dignity and pride and a lot of confidence. And take for instance the Black community, my community actually, we have people that are really afraid to come out in the evenings you know. That's bad because they're part of the community too. And I feel that these particular people should get into the martial arts as soon as possible so that they can gain more of that dignity and pride and self-understanding that they're not afraid. If a man or a woman can fight back, sometimes they can live longer. So, I think the martial arts is like a partner walking down the street with you. In the Black community you should have it.[34]

Similar to the martial arts, the NOI's presence in urban communities was not only a model of Black political empowerment but also a form of Black economic enfranchisement. The NOI engaged in small business enterprise and purchased property—a strategy that it saw as fundamental to the right of self-determination, stability, and sustainability. Of course, the Harlem community had its own renaissance during the 1920s that, again, resulted from the movement of Black people out of the agricultural South. The community of central Harlem was pivotal to the creation of Malcolm X's career as he guided the NOI's "mecca" known as Mosque Number Seven during the late 1950s until his split with the NOI in 1964.

Sanuces, in name, is the personification of reinvention of identity, again, a rasanblaj and a practice of survival that grew out of an appropriation of Asian cultural aesthetics and philosophy. Again, similar to the conversion to Islam and the transformation of Malcolm Little into El-Hajj Malik El-Shabazz, the renaming and reinvention of self were catalytic tools for social change and opportunity for agency not only for the individual but for the legacy that Powell envisioned and the communities that formed through grounding in martial arts practice.[35] It was through this symbolic language that Powell was able to transform or, if we will grant it, "transculturate," Professor Vee's amalgamated system into his own interpretation of a practical system for self-defense, as well as an organization of students and teachers. The Sanuces Ryu system is often represented through an insignia on patches, worn by many practitioners, and is indicative of the way in which sartorial presentation or the adorning of the body with a particular ornamentation and clothing was significant to creating a new body of Afro Asian martial art.

---

34. Abbott, *San Nukas* (1969).
35. Turner, *Dramas, Fields, and Metaphors: Symbolic Action in Human Society*, 55.

There are other iterations of the emblem that Sanuces Ryu disciples have used, each one generating its own meaning to represent a practitioner's particular interpretation of the system. The pyramid with the eye is associated cross-culturally with many organizations, including Free Masons, as a sign of intelligence, knowledge, and knowledge as power. The inverted image of a body wearing a gi and hakama is symbolic of Powell's signature "one finger roll-out" that he often executed during demonstrations. The patches were placed on the gi and hence marked the body as part of the Sanuces Ryu jujitsu community. The emblem and the patch were never sedentary. The patch was "trans" always moving and signifying on the body through stylized acts, gestures, and routines, and the sartorial presentation marked the body as belonging to a community of practitioners.

In Japanese martial arts such as judo, jujitsu, and aikido, the art of falling, rolling, and landing is a major skill of ukemi. As Van Clief states about Powell's ukemi, "He could handstand on one finger and then rollout and you couldn't hear the rollout. It was silent, like he was able to defy gravity. It was amazing."[36] Powell became well known for his trademark style of ukemi as his body leapt into the sky so that his body was completely inverted. Facing head down, he balanced on one finger before rolling forward across the forearm and then the rest of his body. Powell popularized the signature one finger rollout when performing in demonstrations such as the World's Fair (1964/1965) and Aaron Bank's Oriental World of Self-Defense in Madison Square Garden (1975).

Hence it is imperative to examine the repertoire as an archival materiality that is manifested in the kinesthetic practices of martial artists such as Van Clief who studied with Powell and developed his own particular repertoire style. His techniques were based on both his interpretation of Asian martial arts and the political economic conditions that shaped his life. As Diana Taylor suggests, "The repertoire allows for an alternative perspective on historical processes of transnational contact and invites a remapping of the Americas, this time by following traditions of embodied practice."[37]

Ron Van Clief and the Chinese Goju Ryu System

Born in 1943, Van Clief grew up in the Bedford-Stuyvesant neighborhood of East Brooklyn and attended the Boys High School, where he was captain of

---

36. As stated by Van Clief in the documentary film by Burr and Chen, *The Black Kung Fu Experience* (2013).

37. Taylor, *Archive and the Repertoire: Performing Cultural Memory in the Americas*, 20.

the gymnastics team. In his own words, "the Van Cliefs were poor," and they lived in an old rail car that had been turned into a flat that was in a row of flats upon rows of flats.[38] Yet, it was in the backyards of these Brooklyn tenements where Van Clief would let his imagination run wild as a child, scaling buildings, and creating his own world of fantasy with the other children in the neighborhood, including his cousin who lived next door and his older brother Pete. Without any money in their pockets, Ron and Pete would "hop the train [to] Canal street" to the downtown cinemas of Manhattan's Lower East Side, where the ten- and twelve-year-old would wait outside of the movie theater for an opportunity to sneak in. Once inside, they could consume the films produced by the Hong Kong–based Shaw Brothers production company, which began producing kung fu cinema in 1925. The Shaw Brothers films that were exported to US screens became an inspirational site for constructing a non-white body of fantasy for many Black and Latinx youth of New York City's urban enclaves, and the choreography of these films provided a template for imagining and then practicing a bodily discipline that they saw in Hong Kong cinema. Youth could watch the movements within these films, memorize them, and then practice or at least attempt to reconstruct what they saw on the screen once back at home in Brooklyn.

However, Van Clief needed more than what was offered in the movies. He needed the nourishment of the martial arts programs at the St. Johns Community Center in Bedford-Stuyvesant, where he began training with Powell and the aforementioned Ronald Duncan. Under their tutelage, Van Clief engaged in a form of grounding where he sculpted his identity through the Asian martial arts, which in turn provided him a sense of agency and a form of self-expression within a defined structure. In his own words Van Clief articulates his zealousness for the practice. "I did various odd jobs to collect the money to pay for my martial arts classes which were ten dollars a month. I was collecting soda bottles. I was doing all kinds of things. And for ten bucks, I was there every day."[39] Like the transcultural training of the Harlem dojo, the classes at the community center provided a sense of mutual respect between himself and the martial arts community, most importantly, the more senior instructors, Powell and Duncan. Van Clief was in need of such practice and healing because he had been disassembled by the impact of watching his father's har-

---

38. See Ron Van Clief's self-published autobiography, written with Sparky Parks, titled *The Hanged Man*. I have relied on this text for much of my discussion on Van Clief. In addition, Van Clief has published and produced many training videos as well as provided interviews that can be found online in the public domain.

39. As stated by Van Clief in the documentary film by Burr and Chen, *The Black Kung Fu Experience* (2013).

rowing heroin addiction that left him disfigured when he singed his flesh on a radiator.

While the goal may have been liberation from the dismembering effects of colonialism, the crossbordering and grounding practice of martial arts kinesthetics were also implicated in and inculcated into US military and domestic policing. Powell trained the FBI, a profound contradiction since the FBI also surveilled the NOI through counterintelligence programs such as COINTELPRO. At age seventeen, Van Clief joined the Marine Corps in 1960, a decision that amplified the levels of violence he experienced as both soldier and veteran of the US aggression in Vietnam.

Entering the military echoed the profound contradictions of double-consciousness. Throughout the twentieth century, the US had a history of not tolerating Black soldiers in uniform, especially those Black soldiers who returned home after World War II. Thus, Van Clief was still under assault even in the Marine Corps. Upon his arrival at boot camp in North Carolina, white Marines refused to sleep in the same barracks as "niggers," and white soldiers would harass Van Clief by urinating on his face while he was sleeping.[40] This disavowal of Black soldiers came to the forefront when Van Clief refused to move to the back of the bus on a ride back from town to the Marine base in Kingston, North Carolina, in 1963. This refusal resulted in Van Clief's being jailed by the local police and nearly killed. As he states, "I go outside and I am confronted by about twenty like farmer type guys with shovels and pitchforks all that kind of stuff. They beat me up. They knocked four teeth out. They broke my jaw. They broke my left arm at the elbow and turned it around backwards and stomped on it. I almost lost my left eye. And then they hung me."[41] The angry white North Carolinian mob put a rope around Van Clief's neck and pulled him up in the air. The last thing that Van Clief saw was someone swinging a shovel toward his face. When he woke up in the hospital, his Captain told him, "We didn't get ya, but we'll have the gooks get ya."[42] He would then spend four months in the hospital recovering from his injuries, after which he spent two months doing light active duty and was then shipped off to the killing fields of Vietnam.

Yet, the martial arts proved to be a practice of repair during his first overseas tour of duty, which took place on the island of Okinawa where he prac-

---

40. As stated by Van Clief in the documentary film by Burr and Chen, *The Black Kung Fu Experience* (2013).

41. Van Clief recounts this story in numerous sources including his *Black Heroes of the Martial Arts* and *The Hanged Man,* as well as the documentary film by Burr and Chen, *The Black Kung Fu Experience* (2013).

42. Burr and Chen, *Black Kung Fu Experience* (2013).

ticed karate, Okinawa-te and shorenji-kenpo.[43] Both of these practices were tethered to the legacy of Japanese colonialism as well as US imperialism. Okinawa had its own indigenous language and customs, and shared a tributary mercantile relationship between China and Japan. The island of Okinawa had served as a site of trading of goods, languages, and practices such as martial arts. Much of contemporary Okinawan karate or shorenji-kenpo were derivatives of Chinese kung fu, which were initially used to repel invading Japanese incursions from the southern island of Kyushu. These practices were subsequently appropriated under Japanese colonial rule and then incorporated into the modern Japanese state as expressions of Japanese nationalism. In many ways, Van Clief's experience with Japanese martial arts mirrored that of many US soldiers and sailors who found a dojo to call home while overseas.

The experience with racism of the US military did not end in North Carolina. As Van Clief recounts, "I saw a lot of racism in Vietnam, a lot more than what I thought I would. Because the same white cracker officers and NCO's [noncommissioned officers] from North Carolina were having Black guys go out on these no return missions, you know what I mean? I served in Vietnam and Vietnam damaged my mind. It took me many, many years, I can't even say to recover, just to not live in survivor mode."[44] Van Clief's military occupational specialty was artillery, and he was assigned to the position of gunner on the Bell Huey helicopter, a position that had him constantly shooting and being shot at as the Huey often had to cruise at low altitudes over the rice fields of Vietnam to assault the Vietcong, retrieve the wounded, and bring back the dead. "I haven't slept properly for decades. Vietnam damaged my mind. It took many years for me [to] just not live in survivor mode."[45] Van Clief was honorably discharged in 1965, and by the time he returned to New York, he was lost and essentially a junkie. Yet, he still had the martial arts. As he states, "The martial arts were my only escape. I knew that with the martial arts, I could always do my best, and it would keep me going."[46]

Individuals such as Van Clief who participated in the crossbordering and grounding practice of martial arts kinesthetics were also inculcated into US military and domestic policing agencies. With his military and martial arts experience, Van Clief used the skills that he had and joined the New York City Police Department where he was employed as a transit police officer and policed New York City's subway, riding the D train back and forth between Coney Island and the Bronx between 8 p.m. until 4 a.m. Here we witness

---

43. Van Clief, *Black Heroes of the Martial Arts*, 12.
44. Van Clief, *Black Heroes of the Martial Arts*, 12.
45. Burr and Chen, *Black Kung Fu Experience* (2013).
46. Burr and Chen, *Black Kung Fu Experience* (2013).

one of the most daunting challenges to Black Americans—a constant striving for liberation, whilst simultaneously being sucked into the gears of American racial structures. The contradictions of double-consciousness could not have been any starker. As the horrors of Vietnam haunted Van Clief, his father also died from an overdose in 1964, and his only brother was killed in action in 1966. Van Clief fought to keep himself from collapse.[47] When not pulling a double shift with the NYPD, he was in the dojo or working security details at the nightclubs that made up the urban cultural landscape of New York City.

By mastering the repertoire of an Asian cultural form that was also a performance art, Van Clief imbricated himself into the postmodernist art scene of downtown New York by working the security detail at places such as the Electric Circus, a discotheque and nightclub on St. Mark's Street in the East Village of New York, which had become one of the most sought-after entertainment locations in the city. In fact, through his connections at the Nisei Goju Ryu dojo, Van Clief developed his own crew who were members of the Black martial arts community.[48] Together they helped grow the martial arts scene in New York City while also creating an entrepreneurial network of security workers that mixed with and charged the frenetic energy of downtown disco, postmodern art, the burgeoning punk scene, and the Black Arts Movement. Van Clief bounced back and forth between the predominantly white Electric Circus on the ground floor and the predominantly Black discotheque called The Dom located in the "lower depths" underneath the Electric Circus. The Dom became a place where Van Clief could rub shoulders with entertainers such as Sly and the Family Stone, the Chambers Brothers, Earth, Wind, and Fire, Santana, the Rolling Stones, and Jimi Hendrix.[49]

The Electric Circus was a concoction of Andy Warhol's critiques of postindustrial performance art where crooked walls that held psychedelic tapestries of Warhol's work "Exploding Plastic Inevitable" set off a hypnosis of "flashing lights and a mega sound system that rocked the house. . . . Neon paintings all around"[50] that morphed into projected movies and photographs. From the loudspeaker echoed the sounds of guitarist Lou Reed's multi-instrumental rock group, the Velvet Underground, as artists, hippies, trippers, and anti-

---

47. As Van Clief recounts in his book *The Hanged Man*, he felt incredible guilt over the loss of his older brother Pete and their father, who had been a semi-pro boxer originally from Virginia and worked as merchant marine.

48. Many of whom Van Clief included in his text *Black Heroes of the Martial Arts* consisted of individuals such as Malachi Lee, Tom "Lapuppet" Carroll, Owen Watson, Fred Hamilton, Ronald Taganashi, Earl Monroe, and, of course, their teacher, Grandmaster Frank Ruiz, who was instructor of Nisei Goju Ryu Karate under Peter Urban.

49. Van Clief, *Hanged Man*, 107.

50. Van Clief, *Hanged Man*, 108.

war activists entertained themselves with dancing and orgies. The clubs were also a confluence of contested intersectionality in which an unprecedented warping of the American social fabric bent the contours of what had been a constrained 1950s sexuality that exploded as various forms of queer countercultural consumption. Warhol's work not only explored themes of mass production but the production of sexuality itself and made space for drag queen performance in the discotheque fused with the avant-garde jazz sounds that emanated from The Dom to produce alternative understandings of interracial sexuality and queerness.

Yet, clubs also drew the attention of narcotic distributors such as the Hell's Angels biker organization, which was white only, often former combat veterans, and more often than not, hostile to the presence of Black authority. As Van Clief recounts, "One particular night a bunch of bikers crashed the door. Bob Chin . . . [my] dojo brother, was arguing with a big biker."[51] The argument escalated, and the place erupted into a brawl of knives and chairs. There were kicks to the groin, punches thrown to the face as "all the bouncers and bikers were brawling as if it were the Klondike westerns with a symphony of voiceovers from a Kung Fu movie and the vocal of a rock band wailing through the floors."[52] While Van Clief's description of the scene at the Electric Circus reads as a comical *manga-esque* moment of chaos and pandemonium, it also reveals the way in which masculinity was continuing to be produced and contested through a form of Afro Asian performance. In the club space, the Black body could operate as enforcer of the rules and regulations as they saw fit. In this particular instance, the orders were given to white males. One can imagine the group of Black and Puerto Rican bouncers with puffed out afros sporting bellbottoms and open collared shirts fighting with the longhaired bikers, tattooed and in t-shirts, jeans, and leather biker pants, perhaps with a giant American Eagle or even a Confederate flag patched onto the back of their leather vests. The conflict was one of race and sexuality in which to lose a street brawl would not only threaten the masculinized identity and security of a "security team" but potentially threaten their reputation of maintaining order and hence undermine their livelihood.

When not performing his security detail at the clubs, Van Clief retreated to the dojo, where he could refine his skill and polish his soul afire. Back at the Nisei Goju Ryu dojo, he grounded with his Black and Afro Latino brothers. As Van Clief suggests, Sensei Ruiz was in charge and "liked to keep the static going between the Hispanics and blacks. On Tuesday night they would have

---

51. Van Clief, *Hanged Man*, 109.
52. Van Clief, *Hanged Man*, 109.

the black belt class.... The students would form two lines facing each other and start fighting."⁵³ On one night in particular, the short and stocky Sensei Ruiz squared off with the students. Again, in an almost comical display of fraternal love, Van Clief reminisces that after giving Owen Watson a real beating, it was Van Clief's turn. He thought he was ready for the elder and more senior Sensei Ruiz, who lunged at Van Clief, "hitting him in the face with a left reverse punch that rocked" Van Clief so hard he stumbled. Van Clief shook it off, but as he started his attack, he could see Owen and Zulu laughing over Ruiz's shoulder "as if they knew what was going to happen next."⁵⁴ Van Clief launched a roundhouse kick that bounced off of Sensei Ruiz's chest, who just smiled and adjusted his black pair of sunglasses "that he wore when he was in a serious mood." Ruiz moved like a bolt of lightning, and suddenly Van Clief was on his back. When he woke, Sensei Ruiz stood over him whipping his face with a wet towel that brought him back to consciousness. Van Clief had been struck in the back of the head with a spinning back kick that he had not seen and now laid on the "mat clearing the cobwebs from his head embarrassed in front of the rest of the class and the great Sensei Ruiz."⁵⁵ The severe training would start to pay off for Van Clief as he continued to gain a reputation for doing private security, found success as a tournament fighter, and turned his sights on acting.

The martial arts proved to be a pathway for Van Clief to explore differing modes of consciousness and identity. The movement practices of martial arts included experimentations with mind-altering states that intersected with both meditation and meditative substances. In the summer of 1969, Van Clief won his first World Karate Championship, which was part of the Japan Expo at the New York Coliseum. To recall the scene in the introduction between Duncan and Uyehara in the same year at the Waldorf Astoria Hotel, martial arts competitions and expositions were moments of contact through which to promote the Nisei Goju Ryu dojo, where Van Clief would assume the role of "chief instructor of sparring and self-defense." His coworkers from the Electric Circus were now his own disciples, and after class they would go to the movie theaters in Manhattan's Chinatown, and like he had done with his brother when they were kids in Brooklyn, construct a body of fantasy that had now become a reality in flesh. Van Clief was living on the edge of the American counterculture, kicking and licking reality—literally—as he dropped LSD before tournaments and experimented with more hallucinogens. Van Clief became friends with Jimi Hendrix (also an Airborne Ranger veteran) and his

---

53. Van Clief, *Hanged Man*, 113.
54. Van Clief, *Hanged Man*, 113.
55. Van Clief, *Hanged Man*, 113.

roommate at the time, folk-rhythm and blues guitarist, Richie Havens. Van Clief taught Havens karate and would listen to him play the acoustic guitar in Thompkins Square Park in the early spring morning as he strolled back to his apartment from the Electric Circus. Students from the local universities in the city were always in abundance and turned Van Clief on to Timothy Leary's "Tune in, turn on and drop out" event, in which one hundred people were invited to drink LSD-laced Kool-Aid in the forest. That same summer was the Woodstock Music Festival in upstate New York. "Dojo brother" Ron Taganashi and Van Clief piled four girls into the back of a van on their way to the festival. High on LSD and marijuana,[56] Van Clief's world of selves was melting into multiple experimentations of bodily contact through drugs, sexual encounters, martial arts competitions, and eventually, theatrical performance.

Transgressing cultural borders, Van Clief collapsed the distance between performer as martial artist and performer as screen actor. In fact, this was what Bruce Lee understood and did so well—martial arts skills became a platform and gateway into the economy of acting and the film industry. To that extent, martial arts filmography (which I discuss in greater detail in Chapter 3) was another contested space and enterprise that individuals such as Van Clief sought to access. The years 1970 to 1975 marked the height of the blaxploitation film era and provided opportunities for Hollywood studios to make money and for Black talent to enter the entertainment industry as never before. Having enrolled in the Negro Ensemble Company and because of the rise of blaxploitation, Van Clief was able to capitalize on his reputation as a martial artist and reframe himself as a burgeoning stuntman. This shift in his career trajectory from formal policing to a focus on the performing arts not only led Van Clief to performances in front of the camera but also enabled him to provide his services as a technical fight director, fight choreographer, and stuntman for some of the top Black talent in the US, including Samuel L. Jackson, Eddie Murphy, and Richard Pryor, and as a personal security guard for others such as Gregory Hines.

Van Clief formed connections with various martial artists within New York City and parlayed them into entrepreneurial opportunities. He had in fact become a Black performer of Asian martial arts capable of choreographing for the camera and could market himself as security for celebrities. With the credulity and visibility of having rubbed elbows with Black entertainers in Harlem at the Negro Ensemble Company as well as the downtown artists of the East Village, Van Clief was able to present himself as a kyoshi (sixth-degree black belt) and shihan (master instructor) of his own Chinese Goju

---

56. Van Clief, *Hanged Man*, 117.

system. In the dojo, Van Clief taught students the accumulation of the arts that he had acquired from Powell, Duncan, Ruiz, and the teachers that he met in Asia during his tours. Van Clief's name became synonymous with American martial arts communities as he was popularized through performances in tournaments, appearances in magazines, and training documentaries such as *The Super Weapon* (1976) that featured many of the martial artists within Van Clief's New York City circle.

In one scene, Van Clief is introduced by the narrator and actor Adolph Cesar,[57] who states, "Martial art is more than a sport, more than a self-defense system. It's a way of life. It does not create athletes with bulging muscles or finely tuned murderers. It creates men. Men like Ron Van Clief."[58] Van Clief stands across from a sparring partner as each bring their hands together in the *musubi* (literally "binding") gesture that forms part of the courtesy before they bow and engage in practice. Cesar continues his depiction of Van Clief and describes him as "unquestionably the most effective empty hand fighter in America . . . the most dangerous man in America."[59] Van Clief receives a series of attacks in the form of a reverse punch to the head and responds with counter strikes. The narrator's embellishment helps position Van Clief as not only a skilled expert in the repertoire that he has mastered but an interpreter of the new formation of his Chinese Goju. The uke punches Van Clief with several reverse thrusts as Van Clief responds each time, initially blending with the attacker's energy, and then delivers high kicks, roundhouse kicks, spinning heel back kicks, crescent kicks, foot sweeps, neck cranks, knife edge hands to the throat, and then finishes with a technique that each time leaves his partner sprawled out on the floor. Van Clief wears his signature afro with a black gi and red belt symbolizing the rank of shihan (master) for his particular repertoire style of Chinese Goju.

While the attacks for the exercise known as *ippon* (cleanly executed tournament technique) are agreed upon beforehand, the speed, fluidity, and precision with which Van Clief responds is kinesthetically indicative of an improvisatory movement that suggests the influence of varying styles (karate, jujitsu, ninjutsu, and arnis) that Van Clief incorporated into his Chinese Goju. Again, like dancing, part of what set him apart from others was their own particular "repertoire style" that identified who they were and what they were about. For Van Clief, it was the diversity and speed of his techniques that never missed a beat. There was also a diversity of bodies represented in *The*

---

57. Adolph Cesar is best remembered for his performances in the films *The Color Purple* and *A Soldier's Story*. He was also a member of the Negro Ensemble Company.
58. Scarpelli and Sotos, *Super Weapon* (1976).
59. Scarpelli and Sotos, *Super Weapon* (1976).

Super Weapon that were emblematic of the urbanity of New York City and pulled together a multicultural ensemble of practitioners to represent the assemblage of performance disciplines.

Van Clief's training partner appears to be Euro American, while other members were Black and Afro Latino (as was the case with Sensei Ruiz). In other words, the martial arts of New York City in the 1970s were transcultural meeting grounds, contact zones, in which bodies of varying complexions, races, and ethnic backgrounds converged. Like Powell and the Harlem dojo, the Nisei Goju Ryu dojo was a predominantly male space, and *The Super Weapon* featured only one woman in the film. Cesar introduces Elsa Roman, a student of Frank Ruiz and a black belt student of Nisei Goju Ryu system. "Ever since karate came to America there has been controversy over the place of women in the martial arts. Some instructors refuse to even allow them into the dojo while others accept them willingly in their classes."[60] Roman performs a *sanchin* (three battles) *goju-ryu* (hard-soft style) karate solo kata exercise that focuses on synchronizing the body with breathing movements while simultaneously contracting every muscle throughout the body. As opposed to the fluid and fast movement seen in karate randori, the karateka focuses on maintaining the tension throughout the musculature and sinews, moving slowly through the pattern of the kata and exhaling with an audible breath with each movement. Similar to Van Clief, who demonstrated the ippon exercises, Roman then receives a series of attacks by a male student and subdues him by executing a series of techniques. As Cesar suggests, Ruiz was fond of articulating a seemingly gendered equality by stating, "In my school we don't have male black belts and female black belts, we just have black belts."[61] However, the disproportion of male to female practitioners featured in *The Super Weapon* suggests that the alliance of schools, styles, and individuals who operated within Van Clief's sphere were still dominated by a kind of male chauvinism. As Cesar's own description suggested, martial arts in the 1970s was committed to "creating men." Within Cesar's quote is a reminder that the martial arts kata and kumite was and is a process of habituated behavior—a form of twice-behaved or restored behavior that produces its own particular citationality and hence performativity. My calling attention to the gendered performative dynamics of a male-dominated community complicates and troubles individuals such as Van Clief, Powell, Duncan, and many other figures that made up the martial arts landscape. As I have suggested, racial kinesthesia makes visible how bodies and communities are constructed through

---

60. Scarpelli and Sotos, *Super Weapon* (1976).
61. Scarpelli and Sotos, *Super Weapon* (1976).

movement. It suggests a form of intersectionality that embodies the contradictory nature of Afro Asian performance as a strategy for liberation that simultaneously failed to recognize its own shortcomings to speak to a more diverse gendered environment.

Van Clief's competing in spaces such as Madison Square Garden put him in contact with individuals such as Bruce Lee, with whom he sparred approximately a dozen times behind closed doors since Lee, as a kung fu practitioner, did not compete in the tournaments. In these transcultural kinesthetic moments of contact, Van Clief was able to exchange the knowledge of martial arts and further confirm that his identity was linked and hence his survival was connected to an Asian diaspora. According to Van Clief, Lee dubbed him the "Black Dragon" and encouraged him to consider a career in the Hong Kong kung fu film industry. Subsequently, Van Clief auditioned for a casting call in 1973 and signed a five-picture deal with the Hong Kong–based film production company, Yangtze Films. Ironically, this was the same year that Lee passed away, and the same year that Lee's magnum opus, *Enter the Dragon*, was released.

At the time, Hong Kong was a colonized territory of the waning British empire, propped up by the continued US struggle for control of the Pacific. In the middle of a burgeoning blaxploitation film epoch that would soon be supplanted by the "summer blockbuster" genre of 1975,[62] Van Clief found himself flashing back to a Vietnam scenario in which Afro Asian masculinity traversed the meandering transnational lines that connected the metropolises of Hong Kong, New York, London, and Los Angeles that fulfilled the desire for martial arts, sex, and race on the screen. Yet, this experience provided Van Clief access to labor markets in which he could perform iterations of Black heroism. As Van Clief remarks:

> In the United States the Black guys were always the bad guys. The pimps, you know it was during that exploitation kind of period, . . . the drug dealer. . . . I wanted to be a kung fu star . . . [and] they needed a Black hero, finally. . . . In Hong Kong, even though you're hagwei, if they respected your work or if you could do your thing, you were very well respected in Hong Kong. I didn't ever feel any of the stuff that I felt in America. That's why I stayed there for ten years. I was never called a nigger or any of that kind of stuff, but *hagwei* is Black ghost, you know?[63]

---

62. Novotny, *Blaxploitation Films of the 1970s: Blackness and Genre*.
63. Burr and Chen, *Black Kung Fu Experience* (2013).

The series of films Yangtze Films produced capitalized on Van Clief's cachet as a known martial artist and the virtuosity of his dynamic spinning heel back kicks. His fighting record legitimized him as an actual martial artist who had developed a following of students and Hollywood clients. Many of the directors and fight choreographers that were producing material for Yangtze Films were practicing martial artists who were already familiar with Van Clief through competitions and *Black Belt*. In blaxploitation fashion, Yangtze was able to shoot fight scenes that could then be reedited and serialized to produce a series of films that featured Van Clief as the "The Black Dragon," a generalized and almost stereotyped moniker for a Black super hero who was hypermasculinized and capable of taking and giving beating after beating.

Still, Van Clief defined his own terms. In many of the scenes, Van Clief appeared wearing his Chinese Goju Ryu emblem on a t-shirt as he performed flying kicks through the air or fought with the local drug dealers that he and his partners were trying to take down. The films that Van Clief made included titles such as *Xian Nan Yang* (1974), which was translated into *The Black Dragon* when repackaged for US audiences, *Bamboo Trap* (1975), *The Black Dragon Revenges the Death of Bruce Lee* (1975), *Way of the Black Dragon* (1979), *Enter Another Dragon* (1981), and *Fight to the Death* (1983). Sometimes these films provided metacommentary on race, Blackness, and sexuality. In *The Black Dragon Revenges the Death of Bruce Lee*, Van Clief played a detective hired to investigate the death of Bruce Lee. His investigation takes him into the underworld of organized crime and into the backstage of a Peking Opera performer's dressing room. In one particular scene Van Clief pays a visit to the dressing room of a Peking Opera actress and engages in banter with another actress as he waits for the return of his guest. On cue, an actress dressed in a light blue Ming Dynasty style Peking Opera costume turns to face Van Clief. However, instead of her face being painted white (as is the tradition in Peking Opera) her face appears to be browned to almost comical effect. There is a moment of incoherence and even absurdity of her appearance next to Van Clief who is dressed in a suit and tie, and sports his signature afro with a bouquet of flowers in hand. Van Clief reaches out and strokes the actress's face, inquiring, "Shoe polish?" The actress smiles and replies in a dubbed British Hong Kong accent, "No, special Chinese makeup." She then reaches and touches Van Clief's face to see if his color will rub off inquiring, "This makeup?" Van Clief smiles, "No, baby. It's the real shit." Such commentary on race and sexuality, especially within the martial arts film genre of blaxploitation and Hong Kong martial arts filmography would converge when Van Clief was hired as a stuntman, choreographer, and advisor on the martial arts parody, Berry Gordy's *The Last Dragon*. While I provide a close reading of Afro Asian performance in martial arts filmography in Chapter 3, I want to now turn my attention to another significant iteration of rasanblaj and the transcultural Third World borrowings of racial kinesthesia.

Fighting in the West: Lineages, Nationalisms, and Black Karate Federations

> I'm not saying there's anything wrong with being a fan of Jackie Chan, but we should also know about the African American superstars that are out there who didn't get as much media.
> —Dennis Brown, *Urban Dragons*[64]

This chapter has rehearsed a politics of transcultural kinesthesia, a process wherein Black men engaged in a form of crossbordering pedagogies and practices by grounding themselves in Asian martial arts. As suggested, this resulted in a theater of Afro Asian performance, a form of rasanblaj, of what were previously dismembered subjectivities. By crossbordering and grounding in the cultural template of an Asian cultural property, Black people attempted to refine the kinetics of what were non-Western and non-Eurocentric based artforms for their own purposes to address the dismemberment of their bodies and the political and economic conditions under which they lived in the US. Transgressing cultural borders signaled a form of decolonization and while the goal may have been liberation from the dismembering effects of colonialism, as was the case with Van Clief, practitioners and individuals who participated in the crossbordering and grounding practice of martial arts kinesthetics were also implicated in and inculcated into US military and domestic policing agencies, especially the Vietnam War.

The Southern California–based BKF was organized by two veterans, Steve Muhammad (formerly Steve Sanders) and Donnie Williams, during the late 1960s and early 1970s. The BKF was a response to what Muhammad and other Black karateka perceived as discrimination within racially mixed and predominantly white organizations and tournaments, many of which were controlled by Ed Parker, the white Hawaiian-born Mormon who established himself as the head of American kenpo and helped popularize martial arts through the Long Beach International Karate Championship beginning in August 1964 as well as his inroads into the entertainment industry, which included bodyguarding for Elvis Presley. Presley (an egregious appropriator himself) was

---

64. This DVD is unreleased but was provided to me by Jose Manuel Figueroa, who was most helpful in developing my project.

promoted to black belt and karate master under Parker. Parker notoriously claimed that he innovated the Japanese forms of Nihon karate and Okinawan Ryu that he had learned in Hawaii. In turn, Parker claimed that he dispelled with the formality of certain kata and Oriental traditions and adapted them for "real life" situations. While Parker himself had engaged in a form of cultural appropriation and interpretation by breaking with the Japanese formality of kenpo, Muhammad, who had been a student within Parker's organization, engaged in a form of transcultural transgression when he broke with Parker and began setting up the BKF in predominantly Black communities.

But like the aforementioned Van Clief and Duncan, the BKF's Muhammad and Williams's experience with martial arts was coupled with the US military and the contradictions of negotiating American institutions such as schools, martial arts studios, competitions, and police agencies. Specifically, Muhammad worked for the Los Angeles County Sheriff's Department as a police officer. Like Van Clief, Muhammad's critique of US racism chafed with his own awareness of his doubleness as a Black American in which he operated as an agent of the state (foreign and domestic) and simultaneously converted to Islam and joined the NOI.

Muhammad was born in Topeka, Kansas, in 1944, ten years prior to the *Brown* v. *Board of Education* ruling. He then attended Kansas State University and went into the Marine Corps as a member of the Pathfinders.[65] Muhammad's first exposure to Asian martial arts would not come until he was thirteen when he found a job in a Chinese restaurant in his hometown of Topeka, Kansas. Despite his being under the required age to work, the thirteen-year-old convinced the restaurant's owner to hire him doing whatever was needed to be done: dishwasher, mop the floor, and clean the walls. Muhammad states:

> I actually worked there for five years washing dishes and doing whatever I had to do. After about a month, I came early one day and they were doing martial arts. We had no idea what martial arts were back then, this was in 1953. It didn't exist as far as we knew about it; the word karate didn't exist to us. There was judo, but not karate. So when I saw them doing, what I know is taichi [*sic*] now, I looked at them for about a week. I'd go in every morning and watch them through a fence. Finally, one day I asked if I could do what they were doing. And they said, yes. So I took taichi for about five years. After that I went to Okinawa after I'd gotten into the Marine Corps and I

---

65. Muhammad and Williams, *BKF Kenpo: History and Advanced Strategic Principles*, 9. Pathfinders were special forces in Vietnam who set up drop zones, conducted sling load operations, and provided air traffic control and navigational assistance to rotary-wing and fixed-wing airborne operations.

took a science that is called Goju. I didn't get a good base or foundation even though I got a brown belt I wasn't even a good white belt because I'd go in the field for three or four months and maybe train two weeks at a time.[66]

Muhammad's encounter with *taijiquan* at the Chinese family–owned restaurant began one year prior to the landmark supreme court decision to formally "desegregate" US public institutions. This took place twelve years prior to the 1965 Immigration Act.[67] Within the empire's machinations of racial hierarchy and division, moments of transcultural contact through performance and rehearsal sites carried on unabated, and Muhammad's transcultural introduction to martial arts practice took place well before the martial arts explosion in US cinema. The roots of the Chinese family are unknown. Yet one can infer that they embraced Muhammad as a student. The Afro Asian encounter in the middle of 1950s Cold War Kansas further spurred Muhammad upon his "warrior's path." The path resulted from a combination of transcultural kinesthetic encounters, as in the Chinese restaurant in Kansas and the subsequent pursuit of American kenpo in Los Angeles.

When Muhammad returned from his tour in Vietnam, he continued to study martial arts. This led to his training twice a week in Los Angeles under Parker[68] until he was called up for another tour of duty in Vietnam. Muhammad suggests that fighting in Vietnam "gave him discipline and a first-hand look at the reality and brutal effectiveness of combat."[69] Upon discharge from the Marine Corps in 1963, Muhammad immersed himself in the study of Ed Parker's kenpo system (American karate), and received a first-degree black belt under Parker's instructors, Dan Inosanto[70] and Chuck Sullivan.

---

66. To listen to this interview, see Pedro Bennett's interview with Sijo Steve Muhammad located on YouTube at https://www.youtube.com/watch?v=VwjSNuham8k. To see more about Pedro Bennett's history and pedigree visit http://www.kempojujitsu.us/about-us/.

67. The Immigration and Nationality Act of 1965 represents a significant watershed moment in Asian American history. Reversing decades of systematic exclusion and restrictive immigration policies, the act resulted in unprecedented numbers of immigrants from Asia, Mexico, Latin America, and other non-Western nations entering the US. In the process, these new arrivals, particularly those from Asia, transformed the demographic, economic, and cultural characteristics of many urban areas, the larger Asian American community, and mainstream American society, in general.

68. The late Ed Parker was considered the "Father" of American kenpo. Using this term is problematic as it immediately elevates the white subject to the level of authority and a number of popular sources on American kenpo identify Parker as a practicing Mormon in the Church of Jesus Christ of Latter Day Saints. Born into the Mormon Church in 1931 and graduating from Brigham Young University in 1954, Parker is often framed as a "Native Hawaiian" in popular discourses.

69. Muhammad and Williams, *BKF Kenpo: History and Advanced Strategic Principles*, 10.

70. Inosanto, who is Filipino American, is well known as being Bruce Lee's protégé in the jeet kune do system.

However, in old photos and videos of Muhammad fighting and practicing he was often the only Black. His encounter with another Black tournament fighter, Donnie Williams, provided him with a feeling of community. Williams's biography again recalls the influence of the military as a US cultural institution. Born in 1947 in Savannah, Georgia, Williams had his initial exposure to *shotokan* karate in Texas. His subsequent four-year tour in the Navy took him to Korea, where he trained in taekwondo. Upon returning to the US, he continued to train in taekwondo in California under master Byong Yu[71] and gained a reputation within the California tournament fighting system. It was through competitions that he would meet Steve Muhammad and eventually form the BKF.[72]

The creation of the BKF was as much an entrepreneurial endeavor as it was another instance of "Black brothers grounding together" in an attempt to reconcile being both Black and American.[73] Tournaments, dojos, community centers, and public parks were sites of contact that summoned bodies into practice, competition, and real-world applications of martial arts techniques. Yet, these alliances were somewhat tenuous and not all Black karateka and/or martial arts practitioners were allied through a particular political ideology. Their connections were transcultural in that they shared a familiarity based on common struggle of Black experience, Black masculinity in particular, but did not always result in a monolithic and comprehensive whole.

Like Powell's Sanuces Ryu and Van Clief's Chinese Goju Ryu, the BKF also created their own semiotic system through symbolic self-representation. The patches worn by BKF members (Figure 1.2) were indicative of the kind of visual representation the organization used to create community and identify members.

Red for the blood, Black for the people, and green for the land—the Pan-African colors were meant to embody the struggle for autonomy of people within the African Diaspora throughout the world. Furthermore, it is through the yellow fist that an Afro Asian performative aesthetic is devised with layered meanings of juncture and solidarity. The fist painted yellow is doubled in its meaning. It is at once emblematic of Asia as a "yellow people" within the racial logic of black, brown, and red people's solidarity (people of COLOR writ large). Yellow can also be representative of the gold, the natural resources of Africa, as seen in the African National Congress flag and the flag of Ethiopia. The clenched fist with kenpo and karate written on either side of an ascending

---

71. For a more in-depth description on the Yu, see the website www.yusmartialarts.com.
72. Muhammad and Williams, *BKF Kenpo: History and Advanced Strategic Principles*, 13.
73. See Cornel West's essay, "The Emergence of Modern Racism: The First Stage," in the 2000 edition of *The Cornel West Reader*.

FIGURE 1.2. The closed yellow fist with black, green, and read markings is an example of one of the BKF patches that symbolized a form of Black cultural nationalism through the colors of the African Liberation movement

cobra is yet another transcultural marker, as kenpo translates as fist law and karate translates as way of the empty hand/fist. Lastly, the clenched fist became a symbol for international revolutionary struggles within varying Black Power movements.

The BKF also created training manuals such as *BKF Kenpo: History* and *Advanced Strategic Principles* (2002) (see Figure 1.3) and *Championship Kenpo* (1983) (see Figure 1.4), with covers that featured the cofounders, Williams and Muhammad.

As seen on the cover of the books in Figure 1.3 and Figure 1.4, Muhammad and Williams employed the kinesthetics of their style of kenpo for the purposes of sartorial presentation and further built a particular discourse around their interpretation of kenpo. In *BKF Kenpo* (Figure 1.3), Williams in particular seems to gesture toward Black liberation theory by donning a red, yellow, and green kufi (an irony since he is a born-again Christian). In *Championship Kenpo* (Figure 1.4), Steve Muhammad was still Steve Sanders, but both men are

FIGURE 1.3. *BKF Kenpo* book cover

FIGURE 1.4. *Championship Kenpo* book cover

framed as both fighters and masters of the art of kenpo. To see a person in a martial arts uniform already primes the practitioner for a particular form of movement and it telegraphs to the observer that the other is prepared to move in a particular manner. Adorning the body with clothing, patches, emblems, and weapons/tools in this particular manner is politically charged, and the ornamentation was a process of creating an Afro Asian performative aesthetic.

Unlike the Sanuces system, which emphasized the practice of martial arts as purely a form of self-defense, tournament fighting was an important component of American kenpo and the BKF system. Similar to the current popularity and advertising of MMA sports performance events, full-contact and no-contact fighting of the BKF and West coast karate tournaments more broadly, created a sense of personal identity. The success of particular schools and organizations became directly linked to the success of individual fighters and fighting teams.

Like the tournaments, competitions, and expositions in New York's Madison Square Garden, the Long Beach International Karate Championship began in 1964 at the Long Beach Municipal Auditorium. The 1964 event helped launch Bruce Lee's career when he demonstrated his signature two finger push-up, one-inch punch, and challenged everyone to attempt to block his punch. The event provided a forum for practitioners to display and promote the lineage of a particular teacher and/or style by performing the stylistics within a competition or combat situation.

For the BKF fighters, tournament fighting style was informed by Muhammad's embodied knowledge and real-world understanding of violent confrontation. As BKF members contend:

> Muhammad, as a tournament competitor and teacher, believed that his art was designed for self-defense purposes first. In the asphalt battlefields of South Central Los Angeles through the turbulent 1960s, the techniques were frequently put to the test in real-life situations. This became the catalyst for the need to develop a realistic approach to kenpo. It forced the art to move beyond theory and to application.[74]

Tournament fighting styles became an expression of the lived experiences of Blackness. Moving beyond theory to application required an understanding of what has been a contradictory reality for African Americans. The threshold to direct violence at Black Americans has been far lower than any other ethnic group or racial category. Black people can be killed for simply walking, talking, breathing—existing. Members of the BKF who had served in the armed forces understood the combat of the theater of war and the theater of violence in the US. Martial arts brought together a kinesthetic awareness of one's relationship to the other bodies in the environment, and this awareness meant the difference between life and death. In a potentially violent situation, understanding how to control one's breath, posture, and the perception of one's skin is a part of the kinesthetic training that the martial arts offered African Americans.

White fury directed at the Black body was contextualized in BKF's narrative of the 1960s as a series of assaults on the struggle for Black autonomy. BKF members acknowledged these connections in narrating the history specific to their own form of karate practice:

> These events of the past should not be lost to current practitioners of BKF Kenpo because when several black men met in Los Angeles to form an organization in 1969, the cause for which they fought was much in the spirit of the times. As athletes, the founders of the BKF experienced racism in the martial arts and wanted to gain a stronger and more unified voice in

---

74. Muhammad and Williams, *BKF Kenpo: History and Advanced Strategic Principles*, 47.

sport karate events.... There were times when tournament promoters would intentionally match black competitors against each other and employ other tactics to eliminate black participation. Finally, these pioneering young men who dared to speak up were ostracized and labeled "militants" in the hopes of further discouraging their participation in the martial arts. All of this would continue unabated until the arrival of the Black Karate Federation.[75]

The emergence of the BKF was a critical response to the fact that racism was fundamentally imbedded into the institutions that make up the American cultural schematic. In so doing, new epistemes emerged through bodily disciplines, based on Muhammad's experience. Rehearsing new ways of movement yielded the new corporeal stylistics of Muhammad's BKF fighters, and in turn, a "New Negro" form of twentieth-century martial art emerged as both self-defense and sport combat or *kumite* (tournament fighting):

> Fighters incorporated Mr. Muhammad's signature use of timing, broken rhythm, speed and techniques, which allowed them to engage in each and every competition with intensity as if it were a life-or-death confrontation. Often times, when their opponent would be going for points or swinging wildly—without control or technique in full-contact fighting—BKF kenpo students showed that they were technicians who could execute moves with explosive power, speed, and precisions. This is because their art was designed for street application and not tournaments.[76]

The breaking of timing within fighting combinations and katas (forms) recalls the improvisational innovations of the Black jazz musicians such as John Coltrane, Thelonius Monk, Archie Shepp, Miles Davis, Max Roach—and of course the new literary trajectory of the Black Arts Movement (BAM) embodied in the poetic words of Amiri Baraka. To that extent, BKF were grounding and doing a form of repair that was in fact in conversation with and part of the broader BAM or even Baraka's Black Arts Revolutionary Theater (BART).

As scholar Maryam Aziz has observed, "To talk about these arts as cultural formations will challenge us to look in new places for the evidence of the Black Arts Movements' impacts. Furthermore, it will push Black art scholars to reconceptualize what they view as artistic production."[77] Furthermore, the

---

75. Muhammad and Williams, *BKF Kenpo: History and Advanced Strategic Principles*, 46.
76. Muhammad and Williams, *BKF Kenpo: History and Advanced Strategic Principles*, 41, 42.
77. See Maryam Aziz's essay, "Our Fist is Black: Martial Arts, Black Arts, and Black Power in the 1960s and 1970s," in the online journal titled *Kung Fu Tea*, an online journal dedicated to the discussion of Chinese Martial Studies: https://chinesemartialstudies.com.

new forms of broken movements and broken timing anticipated the changing combinations of breakdancing that emerged in hip-hop stylistics. It would be more than safe to say that the first-generation students of the BKF were or would become the progenitors of the hip-hop generation in the 1970s and 1980s. Again, such innovations in Black cultural expressions would not have been possible if it had not been for the crossbordering and Third World smuggling between Black cultural workers and Asian cultural art forms and practitioners.

Muhammad suggests that many predominantly white martial arts studios deliberately sought to marginalize Black martial artists and eliminate Black studios that they perceived to be competition, regardless of their ability or adherence to orthodoxy. As the BKF suggests, the willingness to keep traditions alive in the US by practitioners who had trained in Asia was not embraced. This was the case with one of the senior founding members of the organization, William Short. BKF members observe:

> As an imposing six-foot, four-inches and two-hundred and seventy-eight pounds, Willie Short became one of the first African-Americans to earn a black belt in shotokan karate overseas, which he did in 1953. Short studied shotokan with Kobayashi sensei while stationed in the Air Force at Tachikawa, AFB, Japan. Upon returning to the United States, Short opened the Kobayashi School of Karate at 8711 South Western Avenue. According to Brian Breye (Short's senior belt), Short was not embraced by the white martial arts community. Many schools that had white owners did not even accept Black students at the time. However, Short, who spoke fluent Japanese, was well-known to the Japanese community. They invited him to perform in Little Tokyo during their Nisei Week Festival in the summer of 1960.[78]

Short was fluent in Japanese and embraced by the Nisei community of Los Angeles. Meanwhile, Parker did not speak Japanese, was not a US veteran, and had not been formally ranked under a Japanese system such as shotokan karate which was one of the main karate ryu ha (styles) that emerged to make up the Japan Karate Association and the World Karate Federation. These two organizations were the sanctioning entities of the karate world. Yet Parker was, by and large, granted authority to speak on behalf of East Asian martial arts in the US.

A further biography on Short is needed, but what is clear was the fact that he had engaged in crossbordering pedagogies and had been able to embrace

---

78. Muhammad and Williams, *BKF Kenpo: History and Advanced Strategic Principles*, 49.

the East Asian philosophy of martial arts, not for the purposes of becoming "Asian" or for domination but to ground with Black brothers for liberation. However, again, as I have articulated, this crossbordering was also bound up in the US military and policing agencies, which would suggest that even in these efforts Black masculinity could not fully reconcile the doubleness of being both insider and outsider within the marginalizing and alienating structures of US racism. And yet double-consciousness was a Third World vision for restoring of Black people—to make them whole again through the repetition of the acts, gestures, and routines of karate.

For many in the BKF and the Black martial arts community of Los Angeles, Short was an elder statesman and was twenty years senior to Steve Muhammad, who at that time was still known as Steve Sanders. Short influenced not only Muhammad's trajectory and development as a karateka but also Muhammad's understanding of pan-Africanism and Black cultural nationalist philosophy embodied in the practice of martial arts. Short has been described as a soft-spoken individual who had majored in African American history and made two trips to Ghana, Africa (1970 and 1973). He returned to the US and began to wear traditional Afrocentric garb at martial arts demonstrations.[79]

Short's transpacific journey is further embodied in Muhammad's accounts of the World War II veteran who introduced many of the predecessors of the BKF to Japanese masters such as Mas Oyama, Morihei Ueshiba, and Gogen Yamaguchi when he accompanied Short on a six-week trip to Japan in 1969. In conjunction with the martial arts, Short also introduced Muhammad to the philosophy of Black nationalism and taught him about Malcolm X, Elijah Muhammad, bean pie, and whiting fish. He was a diverse and international figure whose evolving consciousness regarding his African heritage took place in conversation with his staunch devotion to Japanese cultural templates of shotokan karate. Short made the connections within a broader constellation of multiple diasporas in which he saw beyond the confines of styles and systems. He thereby expanded the idea of solidarity among African Americans in

---

79. Short's, and hence Muhammad's, attraction to Black cultural nationalism may have also come from the influence of Dr. Maulana Karenga, a close friend of Short's who was also the creator of the US Organization, a Black cultural nationalist organization that emerged in the mid-1960s. See Scot Brown's *Fighting for US: Maulana Karenga, the US Organization, and Black Cultural Nationalism* (New York: NYU Press, 2005). The US Organization cultivated and developed its own self-defense component known as the Simba Wachanga (young lions), who practiced a repertoire called *Yangumi* (the way of the fist). It would be safe to argue that Yangumi would have been the Simba's reinterpretation of Japanese karate. Furthermore, like Muhammad, many of the US Organization's members of the Simba were also former US soldiers who had been stationed in Vietnam.

Los Angeles and attempted to extend his knowledge to a younger generation through the embrace of martial arts, regardless of style.[80]

Much like Van Clief, who continued to move back and forth between the US and Asia after his experience with Vietnam, Muhammad's exposure to Short's relationship with Japan meant that he was able to expose his mentees to the progenitors of Kyokoshin Karate, aikido, and Goju Ryu Karate. Tournaments were sites where race, space, and place converged to shape the identity of the BKF, as were the numerous locations in which the BKF practiced.

Classes were initially held on Saturdays at Van Ness Park.[81] The classes attracted dozens of other martial artists, and soon a core group emerged calling themselves the Magnificent Seven after Japanese film director Akira Kurosawa's film *Seven Samurai* (1954). The enthusiasm eventually led to several dojo locations being acquired throughout the existence of the BKF.

In addition to the City Public Parks, the Sheenway Community Center,[82] a nonprofit foundation designed to develop an indigenous teaching and learning center with a concentrated focus on early childhood development and total education, played a prominent role in developing the urban landscape of the southern Los Angeles area. Sheenway provided the home for the BKF from 1970 to 1971, and if the windows did not fog up during a workout, it was not considered a workout. Small community-based organizations such as Sheenway insured that children and adults had spaces in which to commune and develop themselves.

The BKF made efforts toward community organizing through transcultural kinesthesia that included the repertoire of kenpo as well as Muhammad's and Williams's military experience. As the BKF members contended, these two forms of discipline were synthesized as performance strategies during exhibitions:

> In all of the BKF schools, particularly in the early years, the military style discipline and training that the students received—combined with inner city determination and tough street smarts—forged a powerful statement of unity. In the group's first appearance, the Lima Lama tournament in 1971, 150 students walked into the event in single file, with military precision and all

---

80. Muhammad and Williams, *BKF Kenpo: History and Advanced Strategic Principles*, 50.

81. For more on the Van Ness Parks in South Los Angeles, see: http://www.laparks.org/dos/reccenter/facility/vanNessRC.htm.

82. Named after Herbert A. Sheen, MD, the Sheenway Center is a nonprofit foundation that developed an indigenous teaching and learning center with a concentrated focus on early childhood development and total education. For thirty-eight years, Sheenway provided a golden learning environment for toddlers through kindergarten, evolving into subsequent grades through high school, http://www.sheenwayschools.org/.

carrying ... briefcases. Each briefcase contained a fighter's "armor," which was their starched and folded karate gi.[83]

At the 1971 tournament, the BKF youth marched with discipline, order, and control over their bodies, all of which conveyed a message of severity. These performances can be read as counternarrative and counterhegemonic. Corporeal disciplining of the body through martial arts tapped into a similar kind of social-kinetic energy present in gang organizations, especially amongst historically marginalized groups who were most vulnerable to the allure that gang culture presents. As taijiquan practitioner and Hong Kong actor, Stephen Berwick suggests, "Martial arts have a very clear cut [sic] sense of family and that family structure can supplant that structure that young people are finding in gangs. . . . It can appeal to different groups who need to find ways to not only protect themselves, but to find pride within themselves within the groups that they are a part of."[84] The borrowing and smuggling of the kinesthetics of an Asian cultural form offered possibilities for Black practitioners and communities to inhabit a new epistemological framework in which martial arts was a self-expression centered around a defined structure that promoted internal strength, self-respect, and physical skill as well as a strong sense of mutual respect between the individual and the martial arts community.

Combined, Van Clief, Powell, Muhammad, and Williams all embodied varying narratives of racial kinesthesia through Afro Asian performance of martial arts in dojo spaces, film, clubs, and tournaments during the twentieth and into the twenty-first century. Yet each one had to negotiate the perils of white supremacy in their own particular way that never fully resolved the riddle of double-consciousness. Racial kinesthesia and, as discussed in this chapter, transcultural kinesthesia created a third space that allowed modicums of entrepreneurial enterprise while simultaneously providing a certain level of emotional sustenance. However, as will become evident in the next chapter on the Black Panther Party's martial arts program, it is important to consider the political calculations that Black martial arts practitioners have made in terms of how they have opted to perform their identities.

---

83. Muhammad and Williams, *BKF Kenpo: History and Advanced Strategic Principles*, 67.
84. Stephen Berwick as quoted in the unreleased documentary film, *Urban Dragons* (2009), directed by Kamau Hunter.

CHAPTER 2

Black Panther Martial Art

Enter the Black Panthers

"East Oakland, California is not a nice place to visit and you wouldn't want to live there," wrote Jim Hoffman in his article "Reading, Writing, and Fair Fighting in the Oakland Ghetto," featured in the August 1975 edition of *Black Belt* magazine.[1] "Most of what is bad about America is worse in East Oakland and most of what is good about America isn't there at all," continued Hoffman as he set the stage for his brief description of the martial arts program located in the Oakland Community Learning Center (OCLC), which was part of the Oakland Community School (OCS). Founded by the Black Panther Party for Self Defense in 1971, the OCS was a radical model for alternative K–6 public education. The OCLC was the afterschool community center that was attached to and housed in the OCS, located at 8501 East 14th Street (now International Blvd.) in the Samuel Napier Inter-Communal Youth Institute, a building that the Party purchased in 1973. Hoffman went on to state, "Unlike traditional public schools where 'discipline' means a set of rules, punishments and rewards that are imposed by teachers and authority figures, the OCS/OCLC emphasize *internal* discipline."[2] By the time that Hoffman's article was

---

1. Hoffman, "Reading, Writing, and Fair Fighting in the Oakland Ghetto," 40.
2. Hoffman, "Reading, Writing, and Fair Fighting in the Oakland Ghetto," 41.

FIGURE 2.1. Steve McCutchen with martial arts students from the Oakland Community Learning Center

published, two years had elapsed since the passing of Bruce Lee. Lee's influence on the pedagogy of the OCS/OCLC was articulated by Ericka Huggins, then-director of the OCS and member of the inner circle of the Party: "All the children admire Bruce Lee.... We want to show them that what went into Bruce Lee was a lot of hard, hard, work, and that every human being needs internal discipline."[3] Similar to Lee's anticolonial performances in his films, the internal discipline of the Party's martial arts program was one that attempted to foster a revolutionary praxis through what I refer to as communal kinesthesia in an attempt to bring about political change.

Similar to the discussion on transcultural kinesthesia, this chapter is an interdisciplinary ethnographic intervention into the politics of Black and

---

3. Huggins's husband John Huggins, along with his comrade Bunchy Carter, had been murdered in a confrontation with members of the US Organization in conjunction with the FBI on the campus of UCLA in 1969.

Asian cultural collaborations that coalesced through the revolutionary philosophy of the Black Panther Party for Self-Defense (1966 to 1982) and the practice of Asian martial arts for the purposes of organization, mobilization, and politicization. To make this intervention, I draw on a number of sources including interviews, archives, and ethnographic films. As I have already suggested throughout this project, the movements of Black Americans out of the agricultural South and into the industrial North created a new urban cultural geography that hastened creative, and at times, radical understandings of Black cultural expression and political power. Black Panther Party cofounder and primary theoretician Huey P. Newton and his family left Louisiana in 1945 and relocated to California, where they worked in the defense industry. While the wartime boom provided survivable wages, such opportunities vanished during the post–World War II era as the dominant white chamber of commerce, local politicians, private industry, and Oakland Police force harassed and murdered Black Americans. If, as theorist Frank Wilderson has suggested, the ontological position that structures the experiences of Black people within the Western epistemological framework of modernity is "gratuitous violence,"[4] then, as Frantz Fanon suggested, the prescriptive therapy to such violence is revolution. The Black Panther Party emerged as a direct response to gratuitous violence and while the images of armed Panthers confronting the police are perhaps the most dominant images in the popular imaginary, the Party's numerous community survival programs were the revolutionary praxis that sustained the Party and members of the broader community that needed respite from the constancy of white supremacist terrorism.[5]

The martial arts program at the OCS/OCLC was one of such community survival programs. By engaging in and mastering the repeated acts, gestures, and routines of Asian martial arts, specifically the Korean art form of taekwondo (way of hands and feet) and the aforementioned Bruce Lee's amalgamated practice of jeet kune do (way of the intercepting fist or JKD), I argue that the Party's martial arts program was a form of community building through kinesthesia or what I refer to as communal kinesthesia that sought to achieve three objectives: first, to mobilize, organize, and politicize; second, to publicize the Party and sustain the OCS/OCLC community; and third, martial arts provided a pedagogical platform for members of the Party and for the

---

4. See Wilderson's discussion on gratuitous violence and Black (non)ontology in *Red, White & Black: Cinema and the Structure of U. S. Antagonisms*. Specifically, I am referring to pages 17 and 18 in which he suggests that modernity is marked by the emergence of a race of people whose state of being—Blackness—is an ontological condition in which no transgression has to be made in order to be socially dead in relationship to the rest of the world.

5. Newton and Blake, *Revolutionary Suicide*, 117.

students of the OCS/OCLC to engage in self-care through recreation and well-being. Again, to recall Walter Rodney, the practice at the OCS/OCLC was a form of "grounding together"[6] in order to rehearse the political philosophy of the Party that in turn rendered the art of Korean taekwondo as a praxis of revolutionary energy manifested in the movement practice of Black flesh. Again, drawing on Jacqui Alexander's discussion of "crossbordering pedagogies,"[7] this chapter also makes visible the conjunction of Asian martial arts and Black political practice that resulted in freedom dreams for Third World peoples who formed new communities through kinetic practices.

The martial arts program at the OCS/OCLC had an explicit political agenda, which was to organize, mobilize, and politicize Black youth and adults around the political philosophy that Party founder, Huey P. Newton, referred to as "revolutionary intercommunalism," which he articulated in speeches and writings.[8] While the Party first began in 1966 as a Black nationalist organization, it went through a series of rapid ideological transformations engaging Continental philosophy including Plato, Hegel, Nietzche, and Marxist-Leninism, as well as revolutionary writings of Frantz Fannon and the Cuban Revolution. But by 1970 the Party saw the struggles of Black communities in the in US as part of a global movement, what Malcolm X had framed as the conditions of the "Global South," with differences and similarities to territories such as Vietnam, China, the Korean Peninsula, and the African continent in the collective struggle for independence from colonialism. By the early 1970s, members of the Party had made multiple trips to Asia, including a historic trip to China in 1972 at the request of the Chinese Premier Chou En Lai, whom Party leaders such as Elaine Brown and Huey Newton met with over the course of a week. While skeptical of the Chinese Communist Party's application of political theory, revolutionary intercommunalism was in conversation with Mao Tse-Tung's teachings and Kim Il Sun's ideology of *juche* "self-reliance,"[9] and was intended to build a decolonized space beyond the

---

6. Rodney, "Groundings with My Brothers," 64.

7. Jacqui Alexander, "Groundings on *Rasanblaj* with M. Jacqui Alexander."

8. See Newton's speech from the Revolutionary People's Constitutional Convention in Philadelphia on September 5, 1970, as well as his *To Die for the People* and *Revolutionary Suicide*, co-written with J. H. Blake.

9. Throughout the 1960s, China and North Vietnam were emerging as part of the global emancipatory space that threatened colonialism. When the Party linked this struggle in Asia with white supremacist capitalism through meetings with the Democratic People's Republic of Korea (DPRK) and China, it brought the emancipation of Black people in the US into the international folds of global struggle. Despite the formal US policy forbidding its citizens from traveling to North Korea, the Party established relationships with DPRK leadership in 1969.

ideological concept of the nation-state and the corporation that had failed to provide the most basic elements for human survival.

According to Newton, nation-states seemingly no longer existed because global capitalism had, through the US empire in particular, reduced the world to a collection of communities that lack control over their local conditions and, at most, could only become semiautonomous within the larger rubric of imperialism.[10] Revolutionary intercommunalism would be the "time when the people seize the means of production and distribute the wealth and the technology in an egalitarian way to the many communities of the world."[11] Imperfect as it was, OCS/OCLC was a practice of "community control" (local people controlling the politics, economy, and culture within their immediate community), and the martial arts program at the OCS/OCLC was one example of revolutionary intercommunal practice that provided an opportunity to seize control of local state resources.

Through communal kinesthesia, Asian political philosophy of the DPRK[12] and the People's Republic of China filtered into the OCS/OCLC community through martial arts practiced by Black bodies.[13] The impact was that martial arts practice at OCS/OCLC provided new epistemological and ontological frameworks through which to imagine and then practice a Black subjectivity wherein the most marginalized of society organized and mobilized themselves as bodies with agency, as Revolutionaries—as *black dragons*.

However, communal kinesthesia not only organized and politicized members into the Party, but by participating in local and regional martial arts tournaments and demonstrations, communal kinesthesia functioned as a performative strategy that enabled the Party to have a greater visible presence beyond the immediate confines of OCS/OCLC. As Amy Abugo Ongiri has observed in her work on the Party's performativity in her book *Spectacular Blackness*, "The Panther's successes would lie more in the influence they wielded in the arena of popular culture than in military culture," and

---

10. Vasquez, "Intercommunalism: The Late Theorizations of Huey P. Newton, 'Chief Theoretician' of the Black Panther Party," *Viewpoint Magazine,* June 11, 2018. https://viewpointmag.com/2018/06/11/intercommunalism-the-late-theorizations-of-huey-p-newton-chief-theoretician-of-the-black-panther-party/.

11. Newton, *The Huey P. Newton Reader*, 170.

12. While McCutchen would not begin formal martial arts training until he relocated from Baltimore to Oakland, he was exposed to Eastern political philosophy through the Party's compulsory Political Education (PE) classes. PE classes incorporated the teachings of Kim Il Sun, the founder of the DPRK.

13. Party members such as Elaine Brown, Cathleen Cleaver, and Eldridge Cleaver traveled to the DPRK in 1969 and 1970. In the spring of 1971, Elaine Brown, Masai Hewitt, Emory Douglas, Huey P. Newton, and members from the Party from across the US made a journey to China at the request of Premier Chou En Lai.

thus the Panthers "self-consciously presented individuals and images whose revolutionary representation would provoke the possibility of radical social change by creating an identification between the visual representation and the viewer."[14] The Black Panther Intercommunal News Service, which produced the Party newspaper, published articles about the martial arts program's performance at tournaments and demonstrations. Classes at the OCS/OCLC provided an opportunity for the community to see what kind of work, instruction, and education the Party provided to the community, much of which was initially free for youth participants. As Ongiri suggests, these tactics were significant because the actual number of Black Americans who joined civil rights and Black Power organizations as rank-and-file members was scarce. Groups such as the Party relied on artistic and cultural production for viability. As former Black Panther Party member William Calhoun observed, "During the entire Civil Rights episode, there probably was never more than ten percent of the Black population involved in any of it at any given time."[15] By 1974 formal Party membership had contracted to about one hundred members, almost all of whom were located within the Oakland Chapter as many of the chapters had been shut down and members had either left or had been purged. Beginning in 1966 and throughout its evolution, the Party was able to maintain visibility and support through varying forms of performance strategies such as the printing and circulation of the Party newspaper, media engagements, and press conferences with the charismatic leader Huey P. Newton; sartorial presentation such as berets and leather jackets; musical concerts; and community survival programs run through the OCS/OCLC, which by 1974, had become the primary focus of the Party.

Lastly, and perhaps most importantly, communal kinesthesia was a pedagogical platform for teaching children how to move and organize their bodies for the purposes of health and wellness, confidence, and self-defense. The community center also provided physical education and community outreach to adults and teenagers. With Bruce Lee or Kareem Abdul-Jabbar as popular iconographs of inspiration, the children and adults who participated in the martial arts program were able to reinvent themselves in the image of anticolonial heroes who could create their own counternarratives. Lee's style of jeet kune do admittedly borrowed from Black boxers such as Muhammad Ali, and hence, Lee's own Asian masculinity was marked with a sense of Afro

---

14. Ongiri, *Spectacular Blackness: The Cultural Politics of the Black Power Movement and the Search for a Black Aesthetic*, 35.

15. Interview with Nishat Kurwa, Studio 360, "The Black Panthers House Funk Band," WNYC. January 31, 2014.

Asian performativity that functioned as anticolonial choreography and was on display when his character Tang Lung (Lee) defeated the white character Colt (Chuck Norris) in the film *Way of the Dragon* (1972). Norris wore white *a la* the Japanese imperialist, Lee was dressed in all black *a la* a Vietnamese guerilla, as he circled and danced around Norris in the style of Muhammad Ali, as he outmaneuvered Norris in what M. T. Kato referred to as the "dance of infinity." Kato likens Lee's kinesthesia to a guerilla tactic and "counteroffensive . . . characterized by creativity of movement, broken rhythm, accuracy, unpredictability, and the overall sense of flexibility. The creativity of movement restores the sense of subjectivity to the 'disadvantaged' one."[16] Hence their fight choreographed Lee's own racial kinesthesia in which the Chinese art form surreptitiously defeated the Western imperialism, represented in the film as coming from both Japan and the US.

Furthermore, aside from physical education the OCS offered a variety of curricula, including math, reading, history, and social studies. An artform such as taekwondo or jeet kune do offered a cost-effective method for providing physical education for the children. Students could conveniently wear street clothes for class and unlike basketball or soccer, all that was required as a training space was the school's auditorium, which also a had a stage for plays and martial arts demonstrations. A member of the core faculty, Steve Steve McCutchen taught math and physical education and led the martial arts program at the OCS/OCLC from 1974 until his departure from the Party in 1979. Party leaders Elaine Brown and Erica Huggins placed a keen emphasis on the pedagogical aspects of the OCS/OCLC and the martial arts program flourished because the kinesthetics of the communal practice was endowed with a conjunction of Asian and Black American political philosophy while simultaneously undergirded by Black feminist practices that took seriously the possibility of an Afro Asian performative masculinity. This is not to suggest that the Party was perfect. Internal fighting in conjunction with the FBI's COINTELPRO and Newton's own paranoia, drug use, and violence forced the Party's demise. Yet, flawed as the Party may have been, it was at the vanguard for pushing for Black political and economic power of which the most obvious and well documented was the Party's voter registration drive that helped elect Oakland's first Black mayor, Lionel Wilson, in 1977. To that end, the Party's martial arts program was part of its portfolio of community survival programs that sought to both corral Oakland residents and heal the community.

---

16. Kato, *From Kung Fu to Hip Hop: Globalization, Revolution, and Popular Culture*, 56, 57.

Steve McCutchen: A Dragon amongst Panthers

On May 2, 1967, Steve McCutchen saw the images of "a delegation of panthers led by Chairman Bobby Seale, Minister of Culture Emory Douglas and first panther member, Bobby Hutton, walk[ing] into the California State Assembly in Sacramento"[17] armed with rifles, shotguns, and side arms. That same year Muhammad Ali had refused to be inducted into the US Army and declared his solidarity with the Vietnamese people. These images helped form McCutchen's purview as the threat of being shipped off to the theater of war loomed, and he saw the results of young Black men returning with the physical and mental wounds of Vietnam as well as the many peers who did not return at all. Originally from Baltimore, Maryland, McCutchen joined the Baltimore chapter of the Party when he graduated high school in the summer of 1968. As chapters continued to open across the US, more young Black women and men found themselves becoming involved in the Party. McCutchen was radicalized by the Panthers' newspaper *The Black Panther: News Service*. As a young Black eighteen-year-old male with near perfect grades who had lettered in track and had been a runner-up in Maryland's state wrestling championships, McCutchen was perfect draft material and categorized as 1-A "available for military service."[18] However, McCutchen had read the Party's Ten Point Platform's Point Six. "We want all Black men to be exempt from military service" and joined the Baltimore Chapter.

In March 1972, the Baltimore Chapter closed, and McCutchen relocated to the Oakland Central Headquarters[19] where he was assigned to work at the Party's printing press. Subsequently, Party members were sent to the college campuses to become involved in student activities as a means of organizing and mobilizing commuter students who came from the greater Bay Area. Some members enrolled at Laney College and other students at Grove Street College, formerly Merritt College. "We were told that we could have a twelve-course limit. When I was looking through the catalogue, one of the courses that was offered was karate. I jumped on that. Master Ken Youn was the primary instructor then. I think there were about a half a dozen of us Party members who enrolled in that same class. Most of them were in the security cadre and some of them had some martial arts background."[20] Merritt College

---

17. McCutchen, *We Were Free for a While: Back-to-Back in the Black Panther Party*, 11.

18. Despite his father being a veteran of World War II who had been stationed in Japan under the US-Japan occupation for four years, McCutchen was resistant to the thought of military service. His father had "literally dragged" him down to the Selective Service office to register for the military draft.

19. McCutchen, *We Were Free for a While: Back-to-Back in the Black Panther Party*, 134.

20. Author interview with Steve McCutchen, May 19, 2016.

was also the campus that Party founders Newton and Seale had attended during the early days of the Party's formation where they studied both political theory and constitutional law.

What emerged from his experience at Laney College was a blueprint for communal kinesthesia, a pedagogical platform to organize, mobilize, and politicize utilizing taekwondo that formed the core component of the physical education program at the OCS/OCLC. The martial arts program was less about physical self-defense than it was about creating a pedagogical platform that promoted health and well-being. To be sure, the Party had numerous survival programs, the most popular of which was the Free Breakfast Program, which provided breakfast for children at school, and the George Jackson Medical Clinic, which provided screening, treatment, and research for sickle cell anemia.[21] While Hoffman had contended in his article that the "Oakland ghetto" was worse than any other place in America, and Daniel Patrick Moynihan opined that the "Negro problem" was one of "pathological dysfunctionality,"[22] the most generative and transformative ideas and movements that have been part of the American cultural landscape emerged from places like the working-class communities of Oakland. The most vulnerable of America's populations, the US Third World, provided the surplus labor that built the postindustrial technological economy and simultaneously attempted to reconstitute itself in the face of US abjection. The contributions of the OCS/OCLC were not only limited to the martial arts but they also provided tutoring, arts activities such as plays, and birthed a traveling funk band called The Lumpen.[23]

Afro Asian Connections and the Martial Arts Imaginary

With the knowledge that he gained from training taekwondo at Grove Street College under Master Youn, McCutchen applied martial arts practice to teach the technical aspects of body mechanics through a system of sport and self-

---

21. Additional survival programs included the following: George Jackson Medical Clinic, Sickle Cell Anemia Research Foundation, People's Free Dental Program, People's Free Ambulance Program, Free Food Program, Free Breakfast Program, Food Cooperative Program, Intercommunal News Service, People's Free Community Employment Program, People's Free Legal Aid and Educational Program, Free Busing to Prisons Program, Free Commissary for Prisoners Program, Seniors Against a Fearful Environment Program, People's Cooperative Housing Program, People's Free Plumbing and Maintenance Program, Free Pest Control, People's Cooperative Housing Program, and Child Development Center.

22. Moynihan, *Negro Family: The Case for National Action*, 40.

23. For more about The Lumpen, see Ricky Vincent's *Party Music: The Inside Story of the Black Panthers' Band and How Black Power Transformed Soul Music*.

defense. Students and parents were also exposed to, and had an opportunity to participate in, other programs that the Party offered. Once class ended, students gravitated toward the programs and learned about the preparation for breakfast, lunch, and dinner at OCS as well as OCS's classroom procedures. Students and parents were able to mingle with members of the Party outside of the martial arts and were in turn educated in the various principles and platforms that were the core of the Party. As McCutchen suggests:

> Through the martial arts education process we were mobilizing participants toward activities. . . . We needed bodies for community events, for rallies, protests, marches, and preparations for other programs. . . . They were mobilized to help participate in those events. I could rally them because they were students of my class. So, I could organize them, call, reach out and say, 'hey we need you at the school to help with this project.' Then as they learned to do that . . . they asked what was next. They would go to other programs. So, they learned how to become young community workers through their relationship with the martial arts programs and then other programs that were hosted at the Oakland Community Learning Center.[24]

McCutchen first introduced martial arts in September 1974 to the OCS as part of the physical education course. Initially, only students who had enrolled in the prekindergarten to sixth grade program at OCS were allowed to participate.

However, as more members from the greater Oakland community learned about the OCS martial arts program, older students made requests for an expansion of the martial arts activities and resources. Throughout 1974, McCutchen continued to teach the same group of students, but in early 1975 older students (such as Byron Aldridge and Fred Moorehead) who had previous martial arts experience, began to express interest in training at OCS/OCLC. While Aldridge and Moorehead never became Party members, they would wind up becoming two of McCutchen's top students and still live in the Oakland area today. But then what of the art form, taekwondo, that McCutchen practiced and taught? What did McCutchen's performance of Afro Asian masculinity reveal about the history of an Asian diasporic tradition and the performance of Asian masculinity in the particular historical political moment in which it first emerged?

In fact, the history and development of Korean taekwondo has a complicated relationship to the emergence of modernity on the Asian peninsula.

---

24. Author interview with Steve McCutchen, May 20, 2016.

FIGURE 2.2. Steve McCutchen leads students from the OCS during the physical education program utilizing martial arts circa 1974. From the "It's About Time" archives.

According to scholars such as Ahn, Hong, and Park, taekwondo is caught up in the legacy of Japan's fifty-year annexation of Korea and the influence of Japanese karate, which became the dominant cultural practice. The formation of modern taekwondo occurred under the direct influence of Japan's karate during Japanese occupation period (1910–1945), which effectively suspended Korean culture for thirty-six years. While taekwondo should be acknowledged as a martial art native to Korea, it cannot deny its Japanese influences and subsequent transformations by Koreans into a martial sport recognized around the world.[25]

However, taekwondo was also a form of modern state building that redressed Korean masculinity after Japanese imperialism. The former president of the International Taekwondo Federation (ITF), Choi Hong Hi, first used the term *taekwondo* in 1955 to refer to the martial arts system that he created. Choi also acknowledged that he had been trained in Japan in karate

---

25. Ahn et al., "Historical and Cultural Identity of Taekwondo as a Traditional Korean Martial Art."

do, returned to Korea, and from 1946 to 1955 he was a divisional commander in the recently formed Korean army and trained troops in *tang soo do*, the Korean term for the form of Japanese karate that Choi had learned under Japanese occupation. Taekwondo became a performance of Korean ethnic and cultural identity and, through its eventual inclusion in the Olympic games, a source of national pride. After 1955, South Korea had to contend with the DPRK. Few practitioners were more zealous in adopting the taekwondo into a national body politic. Choi sought the permission of the state to ratify and officially recognize the new name of his repertoire, the performative practice of reinventing and naming through taekwondo developed a discursive power as a form of Austinian performative utterance in which "the issuing of the utterance is the performance of an action."[26] Martial arts rehearsal and performance become a stylized form of recursive practice, creating citational effects to produce "the repeated stylization of the body, a set of repeated acts within a highly rigid regulatory frame that congeal over time to produce the appearance of substance, of a natural sort of being."[27] Taekwondo was a form of communal kinesthesia developed as a form of creating a particular political genealogy in the recently liberated community of Korea in 1945.[28]

Choreographing the Politics of the Local

Like the South Korean state, the Party was strategic in sculpting the narrative of its martial arts program by creating news and advertising through public access television as well as framing the kinesthetic aspects of martial arts practice as a community building project through the Party newspaper. As I have suggested, communal kinesthesia suggests the way in which organizations such as the BPP mobilized and organized themselves around political movements through acts, gestures, and routines that summoned and mobilized bodies into OCS/OCLC. The process of building community within the OCS/OCLC was captured in a 1977 documentary titled *Rebop*, a show that

---

26. Austin, *How to Do Things with Words*, 6.
27. Butler, *Gender Trouble: Feminism and the Subversion of Identity*, 25.
28. Then, "in September 1954, at the inaugural ceremony of 1st Corps, the troops demonstrated Tang Soo Do" in front of President Syngman Rhee, who after the performance remarked, "That is *taekkyeon* that has existed since ancient times in our country. Taekkyeon is good, all troops should learn this." After this event, the term taekwon was adopted unanimously, as it has a pronunciation similar to "taekkyeon," a general term from the history of the Goryeo Dynasty for all barehanded martial arts in which one aims to kick high to either kick the other's topknot or force them to topple over. Ahn et al., "Historical and Cultural Identity of Taekwondo as a Traditional Korean Martial Art," 1716–34.

was part of a children's television series from 1976 to 1979 hosted by the actor LaVar Burton and aired on Public Broadcasting Corporation channels.[29] What emerges in both print media and the PBS episode is the manner in which community was constructed through the kinesthesia of martial arts and Afro Asian political syncretism.

Amongst the youth featured in the film is Fred Moorehead, who is shown teaching and practicing taekwondo and engaging in other community survival programs. Burton's prologue offers a brief historical overview before delving further into the operation of the programs as viewed through the lens of Moorehead and an eight-year-old girl named Kelita. There is nothing sensational about the delivery of Burton's introduction as the film transitions to Kelita's story. Kelita sits in a school bus (the Party had its own school buses, as well as dorms for children of Party members who attended OCS) with Newton as he explains why he developed the school and what he likes about it. Kelita then takes over the narration of the *Rebop* piece as she guides the viewer through the different elements, and her experiences, at the OCS/OCLC. These include Kelita playing with her friends, eating breakfast with classmates as a teacher instructs them in Spanish, attending history classes, and an introduction to her younger brother, Eric, who loves the karate classes. In a scene that captures the classes, the instructor counts as the young children practice striking and kicking. They *kiai* (the Japanese term for a vocal utterance that the practitioner uses when executing a technique) with each count. Many children can be seen in the background, along with parents who watch their children practice. Moorehead and another adolescent, Joe, are shown in the class working with younger children like Kelita and Eric. Joe moves back and forth amongst the young martial arts students, instructing them on how to move their bodies so that they can relax the hips and release the front kick straight in front of them.

As an assistant martial arts instructor at the OCS, Moorehead's practice also reflected his growth in the other elements of his life. As Moorehead eats dinner at a kitchen table in his father's house; the conversation reveals the subjectivity of the lumpen community of Oakland from which Moorehead hails. As Moorehead and his father eat the meal that his father has cooked, Moorehead states that his father is a pipe fitter for naval air supply. Moorehead

---

29. Oakland Community School Segment, *Rebop* (1978). The program was produced by WGBH Boston and aired on Public Broadcasting Corporation. *Rebop* was an American children's television series that ran from 1976 to 1979 on Public Broadcasting Stations. It was produced by WGBH Boston and featured actor LeVar Burton, who hosted the final season. Like other progressive programs, including SOUL, that were produced by PBS during the 1970s, *Rebop* was socially conscious and race-based.

has three sisters that live with his mother nearby. An awkward flatness permeates their exchange as Moorehead reveals that he has only been living with his father for a year. The two joke about the taste of the food and whether the younger Moorehead will be doing more cooking in the future. The presence of the camera, the awareness of the bond between father and son, and the hope of a future in Oakland may be the cause of this awkward flatness; despite the seeming tension, Moorehead flashes a gregarious smile throughout, and his enthusiasm for the martial arts program shines through.

The next scene cuts to a classroom where Joe, the other adolescent instructor in the film, helps Moorehead with his reading. This scene is intercut between the classroom and the martial arts class at the OCLC. Joe assists Moorehead in correctly pronouncing the words on the page as Moorehead explains his efforts at improving his reading skills. The relationship between the two young men is one of both community and trust; Moorehead articulates his appreciation for Joe's ability to translate his skills as a taekwondo instructor/practitioner at OCLC into his abilities to tutor one of his seniors.[30]

> Joe is a teacher too. Some people think that because he's a blue belt he shouldn't be teaching. But that don't have nothing to do with it. I don't know how to put it. His mind, he can teach real good and he likes little kids and I think that has a lot to do with it. Sometimes I coach Joe on his Taekwondo technique and that's kind of nice because sometime he helps me on my reading and stuff and then I don't feel so bad, like he's taking all the time for me and I can't do nothing for him.[31]

The *Rebop* film is but one archive that documents the Party's commitment to educating, mobilizing, and organizing youth within the Oakland community. Taekwondo became the medium through which individuals such as Joe and Moorehead were brought together to help one another and to form bonds of friendship and fraternalism. An art form such as taekwondo requires conditioning of the body—a form of corporeal discipline that is about both self-care of the flesh and conditioning the mind—and thus, the broader culture of community.

Ericka Huggins suggests that the roots of the Intercommunal Youth Institute (which would ultimately become the OCS/OCLC) can be found in the

---

30. When I say that Moorehead is Joe's senior I am referring specifically to the senior rank of black belt that he holds in relationship to Joe's junior blue belt rank.

31. Oakland Community School segment, *Rebop* (1978).

Children's House, which was founded in 1970.³² The creation of the Children's House was a "decision by then chairman Bobby Seale and Party chief of staff David Hilliard to remove Party members' children from public schools," because the FBI was harassing the teachers of the children of Party members. The new school was intended to be a safe place for BPP members' children at a time when BPP offices and homes were subject to raids, shoot-outs, fire bombings, and COINTELPRO surveillance.³³ Huggins elaborates on the development of the OCS: "The trajectory of what we came to call Oakland Community School, started with an idea of Huey's. He bought the building. . . . He put the non-profit incorporation in place that supported the school financially, and at the fundraising and promotion level, his ideology in general about humanity was the underpinning of the school's pedagogy."³⁴ Newton's idea of creating a self-sustaining organization through nonprofit enterprise is embodied in a photo advertising the martial arts program in the Party newspaper.

At the top of the advertisement (Figure 2.3) is contact information for the Educational Opportunities Corporation (EOC), "a nonprofit (tax-exempt) association of civic-minded Bay Area residents."³⁵ The OCS/OCLC fell under the parent organization of the EOS. To the left of the photo, the advertisement reads, "We are launching a campaign to gain financial support for the students at the Intercommunal Youth Institute through the 'each one teach one' tuition association. We are asking you to donate a nominal amount per year. All monies are for direct support [of] the children. (All monies are tax deductible)." Immediately below the photo of McCutchen and other students in the class sits a perforated pledge form that provides information on how to make the contribution and become part of the community.³⁶

With the many community survival programs operating throughout the 1970s, the Party needed bodies to sustain its mission of serving its constituency. Martial arts practitioners such as McCutchen and Moorehead performed the role of caretakers for elderly people within the community. Moorehead worked for the OCLC's Safe Transportation Program, which utilized the Party's buses to transport senior citizens to the George Jackson Free Clinic, hos-

---

32. Wong, "Pedagogy and Education of the Black Panther Party: Confronting the Reproduction of Social and Cultural Inequality," 21.

33. More resources were added; the Intercommunal Youth Institute emerged as a genuine alternative to Oakland public schools after Newton was released from prison in August 1970.

34. Ericka Huggins as quoted in Wong's "Pedagogy and Education of the Black Panther Party: Confronting the Reproduction of Social and Cultural Inequality," 22.

35. See page 10 of The Dr. Huey P. Newton Foundation's *The Black Panther Party: Service to the People Programs.*

36. The Intercommunal Youth Institute was officially established in January 1971, with Brenda Bay as its first director until Huggins took over as director in 1973.

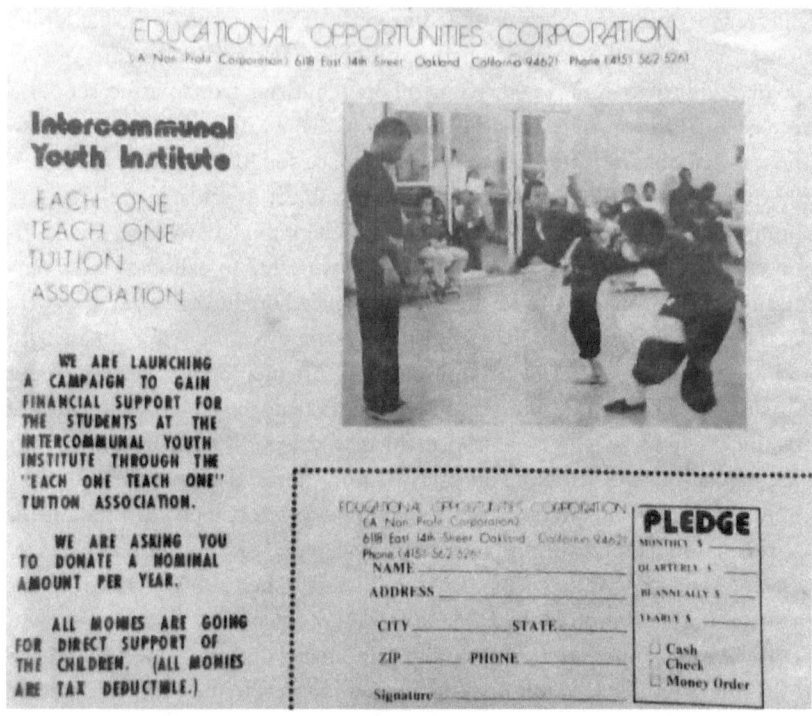

FIGURE 2.3. An advertisement from the *Black Panther Party* newspaper for the martial arts program at the Intercommunal Youth Institute

pitals, banks, meal programs, and shopping. As Moorehead states, "We try to be there to stop the muggers from snatching their purses and mugging them and things like that."[37] The OCLC martial arts program aimed to intervene in two of Oakland's most vulnerable populations; the youth and the elderly, and in engaging youth such as Moorehead through taekwondo, the Party was able to create a needed intergenerational connection. If Mao had sought to close class and generation gaps during the cultural revolutions (albeit imperfectly) the Party's attempt at bridging intergenerational gaps can be read as another gesture toward Mao's looming impact in which the philosophy was actualized in the practice, in the disciplining of the mind through corporeal discipline of the flesh.

> Cognition starts with practice and through practice it reaches the theoretical plane, and then it has to go back to practice. The active effect of cognition

---

37. Oakland Community School segment, *Rebop* (1978).

not only manifests itself in the active leap from perceptual knowledge to rational knowledge, but also, what is more important, manifests itself in the leap from rational knowledge to revolutionary practice. After having grasped the laws of the world, we must redirect this knowledge to the practice of revolutionary class struggle and national struggle as well as of scientific experiments. This is the process of testing and developing theory, the continuation of the entire process of cognition.[38]

Training in taekwondo was a way of applying a theory of class struggle to a daily bodily practice—a communal kinesthesia. This was true both in terms of the Party's use of the martial arts, and in inscribing philosophy into the organization of the community. While Mao and Choi were diametrically opposed in Cold War political economic strategy and ideology, Choi attempted to proliferate state ideology through practice. Martial arts have always cut both ways in terms of their availability for particular political projects and processes; even Choi had solidified the term of taekwondo at a site of nationalist performance—a military demonstration in front of the president.

These transcultural relationships form links that Richard Raya describes in his essay "Martial Arts as a Way to Understand the Black Panthers." As a self-identified "man of color"[39] and Mexican-American youth from Oakland with training in taekwondo schools in the Bay area, Raya's analysis is helpful in building a nuanced lens of analysis that is malleable enough to move transoceanically to both sides of the Pacific Rim. Raya suggests that McCutchen's first teacher, Master Ken Youn, was a Korean immigrant who adapted his own understanding of taekwondo into what he referred to as tiger style taekwondo. Saya writes that "after witnessing conditions present in street fights (not the controlled systemic fights present in many studios), as well as after suffering many injuries which inhibited his kicking capabilities,"[40] Youn broke with the prescribed taekwondo system and modified it to create tiger taekwondo, a style that incorporated multiple hand techniques. A direct student of Youn's, "James Noel of the San Francisco Theological Seminar, also noted that tiger taekwondo incorporates techniques reminiscent of Wing Chun Kung Fu."[41] Together, McCutchen, Lee, and Youn form an imaginative triumvirate, and Lee's jeet kun do is a constant philosophical and corporeal interlocutor between varying diasporic experiences. Through the practice of the corporeal discipline, the imaginative possibilities of the mind are brought

---

38. Tse-Tung, On Practice, 11.
39. Raya, "Might for Right: Martial Arts as a Way to Understand the Black Panthers."
40. Raya, "Might for Right: Martial Arts as a Way to Understand the Black Panthers."
41. Raya, "Might for Right: Martial Arts as a Way to Understand the Black Panthers."

into material reality through the movement of the flesh, and the movement of the body during martial arts practice offered a practice to sustain the political movement of the Party. Huey Newton and Bruce Lee each articulated their own philosophical understandings of the nature of contradictions inherent in any movement system. Or as Newton suggested:

> One of my principles is that contradiction is the ruling principle of the universe, that every phenomenon, whether it's in the physical world, the biological world, or the social world, has its internal contradiction that gives motion to things, that internal strain. Much of the time we Homo sapiens don't realize that no matter what conditions we establish, no matter what government we establish, there will also be that internal contradiction that will have be resolved—and resolved in a rational and just way.[42]

Kinetics (movement) is the essence of life and everything else flows from it—be it political philosophy, revolution, or the repertoire of taekwondo (martial arts writ large). Bruce Lee's philosophical approach moves from wing chun to jeet kune do, in which the opponent's violence is turned back on him or herself, through the redirection of force, strikes, immobilization (joint locks), or any combination thereof, and the dialogical philosophy is embodied in the repertoire—in the movement and in the moment of the practice. Lee recognized within his jeet kune do system a recursive process of inextricably linked and opposing forces that gave rise to the spontaneous improvisatory play between practitioners. No action "occurred without an equal, opposite, and immediate reaction, a principle that he asserted held true everywhere, from physics to fighting and beyond."[43]

Communal kinesthesia allows us to comprehend the connections between the taekwondo as practiced at the OCS/OCLC and the countercolonial and counteroppressive histories and traditions that exist when communities or individuals run up against the "hit" of the oppressive force and are "contracted" by the energy of the blow. Dominant mediascapes shaped a narrative that portrayed the Black body as armed and dangerous—one that had to be constantly put in its place through state-sanctioned anti-Black police violence. Again, as John O. Calmore writes, "The black man is the paradigmatic representation of unwanted traffic."[44] However, oppressed people have proven

---

42. See the transcription of Huey P. Newton's interview with William F. Buckley from *Crossfire* in *The Huey P. Newton Reader*, 268.

43. Raya, "Might for Right: Martial Arts as a Way to Understand the Black Panthers."

44. Calmore, John O. "Reasonable and Unreasonable Suspects: The Cultural Construction of the Anonymous Black Man in Public Space (Here Be Dragons)," 138.

resilient by adapting, with and to the "hit," redirecting, trapping, and in some cases leveraging force itself and thus transforming their marginalization into something venerable. What was once hard (the assailant's attack) becomes soft (non-injurious), and what was soft (the defender's passivity) becomes hard (an effective way to counter a potentially dangerous assault), allowing balance to return.[45] Lee's philosophy of jeet kune do embodied the practice of what he referred to as a formless art form or an expression of self that, like guerilla tactics of the Vietcong, attempted to utilize whatever resources were available outside the grasp of colonizers. As Lee wrote, "Jeet Kune Do favors formlessness so that it can assume all forms and since Jeet Kune Do has no style, it can fit with all styles. As a result, Jeet Kune Do utilizes all ways and is bound by none and, likewise, uses any techniques or means which serve its end."[46] It provides the opportunity to probe, understand, and reconcile the contradictory nature of harmony and the harmony of nature, a contradiction that McCutchen attempted to resolve through the art form that he would develop called *wondotaekwon*, or "the spiraling or returning way of hands and feet."

While McCutchen's base repertoire was the taekwondo that he learned from Master Ken Youn at Grove Street, he acquired additional skills form Kim Chon Yun, who ran a taekwondo school located on 60th Street and Telegraph Road. McCutchen had been suspended at one point from Grove Street College for assaulting a professor who allegedly claimed in front of the class that McCutchen was a government informant—an assertion that arguably could have put McCutchen's life in danger given the political climate at the time. His suspension prevented McCutchen from taking several exams that would allow him to achieve black belt. McCutchen stopped at red belt, one belt before black belt, while training with Master Ken Youn. He also had to contend with full-time Party responsibilities such as working at various survival programs and events, and helping to run the printing press for the *Black Panther Party* newspaper and selling the papers in the community.

Nonetheless, McCutchen managed to launch the martial arts program at OCS/OCLC and began teaching without consent from Ken Youn. Another taekwondo instructor in the area, Kim Chon Yun, accepted McCutchen as a private student. Yun observed him for several months, and eventually McCutchen attained his black belt as well as status in the World Taekwondo Federation (WTF), the official world organization that sanctions the rules and regulations for taekwondo. To expand his training, McCutchen also studied with a second-generation student of Bruce Lee's named Ken Yee who ran a

---

45. Raya, "Might for Right: Martial Arts as a Way to Understand the Black Panthers," 8.
46. Lee, *Tao of Jeet Kune Do*, 12.

school in Berkeley. Yee had developed a system based on Lee's jeet kune do, called jeet gak kune. This was not a traditional form of jeet kune do, but rather a method of training adopted from the core principles of jeet kune do, which itself was a derivative of wing chun. The exposure to jeet gak kune catalyzed McCutchen to further deviate from the more orthodox approaches to movement that he learned through taekwondo.

> What I was seeing between that and taekwondo and his method of Jeet Kune Do, I was learning at a faster pace than what I had learned in traditional taekwondo. It was easier to move from learning the formal sets into free sparring. It was easier to relate between free sparring and multiple areas of combat. He would teach the philosophy of Jeet Kune Do. All of that was being incorporated into the classes that I was teaching. That's when I started stripping away the things that I'd been taught in taekwondo and started adding in the things that I'd learned in Jeet Kune Do/Jeet Gak Kune. I stripped away the one, two, three step sparring and started identifying techniques that emerged based on the attack. When the students learned that there were six methods of attack. Take any technique and I could apply it six different ways. I had six different techniques. That became a regular part of the training that was incorporated into the classes. As I began doing that in mid-'75 that's when interest in tournament competition came out.[47]

McCutchen's martial arts journey and development was not monolithic. The responsibilities of being a Party member meant that he had to sacrifice training time for commitments to Party programs. This experience hastened a creative approach to alternative forms of training and martial arts pedagogy and philosophy. Like Bruce Lee, McCutchen developed his understanding of his own bodily practice based on what was needed, what was available, and what was practical.

McCutchen's amalgamation of freestyle wrestling, boxing, taekwondo, and jeet gak kune, which he weaved into his own training method of wondotaekwon, put on display a diverse set of skills in the *Rebop* film during Moorehead's discussion about the training at the OCLC. In another scene in the film, the students line up across from each other. As Moorehead counts, one group of students charge forward as the other student delivers a sidekick to the chest. The exercise is repeated as the students practice both delivering and receiving the kick. Such practice disciplines the body for taekwondo tournament fighting, which was the popular tournament style of the 1970s. Taekwondo places

---

47. Author interview with Steve McCutchen, May 20, 2016.

heavy emphasis on kicking; punching, takedowns, and submissions are rarely performed or rehearsed. The rehearsal process, like theater, is a practice and preparation for the tournament performance or a performance demonstration for an audience. The exercise of kicking to the chest was related to winning the tournament, but it was also about disciplining and training the body and mind to receive the pressure of violence. In this context, martial arts is the rehearsal for preparing to deal with other types of aggressors—the racist, the rapist, the colonizer. Furthermore, the *Rebop* film also shows the OCLC students, Moorehead in particular, practicing nontournament sanctioned techniques such as catching kicks to the abdomen—locking the ankle in order to take the person down to the ground before finishing them off with a strike to the face. Another technique, more common to jujitsu, judo, or aiki-jujitsu is the flying scissors, in which Moorehead jumps onto his opponent's midsection, using both of his legs to subdue the opponent by scissoring them in between the legs, and taking them down to the ground in order to submit or strike. Such techniques, while common in mixed martial arts today, are usually considered unorthodox in tournament fighting, where points are awarded for kicking the opponent in the head or abdomen. The fact that students at the OCLC were practicing flying scissors and ankle locks elucidates McCutchen's penchant for innovation and his aim to expand the repertoire and odds of survival for his students beyond simple point fighting.

The martial arts program at OCS/OCLC benefited greatly from performances at tournaments and demonstrations. Such events provided an opportunity for students to test their skills in a controlled and safe environment and to show members of the community what they had learned, and what others could learn in the martial arts program. Tournaments and demonstrations were spaces in which to organize bodies through performance for the purposes of fundraising for various projects of the Party. The tournaments were also sites in which various practitioners could observe as well as compete with each other, and thus enhance their own techniques. Through the process of a kind of participant performance observation of an opponent or team member, practitioners could refine their technique and skills. As students at OCLC became further accustomed to tournament preparation, McCutchen began to search for tournaments for students to enter.

The first competition that the OCLC team participated in was held at the Oakland Auditorium. The tournament was a Korean-style tournament emphasizing high kicks to the head. Three students signed up: Two teenagers and an eight-year-old named Derek Nokem. Nokem performed exceptionally well and won the championship for his age group. Nokem was the first tournament winner from the OCLC martial arts program, and blazed a trail for the OCLC to compete in more tournaments throughout California. The shift to tournament competition also shifted the pedagogy at OCLC, not only in terms of the focus of the repertoire but also within McCutchen's grading and ranking system. Rather than using the traditional white, yellow, green, red, and black belt ranking system that McCutchen had been exposed to through taekwondo, McCutchen began adding additional colored belts such as purple and blue in order to provide more specific demarcations for students who were progressing, but had not reached the next level. However, material such as belts, entrance fees to tournaments, protection equipment, and uniforms required resources for students, many of whom might not have been able to afford them on their own. In the middle of 1975, the Party began providing the money to buy equipment, and while the Party was never invested in promoting McCutchen's career as professional martial artist, the program became one of the most popular programs throughout the mid- to late 1970s.

While many within the broader martial arts community may have first become aware of the martial arts program at OCS/OCLC through Hoffman's 1975 piece in *Black Belt*, the *Black Panther Party* newspaper also played a significant role in chronicling the program. An edition of the *Black Panther Party* newspaper on the Youth Institute dated Saturday, October 5, 1974, is titled "Martial Arts Develop Hidden Skills" (Figure 2.4). A photo shows McCutchen in the lower left-hand corner leading a group of students between three-and-a-half and eleven years of age. The students are not dressed in gis; the fact that they are dressed in regular athletic clothing suggests that the photo was taken in the early moments of the OCS/OCLC martial arts program. McCutchen articulates his understanding of both wing chun and taekwondo, stating that "Martial arts is geared toward building harmony between the mind and body and developing the mental and physical confidence of an individual in relationship to his or her attitude toward the social order. It not only strengthens the person's respect for himself but contributes to his respect for all life."[48] The article was published a full year before Hoffman's article appeared.

The article featured in the *Black Panther Party* newspaper (Figure 2.4) narrates the success of the OCLC martial arts team at the Long Beach International Karate Championship, the largest karate tournament to emerge out of the '60s and '70s West Coast Fighting scene. Aside from propagating the Party's ideology and advertising the survival program, the article also enabled the practitioner to articulate the synthesis of martial arts practice in which taekwondo and wing chun are combined and that the two systems are "further

---

48. See page 4 of the *Black Panther Party*, Saturday, October 5, 1974. The copy that I obtained was part of Steve McCutchen's own personal archive of Party martial arts.

FIGURE 2.4. McCutchen teaches at the OCS/OCLC

broken down into exercise, forms, speed development of rhythms and coordination and technical applications."[49] Taekwondo emphasizes power emanating from the hips for kicks, whereas wing chun emphasizes the economy of movement and four corner theories (outside high gate, inside high gate, outside low gate, inside low gate).[50] The intent of four corner theory is to minimize any unnecessary movement of the arms and hands as one prepares to defend from attack. The center-line concept of wing chun holds that regardless of the position of a person's body when attacked, one hand, determined by the position of the body, will always defend the center of the body, as the other hand is geared toward protecting the right or the left side of the body. After going through these wing chun movements, the youth then practice taekwondo, which emphasizes kicking movements and the use of the legs and feet.[51]

Bruce Lee was obsessed with economy of movement. Jeet kune do was intended to evolve Ip Man's teachings and eliminate unnecessary movement when dealing with opponents. Hence Lee was less concerned with forms such

---

49. See page 4 of the *Black Panther Party*, Saturday, October 5, 1974.
50. Lee, *Wing Chun Kung-Fu*, 24.
51. Lee, *Wing Chun Kung-Fu*, 24.

as *chon-ji* (the basic form in taekwondo) or its equivalent *kihon kata* (the basic form in Japanese karate).⁵² While chon-ji has thirty-five movements, as opposed to the twenty movements in kihon kata (basic form), the similarities can be seen in the 'H' shaped pattern, which is made as the practitioner moves through space, first blocking and punching to the left, then to the right, traversing forward, then to the left, to the right, returning in the direction from which the practitioner came, before performing the same exercise to the left, and to the right once again before returning to the point of neutrality from which the performer started.

In many martial arts tournaments such as karate, judo, taekwondo, and varying forms of kung fu, the presentation of the "forms" is an important component of the overall practitioner's performance under the gaze of an authority. In this case the authority is not the state, but rather a teacher, competing schools, and perhaps a body of judges. To perform in this context meant to celebrate the life of those practitioners who represented the OCLC. Kata (or forms) was another way of performing discipline and control over the body and hence a pathway for disciplining and calming the mind.

As suggested by the aforementioned connection between Korean and Japanese forms, communal kinesthesia is embodied within a repertoire that transgresses political borders of the nation-state. Through the kata, knowledge can be retained and perhaps even disguised within the movement of the form. McCutchen perhaps saw a subversive possibility in the practice of kata, whereas Lee wanted to get right to the point and dismiss forms and formalism in exchange for the moment-to-moment improvisatory spirit of an actor's performance. The improvisatory nature of Bruce Lee's approach to jeet kune do was embodied at the beginning of *Enter the Dragon* in response to his teacher's inquiry about his "thoughts when facing an opponent."⁵³ Lee's character responds, "There is no opponent because the word I does not exist.... A good fight should be like a small play, but played seriously."⁵⁴ In this moment, Lee collapses the relationship between the performance of the martial artist's body and the actor's body into an aesthetic quality that can only be achieved through practice. The very nature of the practice of martial arts is a graphy written with the body in which the intention of the player on the stage, screen, ring, or street maintains her or his super objective: to outperform their opponent in some fashion. In this context we can think of martial arts performance as a heightened form of acting—calling forth all of the sensorial awareness that

---

52. Note, in this particular case, when I say Japanese karate or nihon karate do, I am referring to the four major ryu-ha that make up the Japan Karate Federation: shotokan, shito-ryu, goju-ryu, and wado-ryu.

53. See the introduction to Clouse, *Enter the Dragon* (1973).

54. See the introduction to Clouse, *Enter the Dragon* (1973).

any method Strasberg, Stanislavski, Chekhov, or Hagen could have demanded from one of their players. When a *judoka* (judo player) throws their opponent onto their back and submits them in a *shiai* (tournament) or when a karate-ka scores a point in the *kumite* (sparring), the referee scores the winner in front of the spectators, and the objective of the performance event is acknowledged by players, judges, and audience.

Choreographing the OCLC

By 1975 the taekwondo classes at the OCLC were growing. By working with youth and adults from the community, McCutchen gained confidence in his abilities as a teacher. He was able to further interpret his own understanding of taekwondo as varying forms of kinesthesia, used not only for physical practice but for building and sustaining community. Initially, classes were held on Sunday for two hours and Monday and Thursday for three hours, and were attended by thirty-five to forty students. An additional class on Wednesday was reserved for students who were preparing for tournaments. Students were responsible for following the training regimen that would ultimately become the template for the Seven Shadows Martial Arts Association, a small organization that McCutchen went on to form after he left the Party. The lesson plans were derived from the martial arts curriculum that McCutchen picked up from his teachers at Grove Street as well as his tutelage under Kim Chon Yun. Like Bruce Lee, McCutchen wrote his own understanding of the philosophy of the system of won do tae kwon, which also contextualized his own understanding of the layered and contested history of taekwondo.

> The origins of the many schools of taekwondo are as rich and diverse as the style itself. Within the house of taekwondo there are rooms with their own particular characteristics, some common, others different. That is part of the variety and the common thread that allows the art to grow and evolve over the generations yet maintain an identity that is distinguishable from other styles, other houses. Wondotaekwon is one of the rooms in the house of taekwondo. It has an identity that at once is recognizable as of the taekwondo family but it carries the features which serve to define its distinction from other rooms, other schools, or systems of taekwondo.[55]

---

55. McCutchen, Unpublished Instructor's Manual: 7 Shadows Martial Arts Association provided to the author. I have copied and paraphrased a transcription of McCutchen's description that he provided for me. I have documented McCutchen's writing using photographs and incorporated them into my own archive. McCutchen shared these documents with me when

Taken from the Seven Shadows Martial Arts instructor's manual, this description explicates how McCutchen's understanding of the varied rooms that make up the greater house of taekwondo meant that the house was constantly being reframed and reconstructed, and that it was flexible and malleable enough to include additional rooms. In other words, the house of taekwondo is intercommunal, constantly absorbing and developing new understandings of the practitioners who contribute, regardless of the practitioner's particular political, cartographical positioning. The repertoire of taekwondo meanders and cuts across the maps of socially constructed boundaries and racial geometries, and extends its family through daily practice, tournaments, and teaching. Teachers and students are able to imagine themselves in conversation with other practitioners through the kata, and then extend that conversation into social-somatic events by engaging each other in the tournament.

> Seven Shadows Martial Arts Association seeks to promote the art, science and philosophy of wondotaekwon; that system or school of tae kwon do which is approached through the prism of the "method of the spiraling or returning hand and foot." Wondotaekwon and 7 shadows are the extension and synthesis of traditional taekwondo and the contemporary experiences and understandings of its practitioners, who see the individual in relation to not just one system but to all systems and styles whose principles reflect and actualize human potentials at the physical, mental and social levels of lifelong learning.[56]

Included within the lesson plans that McCutchen created were outlines for a system of corporeal discipline that consisted of a twenty-step process designed to guide students through a series of exercises and responsibilities for achieving each belt or rank between belts. The categories of the outlines consisted of Teaching Objectives, Learning Objectives, Skills Tasks, and Evaluation Methods. Students were expected to be able to clearly explain and demonstrate their understanding of commands and terminology using expressions in the Korean language such as *charyo* (attention), *chunbi,* (ready/readiness), *parryo* or *goman* (end position), and *sheer* (at ease) as well as counting out loud in Korean. Students were also required to learn and explain the concepts behind additional terms and names for techniques such as basic up/down inside/outside defense or to explain/demonstrate lead/rear sidekick. Students were

---

I interviewed him at his house in Oakland on May 21 and May 22, 2016. This passage is based on the wondotaekwon that McCutchen provided.

56. McCutchen, Unpublished Instructor's Manual: 7 Shadows Martial Arts Association provided to the author.

then required to set to memory and then demonstrate exercises or techniques during the grading period. As with many martial arts, performance is an evaluative process for understanding the development of each student within the program. The centrality and focus on the body mechanics of the student at the center of the evaluation process meant that the mechanics were rooted in "combat principles." While the mechanics and methods of wondotaekwon still incorporated the traditional *hyung* (the Korean term for forms or patterns indicating the belt rank system found in taekwondo or tang soo do) from white belts to upper dan levels, the emphasis in wondotaekwon shifts at the point of applied skills in the combative aspects and the methods of thinking and developing one's practice. The pedagogical approach used both orality and performance in the repertoire, and students learned by both the linguistic and corporeal discipline that McCutchen was developing through wondotaekwon.

According to the written documents that McCutchen provided, the essence of wondotaekwon holds that learning is a spiraling process and that through the repetition of a skill performed at the beginning or intermediate levels of training, practitioners can improve themselves and evolve into the next level.[57] Qualitatively, the skill performed at the beginning or intermediate levels of training is enriched through knowledge of the skill and mechanics, and thus the understanding of the processes that then determine application of skills: "To affect that determination, the practitioner has not merely repeated skills in isolation from actual applications (combat) but has additionally grasped the imperceptible changes in what is appropriate and what is inappropriate."[58] The practitioner comes to understand that timing, distance, and mobility are the key aspects that determine how and when skills can be effectively and successfully used. In contrast, a practitioner who merely mimics techniques and attempts to kick or punch without understanding the mechanics of the body and the mechanics of motion has not spiraled to a higher level of awareness and physical development. Rather, the practitioner has only traveled in a circle on the same plane as where they began. "From the perspective of physical science, the earth revolves around the sun, it moves through four distinct seasons, yet each preceding season must occur to give birth to the next."[59] McCutchen was concerned with the connection between the rotation of the solar system and its relationship to the pedagogical practices of martial

---

57. McCutchen, unpublished Instructor's Manual: 7 Shadows Martial Arts Association provided to the author.

58. McCutchen, unpublished Instructor's Manual: 7 Shadows Martial Arts Association provided to the author.

59. McCutchen, unpublished Instructor's Manual: 7 Shadows Martial Arts Association, provided to the author.

arts, suggesting that the earth never fully returns to its original point in space throughout the three hundred and sixty-five days that it takes to circle the sun. Nor is the earth in the same position year in and year out. Rather, the "earth spirals around the sun and only returns to a point it may have passed only after countless revolutions. Even then, when it does, seasons at that point in time and space will never be as they once were."[60] There is a qualitative difference in the existence of things on the earth when the earth appears to have come full circle. McCutchen links this rotation and this spiraling to the learning process of the student, stating:

> If we stipulate that things in the physical world or universe flow and ebb, rise or fall, we leave and return along the same levels or paths, then by extension it can be seen that learning operates along a similar method. For instance; a student's front kick in the summer of a given year. The next summer that student will still practice front kicks, but something has happened. Either way, the student's skill level has been transformed. If the student has merely imitated the technique mechanically, then the result will be a better kick than the year before which only indicate[s] a level of knowledge applied to perform the technique, but can the kick be utilized? Has the student actualized the technique, and searched for the various unknowns which will make that or any other technique applicable, effective and successful under most combat conditions? The practitioner who has learned to analyze the strengths and weaknesses of their own mechanics and the limitations of any given technique has not come "full circle" a year later, or at any other point. They have spiraled upward and onward to a more advanced level of proficiency and understanding.[61]

The tournaments were a space in which to actualize and experiment with the philosophy that was developed within wondotaekwon. With the arrival of Norman White, a Chicagoan with experience in taekwondo and American style kenpo, the classes and the tournament were becoming more organized. At tournaments, the competing teams identified themselves only as members of the OCLC. With the exception of Sifu Bill Owens and Julius Baker, two prominent Black martial arts practitioners in the Oakland and San Francisco area, most members from other schools did not realize that the OCLC was a Party program.

---

60. McCutchen, unpublished *Instructor's Manual: 7 Shadows Martial Arts Association*, provided to the author.

61. McCutchen, unpublished, Instructor's Manual: 7 Shadows Martial Arts Association, provided to the author.

They were simply known as the team from the OCLC, and they would eventually start hosting Friendship Tournaments in the center's auditorium in 1976. Friendship Tournaments drew competitors from around the Northern California area, including cities such as Sacramento, Stockton, and Fresno. The OCLC hosted three consecutive Friendship Tournaments for children and teens for white belts to brown belts, and the tournament final drew competitors from over twenty-five different schools. By drawing students from different schools, the OCLC Friendship Tournaments created performance sites of transcultural and interethnic mixture and social interaction. The formats for the OCLC tournaments followed the traditional schedule of kata, weapons, demonstrations, and free sparring. The Friendship Tournaments were an excellent way to publicize the OCLC and its martial arts program, and additional community outreach was provided at OCLC performance demonstrations that were held four times a year. McCutchen would let the students know about the demonstrations two weeks in advance, at which point the students would then collaborate and sketch out the routines that would then be performed. Each student had to take on a creative role within the routine. Students were responsible for developing their own choreography and for using their imaginations to determine how their part in the routine would be performed, while McCutchen would choreograph their entrance onto the stage in the OCLC auditorium.

The demonstrations provided opportunities to innovate the OCLC martial arts repertoire and were often inspired by the performances at other schools like Castro's Martial Arts Academy. In one such demonstration, Castro's performers did their routine in slow motion and then in reverse, performing the exact same techniques as if they were part of a film that was being rewound. Impressed, the OCLC adopted the format and added their own techniques. Bruce Lee taught that, like a theatrical production or a dance performance, martial arts demonstrations required the construction of a "well made play" played well, and that martial arts demonstrations must captivate and awe their audiences through a presentation of performative virtuosity while providing an accessibility and self-defense practicality that might entice audience members to join a particular school or organization.

In the OCLC demonstration that McCutchen recounted, the routine included a three-part story that was told through choreography. The demonstration, which McCutchen narrated, incorporated both representational and presentational aesthetic modes of performance that relied upon performers maintaining their objectives throughout the choreographed scenes, and presenting a sense of "realness" without being injured. The demonstrations also fulfilled an important part of maintaining and galvanizing support from

FIGURE 2.5. Members of the OCS/OCLC team perform in a demonstration at the OCS/OCLC auditorium

the broader Oakland community. Every Sunday afternoon, the center held its open house, which hosted dances, plays, bands, and movies, and the martial arts demonstrations served an important part in fulfilling the programming content for the OCLC. During these performances, dinners and snacks were served in the cafeteria, which served as another opportunity for fundraising.

Student involvement within the tournament system catalyzed McCutchen's own curiosity and participation in the West Coast Tournament fighting scene, which further developed his interpretation of what worked and did not work in combat situations with opponents who were his size, if not bigger. As McCutchen suggested in his interviews, fighting in organized semiprofessional and professional bouts meant that he was able to keep a small portion of the purse that he won. The rest he gave to the Party.

Eventually, McCutchen registered the martial arts program with the American Taekwondo Association (ATA). By registering with ATA, the OCLC was able to offer their students official ranks that were recognized by a nationally accredited association. This also provided McCutchen the opportunity to compete as a recognized black belt within ATA and non-ATA sanctioned matches. To maintain his competitive edge, McCutchen sparred with his own students, but would also practice with local schools such as Master Byong Yu in Berkeley and boxing gyms in Livermore. Because Master Byong Yu

FIGURE 2.6. Steve McCutchen throws a right cross, knocking his opponent backward as referee Carl Kollar watches

had been a national champion, many students-teacher-practitioners, including McCutchen, would visit Master Yu's studio to prepare for competition. Master Yu undoubtedly welcomed them in order to size up his own students' upcoming tournament competitors. McCutchen suggests that the majority of Master Yu's students were not Korean, but rather were Black, and by this point Master Yu was organizing many of the major full-contact regional tournaments. These kinds of Afro Asian connections were in fact another iteration of transcultural kinesthesia that also influenced McCutchen's individual development as a tournament fighter. In fact, then, Black and Latinx communities made significant contributions to the tournament kickboxing and point fighting system that emerged in the US in the 1970s, which allowed students to absorb as much information as possible from whomever was deemed worthy of improving their skills.

By 1976, full-contact fighting had exploded in the US, and Bill Owens and Byong Yu were responsible for organizing fights in the Bay area. This included matching fighters with each other based on skill and size. McCutchen's school had made a name for itself, which established teachers and promoters such as Byong Yu may have found problematic. Matching a fighter against a bigger and more skilled opponent could present an opportunity for eliminating the competition. McCutchen recalled a fight in San Jose in which Byong Yu offered him a contract to fight in the middle-weight division at 155 pounds. However, on the day of the fight, McCutchen discovered that he had been matched against the number two light heavy-weight fighter in California, who had eight fights under his belt, all of which he'd won by technical knockout. The bout was set for five rounds and, despite being outweighed and fighting in a bout in which the center judge was from the competitor's school, McCutchen still accepted. As McCutchen recounted, the first four rounds were split, two going to his competitor, Brandon Letty, and two going to McCutchen. In the fourth round, McCutchen had Letty up against the ropes, at which time Elaine Brown, then Chairwoman of the Party, sent Phyllis Jackson out of the stands waving her hands for McCutchen to back off. In the fifth round, Letty caught McCutchen with a left hook, fracturing McCutchen's neck—an injury that McCutchen did not find out about until years later. McCutchen was unable to use his left-hand jab, and Letty won the bout in a split three-two decision. When McCutchen asked Elaine Brown and Flores Forbes why they told him to back off, they replied that they were worried that he was going to wear himself out. They did not understand McCutchen's conditioning and level of discipline. Even while instructing and carrying out his other duties as a full-time member of the Party and parent, McCutchen had sustained dominant levels of fitness and power.

On July 3, 1977, Huey P. Newton returned from exile in Cuba. Under the leadership of Elaine Brown, the Party had been able to score political victories in Oakland. The city's political apparatus was no longer under control of rich and powerful, white Republican families such as the Knowlands and Houlihans. Most importantly, the Party had mobilized the Black vote to get the first Black mayor of Oakland, Lionel Wilson, elected to office. However, this success had not come without severe internal fissures and defections, including the departure of founder Bobby Seale and seminal members such as Raymond Masai Hewitt three years prior. In addition, Newton was still facing charges for alleged assault and murder.

While McCutchen was having much success with the martial arts program as the OCLC members entered more tournaments, he also became aware of the reckless way in which the Party was endangering his own students, many of whom, including Fred Moorehead, were minors. For reasons he did not fully understand, McCutchen was told by Party officials to stay out of the 69 Village Projects, a location where many of the students lived, but that was also laden with drug activity.[62] One of McCutchen's students, Danny Simms, informed him that members of the Party's security cadre were going into 69

---

62. McCutchen, *We Were Free for a While: Back-to-Back in the Black Panther Party,* 175.

Village Projects every week and shaking down a major drug dealer.[63] This operation included Flores Forbes, who was the head of the security cadre and the Party's armorer. Then in October 1977, the Party's entire operation became unglued when Forbes attempted to murder the key witness in the case against Newton. The incident resulted in the severe injury of Forbes's right hand and forced him to go underground.[64] Forbes reemerged to stand trial several years later.

The media fallout meant that the Party saw a rapid decline in rank-and-file membership, parents withdrawing their children from many programs at the OCLC, and the resignation of Elaine Brown. Furthermore, the grants and money that had been provided to the Party by numerous foundations dried up. Ironically, the martial arts program was able to survive the immediate fallout, but when adult members such as Norman White were busted for possession of firearms, arguably for arms that that were unknowingly being stored at their residence, McCutchen decided he had had enough.

While, the Party's attempt to develop and sustain the community of the OCS/OCLC through the kinesthesia of taekwondo and wondotaekwon had been fruitful, the Party began to crumble. With his students now in jeopardy with the security cadre, McCutchen tenured his resignation. In late January 1979, he held one last class at the OCLC. He addressed the membership, including the beginning, intermediate, and senior students as well as the parents and community members. "I have appreciated the time that you shared and I had to give. Tonight is my last night teaching here. I have resigned from the Black Panther Party. Harold will lead the program and those of you in the back, Fred Jerome, Joe, you can help him. I plan to keep teaching at the school, but this is as far as I can go with all you here."[65] McCutchen called the class to attention, offered one last salute, and then departed out into the January night.

---

63. McCutchen, *We Were Free for a While: Back-to-Back in the Black Panther Party*, 176.
64. Forbes, *Will You Die with Me?: My Life and the Black Panther Party*, 155.
65. McCutchen, *We Were Free for a While: Back-to-Back in the Black Panther Party*, 226.

CHAPTER 3

How Do You Like My Wu-Tang Style?

Enter the *Wu*[1]

At the helm of the nine-member hip-hop group known as the Wu-Tang Clan is the rapper-MC turned kung fu practitioner and actor-director, RZA (Robert F. Diggs).[2] Born in 1969 in the Brownsville section of Brooklyn, New York, RZA and his childhood peers indulged in the martial arts cinema that proliferated throughout New York City's Times Square during the late 1970s and early 1980s.[3] The 42nd Street area was an amalgamation of transnational exchange where locally owned movie theaters screened Asian martial arts cinema alongside adult entertainment and low-budget films for Black, Latina/o, Asian, and Euro American fans eager to see and pick up the latest moves. As

---

1. Not unlike the concept of *bu* in Japanese, which connotes the idea of war and is used in the word *budo*, the character for *wu* in Chinese can convey a similar concept and is most prevalent when referring to *wushu* a particular form kung fu or *wu* style taichiquan.

2. Robert F. Diggs is known as "RZA," which is an acronym for Ruler Zig-Zag-Zig Allah. He also has numerous other aliases, such as The Abbot, Bobby Digital, Prince Rakeem, and the Scientist, which are used interchangeably in his music.

3. For historical readings of the history of the Wu-Tang Clan and RZA's relationship with martial arts see the two written texts that they have developed on Riverhead Books titled *The Wu-Tang-Manual* and *Tao of Wu*, co-written with Chris Norris. Furthermore, RZA and Wu-Tang Clan members have provided interviews for https://www.youtube.com/watch?v=MavHcZOOKzc.

a youth, RZA spent every weekend with his cousin and future Wu-Tang Clan member, Ol' Dirty Bastard (Russell Jones) in mid-town Manhattan watching double-feature martial arts films. Eventually they saw the Shaw Brothers film *Shaolin and Wu Tang* (1983) that provided inspiration for the group's name as well as the performative codes for Wu-Tang Clan's lyrics, narrative structure, and kinesthetic stylistics.

When viewed through the eyes of a young Black man, martial arts films of the "East" provided a persuasive counterdiscourse to the dominant representation of Westernism and Eurocentrism as personified through the white male hero whose antithesis was more often than not a Third World villain rooted in stereotype, such as the savage Indian, the invading Latina/o, the alien Asian, and of course the Black brute. To recall Van Clief's own words about the film industry in which "the Black guys were always the bad guys. The pimps . . . the drug dealer . . . ," Black masculinity was choreographed into negative imagery that functioned in conjunction with racist policy to affirm racial regimes. Yet, the mediated movements found in the images of pop-cultural flows that were consumed in Times Square, at the Cedar Lee Theatre in Cleveland, or on Saturday afternoons on New York City's public access television provided a discursive and somatic possibility for what Black bodies could do. As RZA states, "When it [kung fu cinema] came on TV though, trust me my whole block came outside. Because that's how it was in those days. It came on at three, by five o'clock everybody's outside doing it [the martial arts]. Trying to do the snake, fall back, trying to do everything."[4] There was an emotional resonance that mobilized and catalyzed this particular fan culture comprised predominantly of Black and Brown youth to (re)create themselves based on the mediated kinesthetics of Asian masculinity produced by the Hong Kong–based Shaw Brothers films such as *Shaolin and Wu Tang* or *The 36th Chamber of Shaolin* (1978). The latter film provided the impetus for the Wu-Tang Clan's debut breakout album titled *Enter the Wu-Tang (36 Chambers)* (1993) and was an extension of martial arts fantasy that placed the group on a successful career trajectory that was also a hard-fought battle for control of their own narrative and presentation of self.

The conjunction between martial arts practice and what Fanon Che Wilkins referred to as the "hip-hop imagination" appropriated "kung fu film dialogue, performance, and philosophy into their aural sound scapes [sic] and musical production."[5] Mediated gestures, acts, and routines were restored and twice-behaved as new dance styles, such as B-boying and B-girling, that rein-

---

4. The RZA Interview, 36th Chamber of Shaolin, April 12, 2012, https://www.youtube.com/watch?v=MavHcZOOKzc.

5. Wilkins. "Shaw Brother's Cinema in the Hip-Hop Imagination," 226.

terpreted kung fu moves such as the snake or the dragon and emerged alongside recycled sound styles and rhymed word styles that in turn constituted an Afro Asian performance and a new way of Black urban life.

> These films definitely resonated a lot in the Black community. It's the underdog thing. It's the brotherly thing, and, also I think there was an escapism because you could go over there and watch these movies and it's not even America. It's like a whole other world. . . . The movie *The 36th Chamber of Shaolin* hit me multiple times in my life. The first time that I saw it, it was the first film that I saw that had a history that was outside the scope of American history. In the sense of being a Black man in America, history doesn't ever go further than slavery actually. I never had a true imagination besides Greek mythology and bible studies about what was going on in other parts of the world because I didn't have a clear vision of it.[6]

Kung fu cinema inspired young Black men such as RZA to imagine the possibilities that were beyond the confines of the Western canon, and they were rooted in movements that created new images of self-representation.

This chapter is concerned with the way that the consumption of martial arts imagery catalyzed young people to develop a counterhegemonic world view where they became masters of their own bodies through the mediated kinesthesia of martial arts (kung fu and karate, in particular). As Deleuze contends, "image = movement" and the kinetics of the movement image do not simply remain on the screen, but rather filter through mediated experiences and materialize bodies as they move to other bodies that make new images and hence restored movements, but yet, are "never for the first time."[7] Every punch, kick, and block within kung fu cinema, that is, "every image [that] acts on others and reacts to others, on 'all their facets at once' and 'by all their element[s],'"[8] reshaped the possibility of youths who made themselves through a martial arts mythology that offered an imaginative terrain through which to envision themselves as *invincible warriors,* Black Dragons or The Wu (as they commonly refer to themselves) capable of taking on any challenge. While the Wu-Tang Clan has perhaps been the most visible example of this form of mediated kinesthesia, their journey unfolded alongside a martial arts filmography that anticipated and responded to the construction of Black masculinity as a form of Afro Asian performance in US-based films such as *Enter the Dragon, The Last Dragon,* and *Karate Kid* (2010). These films fea-

---

6. Liu, Jialiang, *The 36th Chamber of Shaolin,* 2009.
7. Deleuz, *Cinema: The Movement Image,* 58.
8. Deleuz, *Cinema: The Movement Image,* 58.

tured performances of Black men either in Asia as part of a heroic fantasy that both celebrated and troubled historically dominant depictions of Black masculinity in relationship to an Asian "other." As I reveal, these popular fantasia have continued to operate as contested sites of Afro Asian performance and a martial arts imagination that at times anticipates, relies upon, and disrupts raced and gendered stereotype.

Jim Kelly and the Promise of a Black Hero

In 1973 the film *Enter the Dragon* catapulted and solidified Bruce Lee's image into the global popular imagination. This was in part because Lee was viewed as a non-white body that could "kick-ass" within an overwhelmingly white film industry. His stature became empowering for people in South East Asia who were fighting imperialism. In his discussion on liberation movements in Calcutta, Vijay Prashad contends, "With his bare fists and nunchaku, Bruce provided young people with the sense that we, like Vietnamese guerillas, could be victorious against the virulence of international capitalism. He seemed invincible."[9] Lee exuded confidence in his films and interviews, galvanizing people of color in the US who adopted Lee as an icon for popular counternarrative and anticipated the transnational cultural practice of RZA and the Wu-Tang Clan. Furthermore, the casting for *Enter the Dragon* was often hailed as a progressive choice that celebrated US multiculturalism. The film's plot revolved around three martial artists, Bruce Lee as Lee (Asian), John Saxon as Roper (white), and Jim Kelly as Williams (Black), who attend a martial arts tournament on a Hong Kong island that is a cover for an underground heroin operation. However, there was a problem with co-star Jim Kelly's performance in the role of Williams that created a conundrum in terms of how martial arts popular culture has been historicized. In *Enter the Dragon*, the framing of Kelly's performance reveals an ambivalence about Black masculinity and Afro Asian performance because his character is the only main character to die.[10] Not only is he killed, but his death is rendered as a pseudo lynching that exposed how dangerous Black masculinity was to the racial order of society and how racial triangulation maintained and continues to maintain racial regimes.

---

9. Prashad, *Everybody Was Kung Fu Fighting: Afro-Asian Connections and the Myth of Cultural Purity*, 127.

10. Jim Kelly passed away in 2013 from cancer. He gave many interviews that can be found online. In one of the more interesting ones, conducted in 1992, Kelly discusses how he became involved in martial arts as well as the film industry, https://www.youtube.com/watch?time_continue=141&v=-j1DPEst7mA.

Originally from Kentucky, Kelly began martial arts as a teenager when not playing football. Kelly subsequently left the university at the end of his freshman year and decided to pursue a career in martial arts and acting. As a strategy to break into Hollywood, he trained in karate intensively and won the middle-weight first place in 1971 at the Long Beach International Karate Championship. He opened a karate studio in Los Angeles and was in turn discovered by a casting agent who worked with one of his students. During interviews, Kelly not only articulated the struggles that he faced as a Black actor who wanted to be an action hero but also gestured toward Lee's own frustration with the film industry, specifically citing the choice to cast the white actor David Carradine in the role of Caine in the television series *Kung Fu* (1972–1975), despite the fact that the script was originally written for Lee. Kelly contended that he and Lee had similar struggles as minorities, "myself as a Black man, Bruce as a Chinese. Bruce caught hell. People don't know that. They didn't even want him in Hollywood because he was Chinese."[11] Knowing that he could not break through the "glass ceiling" of Hollywood, Lee left and went to Hong Kong to launch his film career.

Lee understood race and racism all too well, and he adopted a coalitional approach to dealing with race that enacted his own form of racial kinesthesia. Hence at the beginning of the film Lee adopted a form of Black performativity, employing head-fakes and dancelike movement reminiscent of the Black boxers that he had studied and emulated, Muhammad Ali in particular. In the opening scene of *Enter the Dragon,* he sparred with the actor and Peking Opera performer Sammo Hung in front of their teacher and the other disciples of the Shaolin Temple. The larger and more robustly built Hung portrays an anonymous Shaolin student. Lee's appreciation for Ali's innovative fighting style was articulated when he wrote, "The lead jab is a feeler. It is the basis of all other blows, a loose, easy stinger. It is a whip rather than a club. Ali's theory is to picture hitting a fly with a swatter."[12] Like the nimble Ali, who would "float like a butterfly and sting like a bee" as he danced around his opponents in the ring, Lee's choreography of graceful boxer-like movements made his opponents appear clumsy in comparison. This performative code-switching was immediately echoed two scenes later during the opening credits for *Enter the Dragon* when the very same "whaaa" that is uttered during the fight with Hung is reintroduced over a 1970s music soundtrack indicative of the music of the blaxploitation genre as the screen is filled by a panoramic shot of Hong Kong.

---

11. Walker, David, F. *Macked, Hammered, Slaughtered, Shafted: A Documentary,* (1996).
12. Lee, *Tao of Jeet Kune Do,* 98.

In the following scene, an American Airlines jet glides in over the city's urbanity, and the next shot is framed through the glass window of a busy Hong Kong airport as Williams, dressed in a black jacket and white turtleneck, emerges from the airliner. Williams's identity is marked as a transnational figure as he steps onto the ramp leading to the tarmac. Through a series of shots framed by Hong Kong avenues Williams proves himself to be adept at negotiating the streets as he makes his way across busy boulevards and through the markets as he moves amongst the people, using his feet as his carriage. A quick glance around his surroundings, Williams nods his head and claps his hands together as if to suggest that he knows this urbanity and is confident enough to negotiate the transnational space of the city.

Williams's movement against the backdrop of Hong Kong is a stark contrast to the white character, Roper (John Saxon), who makes his first appearance at the Hong Kong airport dressed in a gray business suit and orders a human taxi driver to collect his dozen or so luxury suitcases. In contrast to Williams, who physically walks the Hong Kong streets, Roper is seen riding in the taxi car, pulled by a Chinese man who appears to be twice his age. Roper's bags are pulled in tow by the five or six other human taxi cars that haul his luggage. The camera angle then switches to Roper's point of view from his seated position of luxury and power—whiteness—and this is yet another contrast to Williams's walk through the city until he finally reaches the river boat that will take him to the island of the renegade Shaolin Monk, Mr. Han.

Just prior to meeting Roper on the boat, we glimpse a view of Williams's recollection of US urban experience through an encounter with his karate sensei, Steve Muhammad (formerly Steve Sanders). As discussed in Chapter 1, Muhammad, who is listed uncredited in the film, was one of the cofounders of the Black Karate Federation (BKF) along with Donnie Williams. Muhammad's brief exchange with Williams momentarily brings the reality of Central Los Angeles to the forefront. The camera tracks Williams as he walks into the dojo toward the front part of the studio marked with red, black, and green coloring of the Black liberation movement. In front of Williams are several rows of Black men who stand in profile, and punch in sync with Muhammad's vocal count, indicating the timing of each strike. Muhammad signals to one of his senior students to lead the exercise so that he can greet Williams, and the two embrace in a handshake as scene in Figure 3.1. The colors on the band of the fist recall the aforementioned Pan-Africanist leanings of many Black nationalist and liberation movements, which began with Marcus Garvey's Universal Negro Improvement Association (UNIA) in 1920.

This moment in the film that unfolds against a backdrop of Afro Asian semiotics briefly captured an alternative discourse to the popular representation of whiteness and Orientalist exoticisms of martial arts.

FIGURE 3.1. Williams and a nameless karate instructor portrayed by Steve Sanders in the dojo. The emblem of the BKF is just behind them. From *Enter the Dragon*, Warner Brothers Entertainment.

Upon leaving the dojo Williams is stopped by two white police officers who confront him as he walks down the street. The patrol car screeches up behind the undisturbed Williams as he remains calm, cool, and collected. Two white police officers get out of the car and approach Williams and begin to physically accost him. While Williams has placed his other suitcase on the ground and stands with both hands in the air, the first cop grabs Williams's bag and begins the interrogation, which quickly becomes physical as the second cop hurls a racial slur.

> POLICEMAN 1: Going on a trip?
> (Policeman 1 frisks Williams and pulls out his passport and plane tickets)
> POLICEMAN 1: Hey, this jig's gotta passport.
> POLICEMAN 2: Where ya' goin,' jig? Where's the plane ticket for?
> POLICEMAN 1: Hong Kong via Hawaii.
> POLICEMAN 2: He's not going to Hawaii.[13]

As Policeman 2 encroaches with his nightstick drawn, Williams quickly readies himself and then strikes the nightstick snapping it. Both policemen attack Williams as he in turn delivers a series of blows to the first cop and disposes of the second one by flipping him into a wooden fence. A dog proceeds to chew on the officer's head allowing Williams to escape in the patrol car. The exchange between Williams and the police was representative of the countless reported encounters between law enforcement and African American men.

---

13. Clouse, *Enter the Dragon* (1973).

While paying homage to the Black Karate Federation's Donnie Williams and Steve Muhammad, the film shows Williams adopting karate as a strategy for surviving the streets of Los Angeles.

However, this maneuver seems to run aground in Hong Kong once he reaches Mr. Han's island. It is also no surprise that Williams's masculinity is framed within the hypersexualized trope of the "Black buck" when the hostess of the island, Tania, played by Ahna Capri, brings an array of prostitutes to Williams's room the evening that he wins the first round of the tournament. Williams's selection of all the prostitutes versus Lee's selection of none, and Roper's selection of only one, reinforces Williams's hypersexualized masculinity, capable of super human "strength."

The following evening, after Williams has defeated Parsons, a fighter from New Zealand, Williams rests in his room surrounded by several nude prostitutes, some of whom are white—none of whom are Black. Williams rises from the bed, dressed in only his briefs. After an evening of intense sexual encounters with multiple prostitutes, Williams has enough energy to go out into the "moonlight" and practice karate forms despite a warning from one of the females not to exit the palace where they are staying. It is a choice that comes with a heavy price as Williams is summoned to Han's office the next day after the morning edification given by Han to the martial arts practitioners. Dressed in the compulsory yellow karate uniform, Williams enters Han's office, unsuspecting of Han's intentions. The following exchange leads not only to Williams's death, but ends in a manner that frames Williams's blackness as strange fruit and then links blackness with the heroin drug trade.

> WILLIAMS: Mr. Han?
> HAN: You fought well yesterday. Your style is unorthodox.
> WILLIAMS: But effective.
> HAN: It is not the art, but the combat that you enjoy.
> WILLIAMS: The winning.
> HAN: We are all ready to win, just as we are born knowing only life. It is defeat that you must learn to prepare for.
> WILLIAMS: I don't waste my time with it.
> HAN: Oh? How so?
> WILLIAMS: I'll be too busy looking good.
> HAN: What were you looking for when you attacked my guards?
> WILLIAMS: Wasn't me.
> HAN: You were the only man outside of the palace.
> WILLIAMS: I was outside, but I wasn't the only one.
> HAN: You will tell me who else.

> **WILLIAMS:** Mr. Han, suddenly I'd like to leave your island.
> **HAN:** It is not possible.
> **WILLIAMS:** Bullshit, Mr. Han-man!
> (Williams turns to see three guards that have entered.)
> Man, you come right out of a comic book![14]

The irony of this scene is that while Williams is killed during his ensuing battle with the "Han-man," in the simulated game of dozens,[15] Williams's euphemism of "Man, you come straight out of a comic book" solidified Kelly's position within a broader pop-cultural imaginary. While fans of the cult classic always seemed to relish in Williams's humor and even "cool" Blackness, Williams had to die and die in a way that reified the positioning of Black masculinity within the racial regime.

The reification of the racial regime is fulfilled when Han, having now fought with Williams in his office, knocks Williams backward sending him crashing through a fake wall, and into a heroin den full of prostitutes who are high and laughing hysterically. Williams is then repeatedly knocked backwards by Han onto the various prostitutes. A fast-paced tempo of the theme song plays over the scene, and it is as if ghosts of Black American heroin dens have somehow descended upon Williams's body in Asia. He is disoriented, confused, distracted, and cannot maintain his balance, making him prey for Han, who then reveals a fake hand that he uses to bludgeon Williams to death. However, Kelly's body (his corporeal flesh) has one last appearance to make in the film. It is this moment that the film confirms one last time Kelly's purpose in the film. The scene erases the gains that the Black liberation movements had made through the appropriation of Asian grammar through martial arts repertoire.

Han leads Roper through the underground factory of his island's heroin operation, interrogating him about his gambling debts in the US until finally Williams's dead corpse becomes visible (Figure 3.2). Williams's body has been stripped naked except for the white boxer pants that were worn in his post-climatic scene with the prostitutes. Chains wrapped around Williams's hands, feet, and neck suggest the bondage of slavery, and remind the spectator of the danger of Williams's Black masculinity despite the fact that he is already dead. As Mr. Han states, "There are certain realities. I want us to have a clear understanding." Looking at Williams's naked body, Roper responds, "No, there's no

---

14. Clouse, *Enter the Dragon* (1973).
15. The goal and pleasure of the dozens is not the viciousness of the insult, but the humor, the creative pun, the outrageous metaphor that emerges through a vernacular rhetorical exchange.

FIGURE 3.2. Han and Roper gaze onto Williams's dead body, which hangs like strange fruit in Mr. Han's dungeon. From *Enter the Dragon*, Warner Brothers Entertainment.

misunderstanding between us." The rope suspending Williams's body is cut loose, plunging it into the water.

In *Enter the Dragon* the Black body was confined within the metacommentary on Black masculinity to that of destruction through castration. Because of the high economic risk inherent in film financing, *Enter the Dragon* could not overreach the color line. Rather the film reified a racial triangulation as Lee and Roper free all of the Chinese workers and addicts that have been kept in bondage on Mr. Han's island as a revolt unfolds against Mr. Han and his heroin operation.

While Bruce Lee died the same year that *Enter the Dragon* was released, the film launched Jim Kelly's career as a martial arts actor, particularly in blaxploitation cinema of the 1970s. However, the end of the epoch of blaxploitation cinema was marked by the advent of the summer blockbuster *Jaws* (1975) that provided a new model through which Hollywood created massive returns at the box office. The year 1975 also marked the formal end to the US war in Vietnam. Hollywood was tasked with the responsibility of waging a culture war on the screen that reconciled the loss in Vietnam and simultaneously repatriated white masculinity.

A "great white" super-hero and leader of the free world was needed, and he first emerged as Sylvester Stallone's character of Rocky Balboa in the film *Rocky* (1976) when he rose up from the streets of Philadelphia to fight the Black boxer Appollo Creed. But Rocky was not a veteran or martial artist. Rather his character was a prelude to the archetypal figure that was embodied in what Yvonne Tasker refers to as the "muscular movies of the 1980s"[16] in films

---

16. Tasker, *Spectacular Bodies: Gender, Genre, and the Action Cinema*, 37.

such as Sylvester Stallone's *Rambo: First Blood* (1982), Chuck Norris's *Missing in Action* (1984), and Arnold Schwarzenegger's *Commando* (1985) and *Norris in Invasion USA* (1985). Kelly critiqued race and gender in representations in Hollywood with the following:

> It's the fear of projecting a Black male in those positions. You take for example a white action hero. Let's take for example this guy by the name of Chuck Norris. . . . I know Chuck. I remember when Chuck was fighting in karate tournaments. He was karate champion, but to me he's never been able to trans(late) that onto the screen. . . . You take Chuck Norris and change the color of his skin, he would be lucky to get a job in Hollywood as an extra. I'm serious. Just change the color of skin to black, I guarantee you he would have problems getting jobs in Hollywood as an extra, but his skin is not black. It's white. And they pushed and pushed and made him a star. . . . There's a fear of projecting Black males in that real strong positive [action hero] image. . . . Hollywood made Rocky . . . Rocky was a great hope. . . . There's a fear of projecting Black males in certain images and that's true no matter if it's the film industry or if it's the corporate world. It's the way it is in this country, in America. . . . It's like trying to destroy any Black man that accomplishes a certain level in this society.[17]

Kelly's attempt to use martial arts as a vehicle through which to access the film industry ran up against the larger challenges of racialized and gendered hegemony. His struggle echoes that of the aforementioned Ron Van Clief who also engaged in a form of self-fashioning by using martial arts to open up various lines of employment opportunities in the film industry, but most importantly "wanted to be a kung fu star" and hence a hero. Kelly wanted to see Black male action heroes who could be victorious and triumphant, but like Bruce Lee, he could not get past the color-line. His critical critique of intersectionality said a lot not only about the particular trajectory of his own career, which was short lived in part because of the end of blaxploitation, but also about the limitations that blaxploitation offered as a genre. Many of the films that comprised the blaxploitation genre relied on stereotypical representations in which the Black men and women were situated as drug dealers, prostitutes, pimps, and law enforcement. Frustrated by the essentialist framing of Black characters, Kelly bowed out of the industry as a whole and continued to reject roles that were offered to him because of their lack of nuance or their reification of negative Black stereotype. Ironically, the confluence of this frustration reemerged

---

17. Walker, David, F. *Macked, Hammered, Slaughtered, Shafted: A Documentary,* (1996).

in a satirical critique of Afro Asian performance in Taimak Guariello's portrayal of "Bruce" Leroy Green in Berry Gordy's *The Last Dragon* (1985).[18]

Taimak's Last Dragon

Set against the urban landscape of New York City's Harlem, Lower East Side, and Chinatown, *The Last Dragon* reimagined the city as a transnational space in which a zealous young martial arts fan and practitioner, "Bruce" Leroy, contests the conventional iterations of Black masculinity through his Afro Asian performance. Unlike Williams's hypermasculinized performance of physical prowess and sexual dominance in *Enter the Dragon*, Leroy is a virginal Bruce Lee sycophant who is dedicated to the monastic perfection of martial arts purity. The plot of *The Last Dragon* revolves around Leroy's search for the one true master after he has completed the penultimate level of training under the tutelage of a ninjutsu Master (Thomas Ikeda) who lives on a boat docked in the East River. Having been given a medallion that supposedly belonged to Bruce Lee himself, the Master sends Leroy out in search of Sum Dum Goy, the oldest and wisest sage in the universe who also happens to reside somewhere in New York City. In his search for Sum Dum Goy, Leroy must venture beyond the comfort of his immediate Harlem community and find "the glow," which is the final stage of his training. Leroy is challenged by Sho'Nuff the Shogun of Harlem (Julius J. Carry III) who aims to destroy Leroy's reputation and manhood in order to prove to the world that he is "the meanest, prettiest, baddest mofo' around town." To complicate matters Leroy must also contend with the mischievous glutton, Eddie Arkadian (Christopher Murney), who aspires to monopolize the video arcade industry by controlling the local club celebrity Laura Charles (Denise Mathews aka Vanity), who is also Leroy's newly found love interest.

Director Michael Schultz negotiated a fine line between blaxploitation and blockbuster feature that would capture the die-hard audiences of the Hong Kong kung fu cinema as well as appeal to the crossover market of those nonmartial artists who were the first MTV (Music Television) viewers of the early 1980s eager to see a Black hero.

---

18. Berry Gordy Jr. was the founder and executive producer of Motown, a Black-owned and -controlled music company based in Detroit, Michigan, that produced and managed a plethora of artists including Michael Jackson, and the Jackson Five, Stevie Wonder, the Supremes, the Temptations, and the list goes on.

> When I first read the script of *The Last Dragon*, it was one of the few projects that I knew immediately was going to be a success. Because in the history of cinema there had been very few Black heroes, but with a young Black hero and gorgeous people, I knew that kids would look at this movie over and over again. So the character of Bruce Leroy, a young unassuming guy who fantasizes that he is Bruce Lee, the Black Bruce Lee, and the adventures that he gets into, I thought would just captivate a young audience.[19]

Not only does Schultz's commentary offer insight into the strategic creation of Leroy as an Afro Asian trope that could fill the lacuna of Black action heroes during the 1980s, but by synthesizing the sounds of popular music produced by Berry Gordy's Motown Productions in conjunction with the imagery of the kung fu cinema, *The Last Dragon* struck gold as a crossover film. The soundtrack incorporated Motown artists such as Stevie Wonder, Smokie Robinson, The Temptations, and of course Vanity whom, like Michael Jackson and Prince, relied upon crossover appeal palatable enough for white suburban audiences, but still flavorful enough for Black and Latinx fans.

Aside from taking advantage of the new technology of the music video format, *The Last Dragon* converged the fan culture of blaxploitation, martial arts, disco, and hip-hop that resonated with an intergenerational and interracial market. As film critic Jeffrey Ressner wrote in the *Hollywood Reporter*, "Berry Gordy's *The Last Dragon* is a fun, frisky R&B/pop musical with touches of such recent hits as *Purple Rain* and *The Karate Kid*, but heavily sugar-coated with the glossy style of video music-movies like *Flashdance* and *Footloose*.... Where else could you see old kung fu footage intercut with a bass heavy R&B tune to create the first-ever Bruce Lee music video?"[20] In a decade that saw the beginnings of a Black independent cinema in the films of Spike Lee and Robert Townsend, there was also a dearth of African American Hollywood film production and distribution. *The Last Dragon* proved to be a commercially successful piece of cinema that occupied a third space with an estimated budget of $10 million that grossed $25 million in the US domestic box office alone.

While the narrative worked hard to parody a wide range of Black and Asian stereotypes, the film's Orientalist framing cannot be dismissed. When Bruce Leroy is not training, he is either teaching classes at his uptown studio or like Ron Van Clief, RZA, and the Wu-Tang crew, consuming kung fu cinema at one of the Manhattan movie theaters, where he eats popcorn with chopsticks. Instead of the hip Western style street clothing or the karate gi

---

19. Schultz, Michael, *The Last Dragon / [videorecording (dvd)]*, 2005.
20. Ressner, "'The Last Dragon': THR's 1985 Review."

associated with Japanese martial arts that Williams wore, Leroy dons a straw canonical hat and a *changshan* emblematic of the traditional Cantonese uniform associated with Chinese martial arts and hence with his idol, Bruce Lee. As opposed to the hip-talking character of Williams who embodied the swagger of the soul/funk era of the 1970s, Leroy is an almost effeminate character who chooses to communicate through vernacular proverbs that border on non sequitur, which render him incomprehensible at times to his foes and certainly somewhat queer to his peers.

However, at the heart of the aesthetic presentation of *The Last Dragon* was Taimak's physique and his ability to actually execute martial arts repertoire that enabled him to become a simulacrum of the Asian hero featured in any Shaw Brothers or Golden Harvest film out of Hong Kong. There was also plenty of sexual energy embodied in his kinetics, or as cultural critic Latasha Diggs suggests, "Oh my god. A brother does something with kung fu (which was really nothing at all) but Jesus he was cute, had good hair and a chest thing going on—a pretty boy who could kick ass."[21] Taimak was not only a New York State kickboxing champion at the age of eighteen, but he was also a student of the aforementioned Ron Van Clief and trained in Van Clief's Chinese Goju Ryu karate school discussed in the first chapter. Van Clief served as technical director and fight choreographer for the entire film. In fact, Taimak did not have any prior acting experience before the film, and it was his connection with Van Clief that actually provided him the opportunity to audition for the role of Leroy.[22] At nineteen and twenty years of age during filming, Taimak was in the physical prime of his training.

In the most scopophilic of contexts, Schultz took full advantage of Taimak's young physique. In the opening sequence, which also serves as the opening credits, the cinematography creates a conjunction of music video and a martial arts training program through Leroy's choreographed movements to the song *The Glow* (1985). Leroy offers a bow toward the camera before performing a series of katas that increase in difficulty and morph into calisthenics. He is shirtless and wears an almost see-through pair of pants and a soft yellow kung fu sash belt tied around his waist which flows with each movement.

His body is backlit using what appears to be three-point lighting that adds a sheen to his body (a prelude to the "glow" that he achieves at the end of the film), further highlighting the muscles as he performs flips, strikes, kicks, and acrobatic rotations on his hands. Leroy's body glistens in the lighting

---

21. Ongiri, "'He Wanted to Be Just Like Bruce Lee': African Americans, Kung Fu Theater and Cultural Exchange at the Margins."
22. Taimak, Interview, 2014, https://www.youtube.com/watch?v=HFvgG_oZhGQ.

as perspiration drips from his chest and shoulders and onto his washboard abdomen.

While Leroy's yellow sash would indicate that he is a novice within the belt ranking system of white to black, the virtuosity in Leroy's performance communicates that he is an advanced practitioner. The opening solo sequence transitions to a paired dynamic test in which Leroy proceeds to catch arrows out of midair with his bare hand that his Master fires at him from approximately twenty feet away. This display of ninjutsu again collapses the distance between martial arts practitioner and actor. As Schultz further reveals during his director's commentary, "This is not a special effect. We actually shot arrows at a predetermined target and had Taimak try to chop them in half out of the air. It took us about two hours before we finally got the timing right . . . the strength right . . . to actually break the arrows."[23] However, the decision to include Leroy catching arrows was also a nod to Van Clief's teacher and ninjutsu practitioner, Ronald Duncan, who taught the technique to his students and performed the technique in demonstrations such as the one described in the introduction. Thus, *The Last Dragon* is also a cinematic cultural expression that contains a genealogical record of Black martial arts practitioners.

Once Leroy successfully passes his test, the Master informs him that he has completed the final level of his training and their journey together has come to an end. Leroy must seek out the wise old sage, Sum Dum Goy, and the first place that he visits is the movie theater that shows *Enter the Dragon*. From the front row of the theater Leroy indulges in the film while consuming popcorn with chopsticks. The theater is filled with a queer multiracial audience of a ganja-puffing man with dreadlocks who talks back to the screen, body builders, break-dancers, drag queens, and of course martial artists. Leroy's obsession with Bruce Lee's *Enter the Dragon* is an intertextual play and commentary on late twentieth-century engagement with the martial arts cinema and echoes RZA's comments about the impact that kung fu cinema had on African American spectatorship. When a b-girl and b-b-boy try to "get down" in the aisle of the theater with their boombox and interrupt the audience's delight, a tough looking Asian man approaches and jumps on the ghetto blaster just as Bruce Lee jumps on his defeated enemy O'hara in *Enter the Dragon*, which is still playing on the screen.

A melee then ensues in the theater when Sho'Nuff shows up and continues the disruption as everyone begins to fight with Sho'Nuff's minions, just as Bruce Lee battles with all of Mr. Han's guards on the screen. It is not Kelly's screen performances over which Leroy fetishizes. Rather, the image of Lee's body is a mediated kinesthetic conduit from Lee to Leroy to the spectator. In

---

23. Schultz, Michael, *The Last Dragon / [videorecording (dvd)]*, 2005.

this scene, Leroy looks referentially to Lee, bypassing Williams. Lee personifies the revolutionary impulse for an imaginary space of Afro Asian liberation as witnessed in other decolonizing performances, such as smashing the sign that reads "No Chinese or Dogs Allowed" or taking on an entire Japanese dojo in *Fists of Fury* (1971).

Leroy's search for Sum Dum Goy eventually leads him to a fortune cookie warehouse factory in Chinatown where he believes the guru Sum Dum Goy will be found. On his first visit, he is confronted by three Chinese American workers who are engaged in a form of yellow-blackface performance. Standing on the sidewalk in front of the entrance to the factory, the workers dance and groove to the R&B sounds of *Suki Yaki Hot Saki Sue* (1985) that blare out of an enormous boombox next to them. Fully ensconced in his Asian performative aesthetic and wanting to know if the master Sum Dum Goy is inside, Leroy's attempt to communicate with the factory workers is thwarted due to a lexical misunderstanding in Black vernacular movements, gestures, and routines. When the first worker asks Leroy what he is looking for, he informs them that he is "looking for the Master." The workers run a linguistic game on him and respond with, "Ain't no master here, dude, ain't no slaves neither." They slap hands giving each other dap. This initial exchange reveals the film's acute awareness of racial kinesthesia, which is doubly coded, and by black-yellow-facing and yellow-blackfacing, the scene calls attention to the very markers through which we do and see race and gender.

> **LEROY:** Is this not his fortune cookie factory?
> **WORKER 2:** Master . . . uh . . . he doing his wisdom thang.
> **LEROY:** I seek only wisdom of the Master.
> **WORKER 1:** You want wisdom, you buy fortune cookie.
> **WORKER 2:** Take a hike, cool breeze.
> **WORKER 1:** Yeah, baby.
> **LEROY:** Please, I must see the Master. I seek only his wisdom.
> **WORKER 2:** Look here, chump. The Master don't see nobody, especially no jive coolies.
> **WORKER 1:** Yeah, he don't see no one who don't know how to get down, baby. You dig, bro? You too square, man.
> **WORKER 3:** Let me say it, so that he can understand it, Jim.
> (taking Leroy's conical hat and putting on his own head.)
> You go now! Haulee ass outta of this place. Am I saying it right my, man?[24]

---

24. As stated by Michael Schultz in the director's cut of *Berry Gordy's: The Last Dragon* (1985).

The dancing at the top of the scene alongside the boombox strikes a nostalgia for the 1980s war of music in which Black blues, jazz, funk, R&B, and rap had entered into the public mainstream through unrestricted speakers of the boombox or as many referred to it, the "ghettoblaster." In the public space, urban and suburban youth shattered the domesticity of the music industry's construction of acceptable style through boom boxes carried on the shoulder. Public dancing can be seen as a form of reterritorializing and contesting the racial geometry of the city.

In the exchanges between Leroy and the Sum Dum Goy factory workers, yellow-blackfacing conceptualizes the physically and socially constructed space of Chinatown and its inhabitants in terms of what is supposed to be the appropriateness of "Asianness" through a Black performativity induced through both the music and the physicality of the Sum Dum Goy factory workers. As Leroy enquires about the illusive Master, the high-low-fives and gesticulating of the factory workers acts to subvert dominant notions of Chinese American identity—that is to say, "Chinese can't get down." The scene would slip into the realms of outright racism if it were not for the contrapuntal response to the factory workers' yellow-blackfacing embodied in Leroy's black-yellowfacing. Conversely, this scene is just as much of a simulacrum as the very stereotypes that it seeks to unsettle. Because of the vacuous variety of Asian and Black roles within the film industry, and because both Black and Asian bodies made their entry onto the screen through blackface and yellowface minstrelsy, the Black and Asian actor is still haunted by the history of race that hovers in the frame. Thus, one gets the impression that the parody is almost running out of air as it reaches for the next laugh. Ironically, the film's nonsatirical humor ends up reifying the very stereotypes that are being called into question.

Unable to locate the Master, Leroy takes a tip from Bruce Lee's *The Chinese Connection* (wherein Lee disguises himself as a telephone worker) and returns to the Sum Dum Goy fortune cookie factory disguised as one of his father's pizza deliverymen in an attempt to enter the fortune cookie factory. As if to suggest that by moving further toward Blackness, their Asian identity will move further away from foreignness, the three factory workers brush up on their Black vernacular by throwing dice in a game of craps—albeit using a craps rule book as a guide. Upon Leroy's entry into the factory, they are sly enough to scheme Leroy and hustle him out of the gold medallion. High and intoxicated, the factory workers instruct Leroy to wait outside while they bring the Master, but then proceed to lock the factory doors and keep Leroy's medallion that they won in the crap throw. But to their dismay, Leroy uses his kung fu strength to bust back into the factory and demands to see the Master.

LEROY: Where is the Master? I want to see him now! (grabbing Worker 2 by the collar and cornering him.)
WORKER 2: Please! Please! There is no Master!
LEROY: You lie!
WORKER 2: No, it's true! We made him up to sell more fortune cookies. Tell him!
WORKER 1: It's true! Show him!
WORKER 2: I'll show you!
WORKER 1: Yeah, show him!
WORKER 2: This is Sum Dum Goy.[25]

The door opens to reveal an odd and antiquated machine that is in the process of manufacturing fortune cookies. A sign flashing on the machine's display reads "He who is color blind must never follow a horse of another color." The double entendre leaves yet another gap to be filled by the spectator's desire to view *The Last Dragon's* cross-appropriation as counternarrative or offensive, and perhaps a little of both. Leroy's legitimacy as the film's protagonist is reestablished through his physicality, simultaneously relieving the audience of having to continue the imagined identity crisis of Asian masculinity performing in a Black vernacular. The audience is reminded that even Leroy's performance is a simulacrum of Black performativity through the machines repetitive production of the object that it manufactures: fortune cookies. Fortune cookies are as much of a simulacrum of America's construction of "Chineseness" as Gordy's construction of Leroy's exotic oriental aesthetic.

By engaging, and yet not engaging, in racialized and gendered stereotype, *The Last Dragon* worked to create a third space that troubled racial triangulation. Through Afro Asian performance, Leroy's attempt to codeswitch between a Black vernacular and an Asian aesthetic enabled him to negotiate the urban terrain in New York City. His stealth like movements recalled Ronald Duncan's postulations about the ninja who moved in and amongst various enclaves and fluidly transgressed community borders. Leroy actually does appear in ninjutsu clothing a la Ronald Duncan when he saves Laura Charles the first time from the evil grips of Eddie Arkadian, who is one of the few white characters in the film. Yet, Leroy was able to codeswitch because he did not attract the ire of US racism that demanded that he die and because he unsettled the hypermasculinzed iterations associated with Williams in *Enter the Dragon* or with the strong the attributes that Kelly described as belonging to the Black super hero. Yet, Leroy is a Black dragon that saves the heroine,

---

25. Schultz, Michael, *The Last Dragon* / [videorecording (dvd)], 2005.

Charles, from Arkadian at the end of the film after she is kidnapped for a second time. In this sequence he also defeats Sho'Nuff and reasserts his position as the softly masculinized "pretty boy" of the film.

Jayden Smith is the Karate Kid Doing Kung Fu Dreams

The Last Dragon anticipated another mediated kinesthetic Afro Asian performance in the 2010 remake of *Karate Kid*. Jaden Smith (son of rapper, hip-hop artist, and actor/producer Will Smith and actress Jayda Pinkett Smtih) plays Dre, a Black fatherless child whose mother relocates from Detroit to Beijing for employment. Jackie Chan portrays Mr. Han, a maintenance man in Dre's new apartment building. A racialized tension is created between the young Chinese boys who physically beat Dre and verbally taunt him about the texture of his hair, which he wears in cornrows, and the presumed attraction between Dre and a young Chinese woman, Meiying, played by actress Wenwen Han. Having been beaten senselessly by his Chinese kung fu practicing classmates who proclaim "No weakness! No Pain! No mercy!" as their academy's motto, Mr. Han takes Dre under his tutelage to teach him "real" kung fu.

On the first day, when training is to commence, Dre enters the backyard of Han's house with skateboard in hand and drops his jacket on the ground in the threshold of the doorway. Han stands next to a wooden pole into which he inserts a dowel. Dressed in a white tank-top and red track pants, Dre proceeds to inform Han of his athletic prowess and natural abilities, describing the litany of talents ranging from Capoeira to jujitsu and why he will make an excellent disciple. Han observes unimpressed before finally instructing Dre to pick up the jacket. In a scene reminiscent of the original *Karate Kid*'s "wax on, wax off," the "pick it up, put it on, take it off," of a jacket becomes a process for training kung fu and a disciplined "attitude."

> MR. HAN: Pick up your jacket?
> (Dre picks up the jacket that he'd dropped on the ground when he entered, and brings it over to the pole where Mr. Han has been working.)
> DRE: Basically, Mr. Han, what I'm trying to say is, I gotta' good foundation here. It might not be as hard to teach me as other people.
> MR. HAN: Hang it up.
> (Dre hangs up the jacket.)
> DRE: Happy now?
> HAN: Take it down.
> DRE: But you just . . .

HAN: Take it down. Put it on. Take it off.
DRE: But I already did all of this . . .
HAN: Take it off . . .
DRE: Can you just tell me why I'm doing this?
HAN: Take it off. Hang it up. Take it down. Put it on the ground. Pick it up. Hang it up. Take it down. Put it on. Take it off. Hang it up. Take it off.[26]

The camera pulls out for a long shot of Chan and Smith standing next to the pole as the routine is repeated and so begins Dre's disciplining process. The seemingly innocuous action of washing a car or putting on a jacket functions as a vernacular methodology to reconstruct the body of Smith's character and is emblematic of an iconographic trope that has circulated in the genre of US martial arts films in which the young disciple is trained by the "little old Chinese man." By accessing a form of corporeal discipline this transcultural engagement moves Dre from outsider to insider status in which he eventually outperforms his foes in a kung fu tournament at the end of the film. Mr. Han is forced to confront his past, reestablishing himself within the community as a teacher of kung fu.

Through Smith's martial arts screen performance, *Karate Kid* (2010) attempts to make a leap toward a utopian Afro Asian performative imaginary in which the Chinese state has embraced the struggle of the Black to carve out an autonomous space. "It's all good in Jackie Chan's hood," because unlike his predecessor Jim Kelly, Smith has found a frontier free of lynching. This frontier is one in which Smith's prepubescent body can not only learn a different cultural template but the conjunction also suggests a Black possibility outside of Detroit. This Black possibility is in Beijing, where Dre is offered license to heroically enact violence upon Chinese bodies without worry of the white subject. American audiences can feel safe in rooting for Dre's struggle without being concerned about the dilapidated Detroit from which Dre and his mother are escaping. In turn, the character of Dre can be read as a deployed strategy to appease US–China anxieties, as if to suggest that Dre's very presence is born out of the necessity to confront Chinese economic and military prowess, and not the result of American inequity. The performance of martial arts as expression of Black masculinity is a vehicle for the stability of US capital vis-à-vis Columbia Pictures, the Chinese state, and the Hollywood machine that must cultivate Black visibility by confining the Black body's movement to one that is not in a confrontation with whiteness within the frame.

---

26. Zwart, *Karate Kid*, (2013).

From Dre's urban dwellings in Detroit, Michigan, the fantasia of China is immediately created at the outset of the film. As Dre and his mother, Sherry, prepare to embark on their flight to Beijing from their quaint apartment, Sherry fantasizes about what the future holds. Looking at the airline tickets, she states, "Oh, Dre, I am so excited! It's like we're three pioneers on a quest to start a new life in a magical new land." China, and the East by extension, is fetishized by the dreams of new prosperity that will lead the Black out of the economic despair of the collapsed automotive industry. After all, they are relocating for economic purposes because she is taking a job in an automotive plant somewhere in Beijing.

Compared to the *Karate Kid* in which Macchio's twenty-two-year-old body was able to negotiate the trials of karate, dating, and driving, Smith's young eleven-year-old body seems infantile.[27] This, in turn, pushes the intimate-like moments between Dre and Meiying as she playfully dances to Lady Gaga's *Poker Face* for Dre while he looks on entranced. As Meiying returns Dre's gaze, the camera reverses to Dre's point of view, and it is the film's spectator who is then watching her prepubescent body. To the left and to the right, Meiying's body is fully framed as Dre watches. It is in the attempt to sexualize her body that we are reminded of her physical underdevelopment as a child. In addition, dancing to Lady Gaga's music, as appropriated Black rhythm and blues, is yet another example in the film in which capital moves through a confluence of black-yellowfacing and yellow-blackfacing in which bodies become fetishized objects.

The "magical new land" that Sherry had fantasized about at the outset of the story is realized in the form of mystical fetishization of the "East" not only as feminine but also childlike. In this film, the East is full of children in teenage roles playing out quasi-adult fantasies. This fetishization is further compounded by the fact that the script, in adherence to the Hollywood formula of the first *Karate Kid,* must also demasculinize the central Asian male character. Similar to Mr. Miyagi of the first *Karate Kid,* Mr. Han is effeminized through his asexual, passive, and nonviolent positioning within the film. While Dre and Meiying as nonprocreative characters are able to pursue a simulated romantic interest within the narrative, Mr. Han and Sherry are not capable of consummating any potential attraction between the two of them on the screen. Unlike Williams and Leroy, the protagonist of this latest film to capture the Afro Asian male encounter is incapable of signifying any kind of

---

27. Macchio was born in 1961, and the original *Karate Kid* was released in 1984. Whereas Jayden Smith was born in 1998 and principal photography for *Karate Kid* (2010) took place during the summer of 2009. The discrepancy in physical development between the two is far from opaque.

sexuality. Even though Sherry makes a gesture to Mr. Han by insisting that he accompany her to the Qixi Festival, the only romantic Black/Asian encounter in this film is vis-à-vis Dre and Meiying. Mr. Han, who is a grieving widower, must maintain the pristine appearance of piety simultaneously reifying the "model minority" for American audiences and not disturbing the myth of cultural purity for Chinese audiences through the possible introduction of interracial children.

Similar to Mr. Miyagi, Mr. Han never shows his physical strength except for when he comically defeats the bullies that attacked Dre, by poking them in the eyes, wrapping them up in their own clothing, and then sending one bully flying into the other. Such antics require acute choreographic skills and reflect the mediated kinesthetics that were a signature of many of Chan's films. As mentioned, the kind of slapstick humor constructed through the choreography is Chan's forte, which he capitalized on as a result of his training as a youth in the Peking Opera. In this respect, Chan and Smith are quite similar to each other as they both have been groomed since children for the entertainment and film industry that relies upon transnational markets to sustain itself. Furthermore, through catch lines such as "the best fights are the ones we avoid," and "kung fu is for knowledge, defense. Not make war, but create peace," Han is able to personify the peaceful old sage. Everything that Mr. Han does is kung fu based, but it is also passive and domestic. Within the scope of global entertainment, Asian masculinity is perpetually tethered to martial arts and becomes almost synonymous with Asian identity. In *Karate Kid* (2010), this masculinity revolves around the passivity of Han and the violent aggression of the rival kung fu school's leader, Cheng, who must ultimately be put down by the fungibility of Dre's performance. In this context, Smith and Kelly are in conversation with each other as they are each deployed to Asia as the vanguard of Americanism.

However, in order for the Black to enact vengeance upon Cheng at the tournament, Dre must be welcomed by China by embracing China. This is achieved cinematically by placing Chan and Smith beside the most recognizable and fetishized objects of the East. The film makes use of, and celebrates, Chinese historical landmarks such as the Great Wall of China and a journey to the top of Wudang Mountains to learn the essence of *qi* (or chi, 気) defined by Mr. Han as, "Internal energy. The essence of life." Han writes the character for qi on the fogged-up window of the train. "It moves inside of us. It flows through our bodies. Gives us power from within."[28] The concept of qi as a

---

28. Zwart, *Karate Kid* (2010).

universal energy that flows through all living organisms is one that has been at the center of Western obsession with Eastern martial arts.

Qi as a fetishized mystical energy can be seen in the production and consumption of products such as ginseng tablets, qi energy drinks, and qigong training media. As a result, an entire industry of simulated Chinese medicine has become conflated with internal medical practices that emphasize continued health maintenance of the body through proper diet and regimented physical exercise. However, this exoticization is further embellished by the mise-en-scène of the film as Dre follows Mr. Han up the stairs to the peak of the Wudang Mountains, during which they encounter kung fu practitioners dressed in Chinese folk training clothing at each successive level until they finally reach the taiji–supreme ultimate–fountain. Dre rests while Han goes ahead of him to the top of Wudang Mountains where Dre drinks from the Dragon Well after Han tells him that it will give him magical power. Just outside, a woman practices kung fu by hypnotizing what appears to be a cobra snake as she balances on one foot atop the perilous but nonetheless cinematically majestic mountain peak. To make this journey all the more climatic, the chamber that contains the Dragon Well with a taiji emblem in the bottom, is also decorated with more taiji emblems. By embellishing Wudang with taiji and kung fu practitioners, the film is able to appease the state's desire to see celebrated national treasures while simultaneously satisfying Hollywood's necessity for the majestic objects that fulfill cinematic cultural expectations. When Chan and Smith are then located within the frame, as Dre endeavors through the training process under Han's tutelage, his character is seen appropriating an Asian folk grammar of kung fu against a backdrop of state-sanctioned scenery. Through Black-yellowfacing, Dre mimetically takes on a repertoire of Asian grammar through kung fu that moves him from the position of outsider to insider within the structure of the film.

The final repositioning of Dre as American Blackness within the racial geometry of twenty-first-century international entertainment as global capital necessitates that he reclaim his masculinity through a final structured performance event: the open kung fu tournament. It is in this controlled environment that Dre, as the personification of America, enacts chivalrous violence upon the Chinese aggressor, Cheng, and the teammates from Master Yi's Kung Fu Academy. Dre delivers a spectacular kick to Cheng's head to win the tournament. It is this scene, in particular, which has drawn the ire from some media critics who view this ending as yet another predictable form of foreigners teaching the Asian a lesson in Asian morality. However, this is an ironic criticism since the majority of Hollywood films have tracked a similar paradigm, only the protagonist has more often than not been a white male.

What is even more ironic, and of particular interest to this project, is the fact that Will Smith, Jayden Smith's father, was able to produce this film in China in collaboration with the Chinese government through the China Film Corporation, arguably one of the most influential state-run enterprises of China. Martial arts, again were a strategy to create an economic opportunity in Hollywood, an industry that is still predominantly white controlled and historically unreceptive to Black creative projects. Similar to rap, martial arts as a genre of popular expression, is a highly importable and exportable form of cultural capital. On the one hand, *Karate Kid* (2010) worked because it was able to plug itself into the Hollywood formulaic structure that is simultaneously oppressive and liberatory. While it provides economic pathways for the US and Chinese economic entities, it simultaneously operates to reify cultural hegemonic institutions that both utilize and perpetuate racial stereotypes. More specifically, by appropriating a grammar of Asia through martial arts, we are able to observe the way in which black-yellowfacing as a form of Black performativity creates contested moments of agency within martial arts cinema. Unlike Williams, who is symbolically lynched in *Enter the Dragon*, Dre is heralded as a champion who fights clean and uses the repertoire taught to him by his master, Mr. Han, to create a space of agency within the tournament's performance fighting ring.

"En Garde! I'll Let You Try My Wu-Tang Style!"

Before Dre ever met Mr. Han in Beijing, the Wu-Tang Clan had positioned themselves as interlocutors of Afro Asian performance from New York to Henan Province, China, where RZA would eventually make his first pilgrimage to the Shaolin Temple in 1999.[29] When Wu-Tang Clan released their first album *Enter the Wu-Tang (36 Chambers)* in 1993, the group was initially recognized for their uniqueness as Black lyricists who mixed dialogue and sound effects from kung fu cinema into their songs. The introduction for the first song "Bring Da Ruckus" on the album *Enter the Wu-Tang (36 Chambers)* began with a sampled dialogue from the film *Shaolin and Wu Tang* before the hard-hitting kick drum and snare accompanying RZA's chorus "Bring da mothafuckin' ruckus" begins. As a prelude, the song commences with the voice over, "Shaolin shadowboxing and the Wu-Tang sword style. If what you say is true, the Shaolin and the Wu-Tang could be dangerous. Do you think

---

29. Xiang Hua, "Shaolin Temple Prodigal Son: Monk Shi Yanming's Return to Shaolin after His Defection."

your Wu-Tang style can defeat me?"[30] When audiences heard the debut album in 1993, the group not only announced their arrival to the hip-hop industry, but like *The Last Dragon*, merged martial arts cinema audiences and Black hip-hop soundscapes.

However, there was a lacuna of understanding in the impact of martial arts and Eastern philosophy on the development of the Wu-Tang Clan. As with much of the mainstream media's coverage of rap and hip-hop, critics focused on the group's "gangster" style that seemed dangerously fascinating.[31] The Wu-Tang's use of martial arts as part of their narrative structure was only one manifestation of the group's martial arts appropriation. Yet, little attention was paid to how the Wu-Tang Clan rendered the art of rap music and the practice of hip-hop as a martial art itself. For the Wu, martial arts was a strategy for surviving in the drug economy and developing their skills as critical entrepreneurs in the music economy, which many have argued bear similarity. Equally neglected was the fact that RZA became an actual kung fu student and that his practice drew from life experience and explorations of Buddhism, Taoism, and the Five-Percent Nation (also known as the Nation of Gods and Earths), which developed as an offshoot from the Nation of Islam.[32]

The confluence of spirituality mixed with the knowledge of everyday experience was articulated in the two books that RZA published, titled *The Wu-Tang Manual* (2004) and *The Tao of Wu* (2009). In conjunction with their lyrics and interviews, these texts form an emergent literary tradition. Embedded within the texts and the lyrics of the Wu was an Afro Asian performance that offered a nuanced critique of global capitalism and a strategy for negotiating intricate networks of the global economy. However, the martial arts were a vehicle for traversing and transgressing these networks while simultaneously developing a Black masculinity that was local and global. The Wu's cultural production oscillates somewhere between the hypermasculine and the humble, and avoids the emasculated stature of Jayden Smith's prepubescent body in *Karate Kid* (2010) while critiquing their own struggles as Black men, which echo Jim Kelly's desire for Black action heroes that are almost always

---

30. Sampled from the film *Shaolin and Wu Tang* (1981).

31. Admittedly, the group had confrontations with law enforcement and the criminal justice system and Ol' Dirty Bastard passed away due to a drug overdose in a New York recording studio in November 2004.

32. Scholars of hip-hop and African American cultural production have written more extensively on The Five-Percent Nation. For development and the evolution of Five-Percenters, see Juan M. Floyd-Thomas's contribution, titled "A Jihad of Words: The Evolution of African American Islam and Contemporary Hip-Hop." See also R. Scott Heath's article, "True Heads: Historicizing the Hip-Hop 'Nation' in Context."

"grotesque" in the Bakhtinian sense and sometimes creep into the comically profane.

RZA first met his kung fu *sifu* (teacher), Shi Yan Ming, at a release party for the Wu-Tang Clan's GZA's (Gary Grice) solo album *Liquid Swords* (1995) in New York.[33] "I felt like I had known him [RZA] forever" wrote Ming in the forward to the second philosophical literary work *The Tao of Wu*. Born in China's Henan Province, Ming was five years old when his parents left him at the Shaolin temple where he grew up and became a thirty-fourth generation Shaolin monk. However, in 1992 during the Shaolin US tour, Ming defected while touring in San Francisco. Soon thereafter Ming made his way to New York where he founded the USA Shaolin Temple. Like Bruce Lee and Van Clief, Ming had many students who were in the entertainment industry, and he collaborated with directors such as Jim Jarmusch in *Ghost Dog* (1999) in which he and RZA had cameo appearances. The two shared similarities in their experiences with abandonment. At the age of three RZA's parents split up, and he was sent to live with his mother's family in North Carolina because his mother couldn't afford to take care of him and his six siblings.[34] When he was seven years old, his mother brought him back from his uncle's house in North Carolina where he'd been living, and the family then moved into the Marcus Garvey Projects in Brooklyn when his mother won the number[35] for $4,000. "I've lived in at least ten different projects in New York–Van Dyke in Brownsville, Marcus Garvey in East New York, Park Hill in Stapleton and Staten Island—and they all taught me something, even if they were lessons no one would choose."[36] Within the Third World spaces of the US such as New York's public housing, there was creativity, hope, and an awareness of an interconnectedness that lay beyond the brick layers of the Marcus Garvey Homes.

RZA likened these experiences of growing up in the shadows of capitalism to that of the mythological story of the Indian monk Boddhidarma (Da'mo in Chinese or Daruma in Japanese), who brought Zen Buddhism to China in 459 AD. Da'mo is thought to be the founder of the exercises for mediation that eventually became Shaolin kung fu and proselytized Buddhism. While RZA found beauty in the teachings of his Uncle Hollis in North Carolina and the ways of Southern folk rhymes, he was also skeptical of the Southern Baptist churches wherein people caught the Holy Ghost. "The screaming and moaning just didn't feel right. The spirit of God sounded beautiful to me, but

---

33. RZA and Norris, Introduction to *Tao of Wu*.
34. RZA and Norris, *Tao of Wu*, 10.
35. Like the mainstream lotteries the "numbers" is unregulated form of organized gambling and has long been an alternative economy in working-class communities.
36. RZA and Norris, *Tao of Wu*, 1.

I quickly separated the experience of God from the church. I just couldn't see God in the fake-ass preachers or people wallowing on the ground. But I could see him in Hollis, my first real teacher."[37] The stories of Shaolin resonated and fulfilled a need to find the beauty of spirituality in the practice of everyday life in the projects. Because Buddhism, and hence spirituality writ large was actualized in the material practice of kung fu, from the point of view of the martial arts practitioner, they could themselves occupy the space of Buddha through the corporeal discipline of their bodies. Buddhism is endowed with the kinetics of bodily practice and is always raced and gendered.

Yet, Buddhism was not the only spiritual practice that would speak to RZA. The Five-Percent Nation was also rooted in the practice of the flesh. Its founder Clarence 13x declared that not only was he Allah but all Black men could become gods if they acquired the Supreme Mathematics that was the foundation of the Nation of Gods and Earths. Like the process of teaching someone martial arts repertoire on the street or in the dojo, the philosophy of the Supreme Mathematics was spread "hand-to-hand" and by word of mouth. RZA's older cousin and Wu-Tang Clan member GZA introduced MCing and Supreme Mathematics to RZA in 1981. By mastering the teachings of the 120 questions and answers and then living one's life according to those teachings, Five-Percenters could gain "knowledge of self" and transform their flesh into gods. Like martial arts sparring sessions wherein students challenge each other and test each other's knowledge and skill, Five-Percenters meet in the "cipher" that can occur anytime and anywhere. The cipher is usually held by other Five-Percenters who want to become gods or who already are gods and engage in schooling aspiring Five-Percenters who are in the process of becoming gods.

As a derivative of the teaching of Elijah Muhammad, the answer to the first question "Who is the original man?" is "The original man is the Asiatic Black man, the Maker, the Owner, the Cream of the planet Earth, the Father of Civilization, and God of the Universe." These riddles that were predicated on the doctrine of the NOI's Muhammad continued to make Afro Asian connections, but more importantly they were taught and spread on the streets of working-class Black urban communities. To recall Stuart Hall, Black people used the body as if it were the only cultural capital they had and worked on themselves as the canvases of representation into the image of God.[38] Heaven was not in the sky, but here on earth. This philosophy of the flesh was made real through practice and resonated not only with working-class Black youth

---

37. RZA and Norris, *Tao of Wu*, 1.
38. Hall, "What Is This 'Black' in Black Popular Culture?," 109.

such as the Wu-Tang Clan, but East Coast hip-hop artists, who have their roots in the Five-Percent philosophy, which is why MCs such as Rakim, Big Daddy Kane, Poor Righteous Teachers, Digable Planets, Busta Rhymes, Mobb Deep, and Professor Griff of Public Enemy were either followers or made reference to the Five-Percent Nation. Furthermore, the cipher also became a site of also engaging in verbal combat or battle between MCs. This impromptu form of wordplay or "freestyling," as it is commonly called, was a temporal space in which wordsmiths challenged each other in rhyme, oftentimes exchanging and rearranging the words of others within the cipher.

While the Wu-Tang Clan's lyrics are full of references to the imagined community of the Five-Percent Nation, the martial arts proved to be a more tangible and compelling discipline through which to cultivate their work. This was most true for RZA who became a student of Ming's, eventually traveling with him to China to practice, rap, and exchange music. The Wu-Tang offered their CDs to the abbots of the Shaolin Temple and in exchange received the music produced by the monks of Shaolin in Henan Province. Inspired by the films about Zen practice and kung fu, during the early 1990s RZA began studying the texts *Tao Te Ching* and *I Ching* in order to further expand his knowledge of Taoism and Confucianism. These texts in conjunction with the filmography formed the basis for *Enter the Wu-Tang (36 Chambers)*, but after meeting Ming, the distance between the screen and the body collapsed.

> We weren't humble warriors in the beginning. Before we would always say, "we ain't about slipping and kicking, we'll flip lyrics and kick your ass." But now we started to see the truth of it. When sifu came to us, I think destiny brought it to us. Then we had a living example of the actual principles. I learned that kung fu was less a fighting style and more about the cultivation of the spirit. ODB and I started to get deep into what they where saying about she energy. We got into the idea of channeling Chi. It rejuvenates your body, but it's also philosophical. It's about finding balance.[39]

The Wu-Tang Clan had already designated Stappleton Projects in Staten Island where they resided as their fictive "Shaolin land." While kung fu cinema had inspired RZA to mimic the exercises (push-up, sit-ups, punches, and kicks) that he saw in movies, magazines, and training videos, it wasn't just enough to imagine kung fu in words. "It's impossible to reach enlightenment solely through the exchange of words," rather RZA took to heart the Buddhist philosophy embodied in the kung fu system.

---

39. RZA and Norris, *Tao of Wu*, 52.

Ming opened his first USA Shaolin studio on the top floor of a building on Broadway just north of Houston Street in downtown Manhattan. Nestled between the East and the West Villages, the location of Ming's school was a rejoinder to the experiences of Ron Van Clief and Taimak. Ming was able to survive in part because he utilized the theatricality of kung fu demonstrations that included bending metal iron rods that were pointed into his throat. Other theatrical displays such as breaking boards across his arms and torso demonstrated the power of Ming's chi. The sensational performances of Shaolin demonstrations drew the attention of celebrities. Actors, writers, and directors who became Ming's students brought both money and notoriety to USA Shaolin as Ming established himself as a teacher who could teach students how to develop their chi. Or as USA Shaolin's motto goes "More chi! Train Harder!"

RZA described his training experience with Ming as both intense and interdisciplinary in terms of the regiment that encompassed the exercises to develop stamina, flexibility, and balance through qigong or standing meditation. In kung fu, these exercises are done to develop internal and external power in preparation for the combat skills that are acquired through empty hand sparring and weapons training. But martial arts also meant disciplining the body to control the mind, something that RZA took to heart in his application of martial arts philosophy and as something that the Wu-Tang Clan embraced in their approach to dealing with the music recording industry as a whole. This strategy meant celebrating a diversity in their approach to cultural production. In the chapter titled "Capitalism" in *The Wu-Tang Manual*, the authors revealed that during a three-year hiatus after their 1997 record-setting double album *Wu-Tang Forever*, the group developed a five-year plan to augment their work in other markets. The "Wu-Wear clothing line hit $15 million in annual sales, the comic book line nudged out *X-Men* for the top spot in the country, and its first kung fu video game sold 600,000 units for Sony PlayStation. And six Clan members recorded successful solo albums."[40] Was this manual a ploy to simply sell more of the group's material goods? The group's writing was perhaps a third vision of double-consciousness. By recognizing that there were market forces that stood beyond the immediate confines of New York, the group was able to extend their own philosophy, knowledge of self, and urban Taoism, again a conjunctive political concept of Afro Asian performance. The *Wu-Tang Manual* placed into circulation the group's literature that mirrored both the transnational writing correspondences of Black radicals such as the poet Amiri Baraka as well as Eastern philosophy.

---

40. RZA and Norris, *Tao of Wu*, 52.

While RZA created the musical scores for martial arts films such as Quentin Tarantino's *Kill Bill Volume 1* (2003) as well as producing, writing, and directing his own martial arts–based film fantasia that took place in a mythical village in China titled *The Man with the Iron Fists* (2012).[41] An example of the convergence of Wu-Tang Clan's martial arts practice and aesthetic presentation was captured in the music video for the song "Chi Kung" from the album *Birth of a Prince* (2003).[42] Similar to Tarantino's martial arts series *Kill Bill* that drew from Bruce Lee's *Enter the Dragon* and kung fu filmography. The music video for "Chi Kung" was Wu-Tang's iteration of the 1970s kung fu cinema that inspired the group. The video tells RZA's version of a kung fu master battling rival families through a series of Afro Asian martial arts vignettes that feature Black and Asian bodies only. Like *The Last Dragon*, which treads in the realms of archetype and stereotype, the video slips into the world of a fantastical farce. The cinematography breaks the illusion of realism by including the members of the film crew, boom microphone, and dolly tracks in the camera's frame throughout the video. The five-minute video is full of martial arts choreography *a la* wushu that Ming taught his disciple, RZA.

In the music video, RZA plays the Prince who has acquired "the knowledge of self" through qigong practice and the supreme ultimate art called taijiquan. In the first sequence of the video, RZA performs what appears to be a taijiquan solo form in between a column of paper lanterns that hang from the ceiling. The vocals for "Chi Kung" articulate RZA's synthesis of the Five Percent Nation with Chinese martial arts that is as much an Afro Asian formation as it is a challenge to master narratives of Western hegemonic discourse.

> The grand ultimate supreme, no extremedies
> We use Tai Chi to deflect off our enemy
> Five poisons, from the Clan there's no Remedy
> We dispell the smell of wickedness in our vicinity
> Bobby, the atomic, Islamic, bomb-droppin'
> appear in your atmosphere like the comet
> Heading to the Western Hemisphere, non-stoppin'[43]

---

41. Shot on location in China, *The Man with the Iron Fists* was developed by RZA himself. The story focused on a mythological village in nineteenth-century China in which RZA portrayed an escaped slave named Thaddeus Henry Smith who finds his way to the village and becomes the local blacksmith capable of manufacturing unique weapons for the local warlords who battle the colonizing British and each other.
42. https://www.youtube.com/watch?v=Fjr3k882waE.
43. RZA, *Birth of a Prince*, 2003.

RZA invokes the imagery of the Supreme Mathematics of the Gods and Earths as well as the supreme ultimate of tai chi and links the kung fu classic film *Five Deadly Venoms* (1978) with his personification of "Bobby, the atomic, Islamic." These strategies for gaining the knowledge of the self through techniques of the body become visible and are further bolstered by RZA's sartorial presentation as he appears shirtless in what seems to be a pair of white changshan pants, a blue do-rag, and a red sweatband with the Wu-Tang Clan logo on it. The logo is also conspicuously tattooed on his shoulder. In the tradition of the Hong Kong kung fu cinema that featured exaggerated sound effects whenever characters punched or kicked. RZA's choreography is accompanied by similar sonic effects that heighten each move and telegraph an audiovisuality of kinetic energy. With sweat dripping from his body *a la* Bruce Leroy in the opening sequence of *The Last Dragon*, RZA is then hit with a large metal club with spikes in it by an Asian kung fu practitioner. Another practitioner appears from offscreen and attempts to cut the Prince with two pliable metal swords most often used in wushu training. The Prince moves with great alacrity and defeats his opponents using tai chi or wushu style techniques.

Every Prince must have a Princess, and in the case of "Chi Kung," the Prince has a Black Princess whose family possesses the secret manuals of qigong. That both the Prince and Princess are Black speaks to Wu-Tang Clan's acknowledgement of African diasporic rites that are essential for building a Black nation an "imagined community" that has been at the foundation of both the NOI as well as the Five Percent Nation. Yet, in the mythical world of the music video for "Chi Kung" the knowledge and practice of martial arts is part of the affective and political economy through which the characters derive their power and their status for both the male and female characters. The jealous Lord Bo (played by the actor Bookeem Woodbine, who is also one of Ming's students)[44] seeks the secret manual of qigong so that he may become all powerful. Lord Bo is also a qigong practitioner who breaks glass bottles that hang from a rope with his forehead without cutting himself as he emerges from a mist sprayed from a spray bottle that is seen within the camera's frame. He spars with his students who attack him with long spears. Lord Bo then bends the spears with his throat by "channeling all of the qi" into his neck. For Lord Bo "all that matters is qigong," and he will stop at nothing to obtain the secret manual that reveals its inner workings. This is, of course, counter to the very nature of qigong because chi can only be developed and mastered through its actual practice.

---

44. See the video for Woodbine's performance, https://www.youtube.com/watch?v=Fjr3k882waE.

In his quest for power, Lord Bo has his cadre of Asian female wushu mercenaries attack the Princess, who is protected at all times by her Maid, who is also a wushu practitioner and student of the Prince. The Princess escapes, but the Maid is taken prisoner and held for ransom by Lord Bo's cadre. In addition to being a master of taijiquan, the Prince is also a skilled calligrapher and instead of the secret manual of qigong in exchange for the Maid, he offers Lord Bo a text written in the style of the *Wu-Tang Manual* with RZA's imprint on the front cover. Upon seeing that this is not the secret manual of qigong Lord Bo becomes irate and "kung fu kicks" the herald who delivered the message out of the screen.

The rapper Kinetic 9 whose vocals can be heard on the track also makes a cameo appearance as a customer in a restaurant surrounded by a group of Asian female courtesans whom also sport Wu-Wear clothing in a moment of product advertising. Kinetic 9's gregarious banter draws the ire of Lord Bo and a comical exchange between the two ensues.

> **LORD BO:** Yo! You should keep quiet before you lose what you have.
> **KINETIC 9:** To a warrior there's no loss in the game.
> **LORD BO:** What about the loss of a life?
> **KINETIC 9:** Well, if you keep this up one of us sure to die.

Kinetic 9 tosses a bright red apple directly above his head at which point one of the courtesans seated next to him throws a series of blades into the air cutting the apple. Perfectly sliced apple pieces then fall into the hands of the four courtesans who have been standing behind him massaging his shoulders. The courtesans applaud as Kinetic takes a bite out of the apple leaving Lord Bo with a smirk on his face. "Impressive," he contends.

Despite Lord Bo's menacing behavior, the Prince seeks the return of the Maid and confronts Lord Bo, who in turn agrees to set her free on the condition that the Prince's best kung fu student is capable of defeating Lord Bo's best student. The fight is on in a winner takes all battle, and the Maid is cut free. She engages in wushu combat with Lord Bo's mercenaries all of whom are Asian females. In this moment, "Chi Kung" shifts the imagery of Asian females from the position of subordinates to that of warriors. While the Maid proves herself agile and an adept wushu warrior as she defeats all of Lord Bo's students, the music video cannot escape its reliance on gendered stereotype from its creation of the "concubine" image to the dubbed sounds of cats fighting as the Maid engages Lord Bo's female assassins.

The final clip for the close of the music video centers RZA in a director's chair surrounded by all of the women who were loyal to Lord Bo, the Prince, and Kinetic 9. The camera pulls back to reveal the lighting for the set, dolly tracks, and a boom mic as a camera assistant snaps a clapboard signaling the end of the martial arts fantasia that has unfolded. However, the camera keeps rolling as crew members check the lighting and move equipment around on the set, and noticeably, all of them are Asian men. While the music video for "Chi Kung" acknowledged that the Black bodies framed in the video were in engaged in an Afro Asian performance that embellished kung fu as both practice and representation, the inclusion of the film crew also suggests that "Chi Kung" was emblematic of a continual negotiation of collaborative Afro Asian cultural production. Not unlike Will Smith's entry into the Asian film market through the *Karate Kid* (2010), the Wu-Tang Clan's framing of Black masculinity through the narrative of kung fu fantasia was a gesture toward the very genealogy of kung fu cinema from Hong Kong that had influenced and mentored the group as youth. However, it is also a gesture toward what I have referred to as an "Afro Asian futurism," a method by which marginalized communities create "new collectivities based not just upon eviction and exclusion" but also on "turning pain into power," and are able to form "new and imaginative uses of technology, creativity, and spaces."[45] While the music video for "Chi Kung" oscillated between the polarity of racialized and gendered essentialism and a new frontier for imagining racialized and gendered collaboration, the music video was rendered as an homage to RZA's kung fu teacher Ming and the broader legacy of kung fu cinema that continues to influence the hip-hop industry.

---

45. Price, "Remembering Fred Ho: The Legacy of Afro Asian Futurism."

CHAPTER 4

The Sound of a Dragon

Fred Ho's Afro Asian Jazz Martial Arts

> What's little known is that Bruce Lee was really, truly a jazz artist.
> —Fred Ho[1]

Sound Movements of Resistance

This project has focused on the way Black Americans, men in particular, took up the practice of Asian martial arts at the beginning of the mid-twentieth century as a performance of Afro Asian theater that, in turn, resulted in new articulations of self-fashioning to survive and cope with the never-ending impingements of US racism and white supremacy. As I suggested in the introduction, racial kinesthesia was a process of adapting cultural practices through the kinesthetics found in an Other's cultural template in an attempt to redress, in this case, a wounded Black masculinity and to claim a sense of agency, control, and sovereignty over their bodies, which had been stolen, mutilated, devalued, and rendered nonhuman. Racial kinesthesia choreographed and also organized bodies into enabling valences of racialized performance, as new communities, and hence new cultural practices, were created during the migrations of Black Americans out of the agricultural South and into the industrialized North for economic opportunity and survival. As articulated in the discussion on transcultural kinesthesia, Black engagement with Asian cultural practice was indicative of a struggle for liberation and not reflective of traditional and hackneyed moments of Eurocentric

---

1. Fred Ho, Interview with the Author, April 23, 2011.

or Westernist appropriations of Third World (Black, Asian, Indigenous, and Latinx) cultural production for the purposes of domination and colonialism. Interesting, and perhaps too often ignored, is the way that other minoritarian people have also borrowed from Black intellectual political movements in order to develop their own critical frameworks through which to critique US racial politics and articulate nuanced forms of identity formation.

However, in this chapter I focus on another iteration of Afro Asian performance as manifested through what I refer to as the sonic kinesthesia of the Chinese American baritone saxophonist, cultural producer, and activist, Fred Ho, who created a series of Afro Asian jazz martial arts theatrical performance pieces that drew upon the musical energy, aesthetics, and political philosophy of the Black Arts/Black Power movements in conjunction with the kinetic energy and mythology of Asian martial arts. My use of the term *sonic kinesthesia* indicates how racially marked sounds can be used to forge new possibilities of coalitional political possibilities as well as how the kinesthetics of instrumentality provide the score for and complement the choreographic harmonies of martial arts as a form of musical and theatrical cultural expression.

To create the Afro Asian theatrical performances, Ho's musical ensembles, such as his core band the Afro Asian Music Ensemble, were intentionally multiracial and multiethnic in order to engage and rehearse a form of revolutionary antiracist coalitional politics. As performance theorist T. Carlis Roberts has observed in their discussion of what they refer to as the *sono-racial collaboration*, antiracist and anticolonial musical collaborators create radical politics by intentionally forging "relationships with artists of other racial or cultural backgrounds, employing sound as a medium for interracial communication and bonding. Artists also collaborate with racialized sounds in order to broaden racial categories. Most surprisingly, racialized sounds themselves collaborate, working in tandem to construct interracial discourses even when bodies are not present (although always implied)."[2] In addition to the sounds produced by the kinesthetic movements of interracial musicianship, Ho's Afro Asian music provided a sonic energetic propulsion for the martial arts movements—the repeated acts, routines, and gestures that made up the choreography within the Afro Asian jazz martial arts pieces that he created. However, the coalitional politics was also organized and summoned through a form of imaginative kinesthesia that started with and emanated from the breath or what he analogized to the principles found in martial arts, such as the cultivation of qi and "kung fu breathing."

---

2. Roberts, *Resounding Afro Asia: Interracial Music and the Politics of Collaboration*, 6.

Cultivation of the breath and the cultivation of qi was a kinesthetic process of creating new sounds, not only harmonic but also rhythmic, and Ho insisted that the stamina required for combat was the same stamina and volatility that was required to create a revolutionary sound. As Ho stated,

> What fascinates me is the relationship between music and martial arts. It's also there in dance and the martial arts, but the music is intuitive improvisation that is magical because similar to Bruce Lee, who was truly a jazz artist, the music and conjunction with arts is [sic] pure improvisation, communication, collaboration, and mobilization. If you ever ask people what is Jeet Kune Do, they will tell you it is not a "form" per se but that it is actually a consciousness, a mentality. It is an appropriative process that is very much like musical improvisation. Musical improvisation is a totality of all that one has ever studied. You have to be formless because the philosophy of jazz improvisation happens in the moment of the movement and the movement of the moment and just like Jeet Kune Do it's about individual style made from amalgamated forms.[3]

By working with the saxophone as an instrument of breath, improvisation, and combat, Ho collapsed the distance between musician and martial artist. Like the Cha Cha dancer, Bruce Lee, who incorporated Afro-Caribbean instruments such as the conga into his Jeet June Do classes[4] to study and teach rhythm and timing, Ho improvised with rhythm and tempo with the saxophone. Much in the likeness of Bruce Lee's martial arts repertoire, the baritone saxophone was a kinetic force that was predicated on the cultivation of qi (life force) through breath—rhythmic breathing—to create the multicultural kinesthesia that signified his Afro Asian performance. The martial artists' movement is always focused on the breath and breathing, and for Ho the saxophone was equally a practice in sustaining breath, concentrating the breath, and focusing the breath to enhance one's qi, again, one's essential kinetic energy and life force, in order to move beyond the normal range of the instrument's sound. Using kung fu breathing to push beyond historic instrumental limitations, and breaking the two-and-a-half-octave register on his saxophone, allowed Ho to create the space that he needed to survive within a complex American system, which while on the one hand celebrates a postracial society, still must essentialize those who negotiate a multivocality of identities. Bending harmonic scales with kung fu breathing was a physical

---

3. Fred Ho, Interview with the Author, April 23, 2011.
4. Polly, *Bruce Lee: A Life*, 199.

technique and political act through which to organize and mobilize both artists and spectators.

However, what then to make of Ho's use of Black musical traditions? Were these not forms of appropriations of an Other's cultural expression and practice? How does this resonate when Asian Americans are often framed as "model minorities" and hence assimilable into American cultural discourse? What does Afro Asia as a political concept, social movement, and musical interpretation have to do with martial arts, and how did martial arts enable Ho to launch his own Chinese American identity and political consciousness?

While there is a historical precedence of appropriations of Black American expressive culture, especially music, as E. Patrick Johnson has suggested in his discussion of appropriating Black sound, "Negotiating any identity is a dangerous adventure, particularly in a postmodern world in which we have come to recognize that identities are made, not given. We also must realize that the postmodern push to theorize identity discursively must be balanced with theories of corporeality and materiality."[5] As I suggested in earlier chapters, Afro Asian performance and the martial arts imagination was a process of Third World borrowings and exchanges that were not always direct, even, or rhetorical similes. Social-somatic practices such as martial arts have afforded historically marginalized people options in negotiating identity. For Black Americans, this meant taking on the racialized and cultural signifiers of an Asian cultural template and rehearsing the repertoire of a martial art (kung fu, aikido, jujitsu, karate) into an aesthetic practice that became an expression of Black political and cultural power.

Born as Hou Weihan in 1957 to Chinese immigrant parents in California, Ho's journey to find an artistic and political space within multiple cultural spheres was driven by transformation, transgression, and contradiction. The greatest impact on Ho's identity was his training as a baritone saxophonist, while in junior high school and high school, in the tradition of the Black Arts Movement by individuals such as tenor saxophonist Archie Shepp and poet Sonia Sanchez. Sanchez, in particular, initiated Ho into Black and Latinx struggles at an early age, introducing him to *The Autobiography of Malcolm X* and the Black liberation movements of the 1960s, respectively,[6] and he was later mentored by Black Arts Revolutionary Theater founder and poet Amiri Baraka. As an Asian American searching for his own identity, he encountered racism and xenophobia in elementary school and into adulthood when he joined the Marines in 1973, but was subsequently dishonorably discharged

---

5. Johnson, *Appropriating Blackness: Performance and the Politics of Authenticity*, 218.
6. Ho, *Wicked Theory, Naked Practice*, 171.

in 1975 when he struck an officer who called him a "gook"[7] during a training exercise. That same year Ho also joined the NOI and became Fred 3X, but neither Black nationalism or US militarism worked for Ho. The contradictions were profound when considering that Ho was also involved in political organizations and movements such as Marxist-Leninist-Maoism, the League of Revolutionary Struggle (LRS), *I Wor Kuen* (Society of the Harmonious Righteous Fist), ecosocialism, and matriarchal socialism.

Like a martial arts master-to-disciple relationship, Shepp provided the tutelage for Ho to develop his repertoire style of the saxophone, the instrument that guided him throughout his career and provided the soundscape for his core band the Afro Asian Music Ensemble (an interracial group), which he formed in 1982, as well as the Afro Asian jazz martial arts performance pieces that he then began creating in 1997. Furthermore, similar to the way that martial arts cinema provided a counterdiscourse to the dominant representation of Westernism and Eurocentricism for Black and Afro Latinx youth (a la the Wu Tang Clan), Ho was also inspired by the mediated kinesthesia of Asian masculinity within the Hong Kong kung-fu cinema of the 1970s, not the least of which was, again, Bruce Lee's display of Chinese cultural traditions embodied in his kinetics on the screen as well as his resistance to Hollywood racism.

The conjunction of Black American expressive culture and Asian expressive culture propelled Ho's work into what Dwight Conquergood referred to as dialogical performance that sought to bring "self and other together so that they can question, debate, and challenge one another. It is a kind of performance that resists conclusions, it is intensely committed to keeping the dialogue between performer and text open and ongoing."[8] The Afro Asian Music Ensemble was already dialogical in name and sought to enter into conversation with Other cultural struggles through the practice of experimentations in sounds to make new polyhybridic sonicscapes. Such articulations were collaborations that integrated traditional Chinese instruments such as the *erhu* (two-stringed bowed lute), *sona* (double-reed pipe), *p'ip'a* (four-stringed plucked lute), *xiaoluo* (small gong), *daluo* (large gong), *muyu* (wood fish idiophone), *ban* (wood block), and *naobo* (cymbals) as well as instruments associated with the African American jazz tradition: alto, tenor, and baritone saxophone; double bass; and hi–hat, kick, crash, and snare drums.[9] However, part of what made Ho's work unique was the acknowledgement that despite

---

7. Brown, "Chords of a Revolution: A Jazz Musician Thrives in Brooklyn."
8. Conquergood, "Performing as a Moral Act: Ethical Dimensions of the Ethnography of Performance."
9. Asai, "Cultural Politics: The African American Connection in Asian American Jazz-based Music."

his virtuosity with the baritone saxophone and composition, he understood that his investment in a Black cultural expressive form was not an attempt to reproduce an "authentically Black" sound, but rather the music was intended to prepare for an antiracist multicultural future.

Similar to the Black Panther Party's attempt to foster revolutionary intercommunalism through the kinesthesia of Asian martial art and political philosophy, Ho's Afro Asian jazz martial arts performances were cultural expressions of his participation in and relationship to various political organizations that were always a rejoinder to the Africa Asia Conference of 1955 held in Bandung, Indonesia, that brought together twenty-nine countries from Africa and Asia to define the direction of recently liberated aligned and nonaligned territories. While the Bandung Conference, as it is popularly called, provided a vision for national liberation, as scholars such as Vijay Prashad have also observed in the subsequent decades after Bandung, with emerging Third World countries becoming indebted to the monetary regimes such as the International Monetary Fund, the foundations for solidarity that had seemed so celebrated and abundant largely eroded, "with Africa and Asia interested in each other's resources and capital, where the bold pronouncements for a radical reconfiguration of the international political economy ha[d] vanished."[10] Similarly, much of the Black and Asian connections consumed in popular culture, such as the *Rush Hour* film series, K-Pop, and J-Pop, may contain junctures of Afro Asian performance, but lack in subtlety and nuance of the political, historical, and economic conditions that structure such cultural production, consumption, and subsequent social impact. Even worse, the solidarity that had perhaps been present during the Third World Liberation Strike of San Francisco State or support between Black Panthers, Asian Red Guards, Puerto Rican Young Lords, and Chicana/o Brown Berets seemingly dissipated from popular discourse as the essentialist images of Korean and Black conflict dominated the imagery and much of the conversation around the 1992 uprisings in Los Angeles without critiquing the underlying conditions that created the dynamics of Los Angeles's racial regime—and for that matter the US as a whole.

While Fred Ho passed away on April 12 2014[11] after a yearlong battle with cancer, his books and essays, music, and musical theatrical martial arts dance pieces, I believe, were visions for developing "a solidarity of politics and cul-

---

10. Prashad, "Bandung is Dead: Passages in Afro Asian Epistemology," xiii.

11. Ho had been diagnosed with stage 3b colorectal cancer on August 6, 2006, just before his forty-ninth birthday. After numerous surgeries and attempts at conventional Western medical treatment, Ho turned to radical alternative strategies such as a raw food diet. For Ho, the elimination of the toxicity that gave growth to cancer cells in the body was a war against capitalism and the toxic conditions that such a system produces. As Ho wrote in *Diary of a Radical Cancer Warrior: Fighting Cancer and Capitalism at a Cellular Level*, "Capitalism . . . is the cancer

ture between people of color in the face of white supremacy, capitalist domination, patriarchy, and old and new forms of colonial imperialism."[12] The three Afro Asian jazz martial arts performance pieces addressed in this chapter each provide nuanced ways of how sonic kinesthesia articulated Ho's interpretation of a radical Asian American consciousness that critiqued colonialism, colorblind ideology, and model minority mythology through racially mixed ensembles, movements, and sounds. In *Voice of the Dragon: Once Upon a Time in Chinese America* (2004), Ho predicated the piece on the Hong Kong martial arts film and television series *Once Upon a Time in China* (1991), which depicted a Canton folk hero, Wong Fei-hung, at the end of the Qing dynasty, fighting against Eurocolonialism and ultimately the establishment of the Republic of China. Like those Chinese who aided the British and European powers during the Opium Wars, *Voice of the Dragon* was intended to be a critique of Asian Americans who settled for model minority mythology in the US in order to gain access to the social privileges of whiteness. *Deadly She-Wolf Assassin at Armageddon* (2006) drew upon the martial arts cinema such as the Japanese epic Lone Wolf and Cub, which depicted a fictional folk martial arts hero embodied as a masterless and disgraced samurai. However, Ho's version employed a female heroine, embodied as the deadly She-Wolf. In *Sweet Science Suite: A Scientific Soul Session Honoring Muhammad Ali* (2011), the Afro Asian Music Ensemble became part of Ho's larger collective called the Green Monster Big Band, which provided music and sonic kinesthesia for Ho's homage to the pugilist and political activist, Muhammad Ali, and further critiqued colonialism, colorblind ideology, and model minority mythology through racially mixed ensembles, movements, and sounds. The kinesthetics of sound emanated from the music ensemble that was positioned upstage from the martial artists/performers who narrated the neomyths through their choreography. Ho composed and conceptualized the work with writers, directors, and choreographers, many of whom were women who, like Sonia Sanchez, shaped and molded Ho's thinking about the politics of gender, race, and class struggle and his own masculinity.

The Voice of the Dragon

Voice of the Dragon was intended to be a critique of Asian Americans who settled for model minority mythology, something that Ho fully repudiated as it was not only antithetical to Afro Asia political performance, but that

---

for Planet Earth; and cancer ... is the exponentially increasing environmental and social toxicity of capitalism assaulting the individual person" (40).

12. Mullen, *Afro-Orientalism*, 165.

model minority mythology was a technique of white supremacy that had been transferred from alien exclusion acts and Asian lynching into a seemingly innocuousness.[13] As Ho wrote, "The rise of anti-Asian racism initially coincided with the need to scapegoat Asians during times of general economic downturn in the United States. In the post–World War II era of economic prosperity and US world empire consolidation, a new form of insidious racism promoted the 'model minority myth' of Asian success in order to divide APIs from other oppressed nationalities, and to foment jealousy and anxiety about Asian advancement."[14] Sonic kinesthesia brought together Black cultural expression and Asian performing martial arts in order to chafe against the ideology of racial triangulation in which Black people are considered constant second-class insiders and Asians are regarded as desirable outsiders. Model minority mythology is a part of anti-Blackness and ultimately anti-Asianness. Hence, by choreographing movement through sound, Ho was also attempting to choreograph change within the broader cultural schematic. As Ho recounted, "Afro Asia represents a different paradigm. Within the context of the performances, these are vision quests to demonstrate that the system is not infallible or invincible. They don't subscribe to the illusion that capitalism has perpetuated."[15] The synthesis of disparate performance disciplines created an expanded vision of socioeconomic justice in which "new forces are exemplified and new forms of struggle are generated."[16] *Dragon* decried Asian Americans who discarded the history of Asian American discrimination and turned their backs on Asian American activists whose efforts dovetailed with other radicals of color.

Ho composed the musical score and cowrote the script with playwright Ruth Margraff; the production was directed by Mira Kingsley, choreographed by José Figueroa, and performed live by the Afro Asian Music Ensemble. Originally envisioned as part of a trilogy, *Dragon* reimagines the mythic story of the formation of the Shaolin Temple and the temple's subsequent betrayal by a renegade disciple, Gar Man Jang. Instead of casting trained dancers, Ho utilized martial art practitioners; Wu Shu fighting forms were the base vocabulary for movement. The story was guided by a didactic omniscient narrator who helped orchestrate the plot and the action onstage by introducing the name of each disciple, along with the particular kung fu form that the disciple represented.

---

13. For my analysis, I used a 2004 video recording of a live production of *Voice of the Dragon* presented at Kean University. I also used supplementary materials provided to me courtesy of Fred Ho and Big Red Media, and Mira Kingsley.
14. Ho, *Wicked Theory, Naked Power*, 339.
15. Fred Ho, Interview with the Author, April 23, 2011.
16. Fred Ho, Interview with the Author, April 23, 2011.

Voice of the Dragon began as the Narrator, dressed in a fusion of nineteenth-century US Southwestern– and Chinese American–style clothing, introduced a multiethnic ensemble of martial artists dressed in kung fu attire. The ensemble then entered from the wings, holding white paper with Chinese *hanzi* that also represented the Shaolin Scrolls. The hanzi and Scrolls served as the scenic frame, making the ensemble seem like cartoon characters. The martial artists moved to the rhythm of the music of the Afro Asian Music Ensemble, located upstage, as the Narrator delivered the prologue, "The Way of Shaolin":

> Once upon a time . . . in a Place beyond History and Fantasy, in a time when Human Conflict was not Waged by Weapons of Mass Destruction but by the Martial Arts . . . and the Martial Artists were much more than Warriors or Fighters, they were revolutionaries . . . the Shaolin Temple exemplified THE WAY!!!" (Ho and Margraff 1999)[17]

The character of Gar Man Jang from seventeenth-century China allies herself with the Manchu imperial forces who had sacked the temple. She discovers the legendary Shaolin secret scrolls, which include all of the accumulated knowledge of martial arts. By absorbing the scroll's deadly power, she becomes an invincible supernatural destructive force. The Five Disciples, who survived the attack on the temple, refine their kung fu skills and reunite in the end to destroy Gar Man Jang. The confluence of jazz and Chinese mythology created a new space in which each martial artist embodied one of the five animals of the Shaolin fighting system. These animal styles distinguish the Five Disciples from each other. We are introduced to Chen Jak:

> First of the Five to escape was Chen Jak, visionary strategist. His philosophy: "Not to resist is to acquiesce to your own oppression. To win one hundred victories in one hundred battles is not the highest skill, to subdue your enemy without fighting is the highest skill." His element: Water. His animal: the Dragon—to ride the wind. His fighting style: T'ai chi ch'uan.

The character of Chen Jak is a play on both Chen-style t'ai chi ch'uan, as well as the Chinese American activist, Jack Chen. The choreography that creates Chen Jak's character is initially fast and utilizes snapping movements throughout the narration. However, when t'ai chi ch'uan is introduced, his movement

---

17. All quotes from *Voice of the Dragon: Once Upon a Time in Chinese America* are from the unpublished playscript by Fred Ho and Ruth Margraff. The script is unpublished and was provided to me by Ho.

FIGURE 4.1. The character of Chen Jak, stage left, battles with a soldier loyal to Gar Man Jang while the Afro Asian Musical Ensemble is led by Fred Ho, who is upstage center in the 2004 performance of *Voice of the Dragon: Once Upon a Time in Chinese America* at Kean College.

changes to a markedly slower tempo that is emblematic of tai chi's stylized slow motion. Chen Jak is immersed in a soft blue light that matches his blue uniform. The melodic sound of an alto sax that flows with jingling chimes suggests the sound of wind. Another player enters and attacks Chen Jak. Chen Jak is no longer solo; he is engaged in a dynamic sparring that metaphorically conveys his story.

The scene illustrates Chen Jak's philosophy: "To win one hundred victories in one hundred battles is not the highest skill; to subdue your enemy without fighting is the highest skill." The opponent is aligned with Gar Man Jang, and metaphorically with the Asian American reactionaries. Chen Jak's victory is thus a metaphor for the desired success of Asian American radicals in their struggle against assimilation.

Each of the subsequent disciples is introduced by the Narrator. "Second of the Five was Miao Hin, Master of Knives. 'A man of peace, armed always to the teeth.' His element: Metal. His animal: the Snake—for suppleness and rhythmic endurance. His fighting style: Snake-style kung fu." Miao Hin slithers snakelike back and forth, hypnotizing his opponents, neutralizing their attempts to attack. The introduction of the Third and Fourth disciples brings about a direct interplay between the musicians in the quartet and the martial artists. "Third of the Five was Gee Shin, the Builder. His philosophy: 'The deeper the root, the stronger the tree.' His element: Wood. His animal: the Leopard—to harness power. His fighting style: Leopard-style kung fu." Gee Shin carries a long wooden staff that becomes an extension of his body, as the drummer and the keyboardist's rhythms synchronize in time to Gee Shin's movement. When Gee Shin's staff hits the staff of his foe, a call and response is performed between the staff and the drummer's rhythmic tapping of shells. The staff transforms from a weapon into a musical instrument, and then into a theatrical prop.

The introduction of the Fourth disciple injects a new feel to the music and choreography. "The Fourth of the Five was Li Wen Mao, the Cantonese Opera artist. His philosophy: 'Opera is warfare without bloodshed. Warfare is opera with bloodshed.' His element: Fire. His animal: the Crane—for grace and self-control. His fighting style: Crane-style kung fu." Li Wen Mao's performance did not imitate Beijing Opera, but rather was an idiomatic expression of Ho's transcultural creation that generates its own authenticity, the origins of which are produced through the movement of the martial artist. Li Wen Mao makes use of an iron fan, which, like Gee Shin's staff, becomes an extension of his body, a weapon to fend off his attacker's sword.

The last of the Five disciples, Ng Mui, holds a significant place in the mythology of kung fu, as it is commonly believed that she was the progenitor of the Wing Chun–style of boxing.[18] Wing Chun became a popular form of close-quarter fighting within southern China and was popularized by Bruce Lee, who adapted Wing Chun into his eclectic Jeet Kune Do system. The Narrator introduces Ng Mui:

> Ng Mui. Teacher, propagandist, organizer, inventor, healer, philosopher, revolutionist, and (*ad libs as boxing announcer*) in the far corner, wearing the yellow tunic and hailing from central China: She's rough, she's tough, she'll knock you out like a jiggly-puff, she's Ng "The Annihilator" Mui, the greatest hand-to-hand boxer of allllllllllllllllllllllll time! Her philosophy: "Uphold principles, spread the glory of kung fu, make revolution!" Her element: Earth. Her animal: the Tiger—to strengthen bones. Her fighting style: Tiger-style kung fu.

Ng Mui is nimble and quick, embodying the boxing tiger form. Her hands and feet move with an agility that her leviathan of an opponent could not

---

18. It is commonly believed that Ng Mui taught boxing to Wing Chun, a peasant woman who used the combat repertoire to defend herself against a forced marriage. For more on the history of Wing Chun and the legend of Ng Mui, see Lee, *Wing Chun Kung-Fu*.

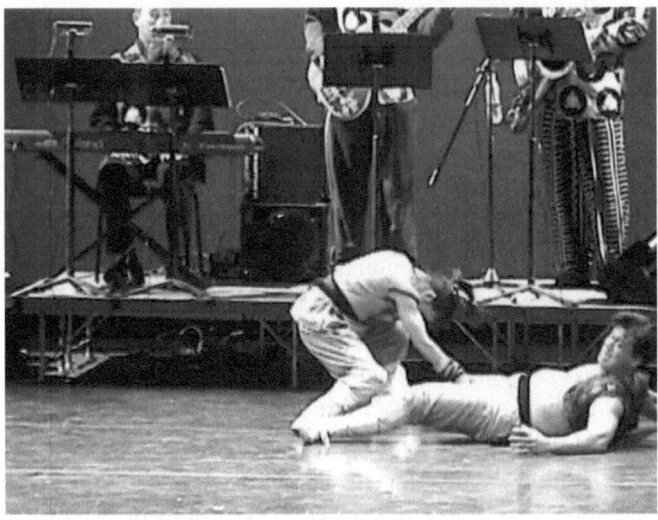

FIGURE 4.2. The character of Ng Mui emasculates her opponent as the Afro Asian Music Ensemble plays directly upstage in the 2004 performance of *Voice of the Dragon: Once Upon a Time in Chinese America* at Kean College

match. His flabby body creates a stark contrast to the "muscularized" body of the actor portraying Ng Mui.[19] This contrast is brought to the foreground when, after having knocked her opponent spread-eagle flat onto his back, Ng Mui reached down, grabbed his testicles, and emasculated him as he lets out a shriek (Figure 4.2).

With the introduction of Ng Mui and the legend of Wing Chun, *Voice of the Dragon* also pointed to a larger metanarrative in which the imagery of Shaolin constantly reinvents history by exploring China's historical–political evolution. Even the permutation of the present-day Shaolin Temple's reinvention through the Chinese Communist Party (CCP) works in conjunction with the West's fascination with martial arts, as evidenced by the guided tours that bring thousands of practitioners every year to the "authentic" birthplace of kung fu. For the CCP, the present incarnation of the Shaolin Temple serves as a vehicle for perpetuating the nation-state by bolstering the "authenticity" of folk heritage as well as capitalizing on the social–somatic process of kung fu, which situates the Shaolin Temple at the nexus of a transnational martial arts network.[20]

19. Tasker, *Spectacular Bodies: Gender, Genre, and the Action Cinema*, 123.

20. For more on the CCP's revitalization of the Shaolin Temple, see Adam Frank's chapter "Through Martial Arts We Will Become Friends," in his ethnography *Taijiquan and the Search for the Little Old Chinese Man: Understanding Identity Through Martial Arts*.

By the end of the piece, the Five Disciples regroup and refine their fighting skills to defeat Gar Man Jang. Forming a circle, the group creates an improvised choreography that coincides with a free-form jam session. The disciples form a circle, and each steps into the middle to perform a reiteration of their fighting system. This style mirrors jazz's improvisatory style; like a musician making a run within a set, the performer explores his or her own interpretation within the moment. In contrast, the Disciples defeat Gar Man Jang, a reactionary figure who reenters dressed in a one-piece spandex costume that suggests her disfigured soul. They carry her body offstage, leaving only the Narrator, who has been watching the final battle.

Voice of the Dragon concludes with the suggestion that others will be complicit in systems of domination. The final monologue points once again to the problematics of revolutionary practice, and the anxiety that an empathetic audience faces when posed with the challenge of understanding the intertwining of race and power within the appropriation of technological innovations in war. This became explicit with the Narrator's closing words:

> After the defeat of Gar Man Jang, the Five rebuild the Shaolin Temple ruins. Firecrackers blaze above another pack of Western bandits, lurking in the shadows, seeking more advantages! These Western Bandits can't exactly reach the next most coveted invention of the Chinese ... the Firecracker ... known today as gunpowder (not as in gunpowder tea, but as in firearms, cannons, and Weapons of Mass Destruction with which we could negotiate our human conflicts instead of hand-to-hand in the cumbersome Shaolin way). So they kowtow low before a new and very, very, foolish little monk, down on his knees and scrubbing at the Shaolin Temple.
>
> (*An apology:*)
>
> And I reached down. I sold the firecracker and my soul. And so on goes the pirating of poisoned souls against Shaolin. Every passing century, every once upon a time, and every ever after.

With the Narrator's closing speech, Ho linked the legend of Shaolin with Chinese technology and the invention of gunpowder. The Narrator's sartorial combination of Western and Chinese clothing emulated the synthesis of Ho's semiotic process and reminded the audience that the Asian diaspora was part of the construction of the West as both a discursive and physically racialized space. Chinese immigrant labor built the transcontinental railroad,[21] yet it was the technology of gunpowder that Western colonial powers used to

---

21. As writers such as Frank Chin have demonstrated, the historical trajectory of the Chinese diaspora cannot be separated from the Asian American experience in the Southwestern United States as laborers of the railroads.

dominate Asia and Africa and maintain a racial hierarchy within the white settler project of the United States.[22] The closing polemic suggests that by having the ability to speak within the world of the play, the Narrator is an agent whose language is fallible because it is not embodied in the form of martial arts movement or music. The Narrator was both an intermediary and a sellout assimilationist, unable to transcend the limitations of didacticism.

Again, these political exhibitions were created through sonic kinesthesia as the breath of the saxophone and breath of the martial artists organized sound into movement and movement into sound. Sonic kinesthesia is a musical energy akin to what Fred Moten describes as a "revolutionary force of the sensuality that emerges from the sonic event,"[23] as an expression of resistance and struggle. Ho's sonic kinesthesia was "the generative force of a venerable phonic propulsion, the ontological and historical priority of resistance to power and objection to subjection, the old-new thing, the freedom drive that animates black performances"[24] that pushed him to conceive of Afro Asian performance as a confluence of disciplines, acculturation, and political strategy in which martial arts and music combined to create liberation movement.

The Deadly She-Wolf

Ho once again collaborated with playwright Ruth Margraff to develop the script for *Deadly She-Wolf Assassin at Armageddon*,[25] which was subsequently produced in 2004. The development of the story was inspired by Margraff's interest in Japanese Noh Theater as well as the Japanese nationalist writer, actor, and martial artist Yukio Mishima's short story, *Patriotism*.[26] Both Margraff and Ho shared a keen interest in Japanese manga, and thus the main plot of *Deadly She-Wolf* was based on the 1970s Japanese manga and film series,

---

22. While it is popular knowledge that China is credited for inventing the mixture of sulfur, coal, and potassium nitrate that became gunpowder, the expansion and appropriation processes of this technology is still very much a contested history.
23. Moten, *In the Break: The Aesthetics of the Black Radical Tradition*, 12.
24. Moten, *In the Break: The Aesthetics of the Black Radical Tradition*, 12.
25. Margraff and Ho, "Deadly She-Wolf Assassin at Armageddon."
26. Mishima and Sargent, *Patriotism*. Originally published as a short story in 1960, Mishima's *Patriotism* serves as a source of inspiration when dealing with contradictory positions of identity. Mishima can thus be seen as a figure whose writing and performances resonate with what might seem to be the least expected of audiences. This further complicates Mishima's contradictory stance on the re-armament of Japan and calls into question whether militarization necessarily leads to colonialism. From this perspective, Mishima is no longer simply a Japanese person struggling with the Japanese condition. Rather, Mishima embodied the contradictory nature of the beautiful and grotesque—love and brutality—being part of the same performance.

Lone Wolf and Cub (*Kozure Okami*). In *Deadly She-Wolf*, martial arts choreography was employed to narrate the internal struggle within Japan just before the Meiji Restoration of 1868. While the catalyst for the Meiji Restoration is often depicted as having been the result of Commodore Perry's "opening up Japan," *Deadly She-Wolf* troubled the dominant master narrative of Perry as the Great White Crusader bringing modernity to the heathens of the East. The cultural memory of Japan's transition from a feudal agrarian system to an emergent industrial state has often been depicted through popular musicals such as Giacomo Puccini's *Madama Butterfly* (1903), which continues to have actors perform in yellowface. As Shannon Steen has observed, these theatrical productions enabled the creation of racial identities to "organize international power, global space, and the bodies within it,"[27] and were often organized around legal acts that worked in conjunction with theatrical productions to construct US race identities.[28] In contrast to such essentialized notions of racialized and gendered performance, *Deadly She-Wolf* rendered Japan as a contested place in which the Shogun is a "despot at the twilight of his imperial epoch" who desperately attempts to cling to power and negotiate with fictional archetypes such as Bok Mei Lotus, Chinese Super warrior; Colonel U. S. A., Ulysses Sam Armageddon; Rogue Assassin, Disgraced *Kaishakunin* (an executioner); and Qaseem the Killing Machine, Black Super warrior, all of whom converge upon a mythologized Japan in the quest for power and control. In this version of Japan's emergence into a "modernity" a female character, She-Wolf, is the arbiter of the fate of many of these characters and hence the political economy of Japan.

While the aesthetics of Noh Drama and *Lone Wolf and Cub* were ostensibly artifacts of Japanese cultural practice and utilized Japanese actors, *Deadly She-Wolf* mobilized a multiethnic cast of performers that, unlike *Lone Wolf and Cub*, placed an ensemble of female martial artists and performers at the center of its work. The production was also a collaboration between Ho and Sonoko Kawahara, a stage director originally from Tokyo who works and lives in New York. In *Deadly She-Wolf*, Ho utilized the sounds of Japanese instruments such as the *shakuhachi* (Japanese flute) in juxtaposition to his baritone saxophone that offered an Afro Asian sonic kinesthesia as music and chore-

27. Steen, *Racial Geometries of the Black Atlantic, Asian Pacific and American Theatre*, 5.
28. For more on the relationship between performance and the law, see Chambers-Letson, *A Race So Different: Performance and Law in Asian America*. Musical theater productions such as *Madame Butterfly* maintained orientalist frameworks, and at times have used Black and white bodies to create Asian identity on the stage in order to support policies such as The Chinese Exclusion Act of 1882 and the National Origins Act of 1924, both of which served to control and subordinate Asian populations in the US.

ography. Kawahara's direction of *Deadly She-Wolf* worked to contest the representation of patriarchy on the stage and challenged Ho's own assumption around gender, power, and collaboration.

At the top of the performance, Iyagu, a conspirator from the brutal Iyagyu clan who is determined to destroy the Shogun, summons the characters Bok Mei Lotus, Colonel U. S. A., and Qaseem in an effort to both undermine the Shogun and kill Rogue Assassin, who until this point has functioned as the executioner for the Shogun. In the third scene of the second act, Colonel U. S. A. attacks Rogue Assassin with his cutlass[29] after taunting him with a recital of his résumé for destruction and colonization. The Colonel promises to demonstrate "West Point brutality" and the superiority of the white man.

The Colonel, played by Aaron Armstrong (white), is dressed in all-white chaps and a button-down collared shirt, while Rogue Assassin, played by Yoshi Amao (Japanese), sports an all-black kimono and hakama. An almost inconspicuous twist occurs in the fight choreography when Colonel U. S. A. parries and thrusts with his US-issued saber, and countering, Rogue Assassin grabs the Smith & Wesson revolver from the Colonel's leg holster. Rogue Assassin's sword has been knocked out of his hand and it seems as if he has been defeated. The omniscient female Narrator (Marina Celander) speaks the role of Colonel U. S. A.

> It's the white man's time now, sorry. Even if it takes a few more ornaments, West Point brutality will always prevail over the eastern goon. So I'll make this easy. I'll just get you in between the—agh!! (Colonel U. S. A. grabs for his holster. Realizes gun is missing. Rogue Assassin reaches in his sleeve, and shoots Colonel U. S. A. between the eyes.)

Having missed the moment when Rogue Assassin steals the gun from the Colonel's holster, the audience is caught off guard and gasps audibly as the Colonel reaches for his revolver only to discover that it is now in Rogue Assassin's hand. This choreography contextualizes the engagement between European and American imperialism with Asia, and the arrival of Commodore Perry in Japan.

In the reversal in power between Colonel U. S. A. and Rogue Assassin, violent domination that is initially reserved for Colonel U. S. A., and thus for white masculinity, is subverted through the aforementioned paradigm shift as Rogue Assassin shoots Colonel U. S. A. between the eyes (Figure 4.4). The character of Rogue Assassin is no longer relegated to the status of effeminate

---

29. A short broadsword or saber used by US cavalrymen for slashing.

FIGURE 4.3. Aaron Armstrong, stage right, as Colonel U. S. A. Armageddon, and Yoshi Amao, stage left, as Rogue Assassin

FIGURE 4.4. Having taken Colonel U. S. A.'s six shooter, Rogue Assassin shoots the Colonel with it

Asian male in relationship to white patriarchal heroism. Through the choreographed movement, created in conjunction with Ho's live music ensemble, Ho subverts dominant narratives of white patriarchal colonialism often seen in mainstream performances such as *The Last Samurai* (2003) or the novel turned film and epic series, *Shogun* (1980).

By refusing the traditional trope of the Euro-American male hero, *Deadly She-Wolf* attempted to decolonize the mythology of an effeminized East. The performance is akin to the bushi performances of Yukio Mishima and the notion of samurai spirit that was incorporated into his personal and artistic process. Like Ho, who was a member of the US Armed Forces, Mishima joined the Japanese Self-Defense Forces. His military training and fanaticism were integrated with his practice as a novelist, playwright, actor, and martial arts practitioner, specifically the art of kendo (a form of sport sword fighting with bamboo sticks). For *Deadly She-Wolf,* Ho and Margraff drew on Mishima's bushido imagery in *Patriotism,* as well as the rogue samurai character, Ogami Itto, from the manga and subsequent film series, *Lone Wolf and Cub.*

Unlike Mishima's hypermasculinized homoeroticism, Ho and Margraff's martial arts jazz operetta inverted dominant male roles like those of Mishima's *Patriotism* and *Lone Wolf and Cub.* Ho supplanted characters such as Ogami Itto (who was portrayed by the Japanese actor Tomisaburo Wakayama) and the omniscient male Narrator in *Patriotism* (portrayed by Yukio Mishima himself) with female characters and lead female actors as seen in the performance of Marina Celander and Ai Takeda. In *Deadly She-Wolf,* the characters of She-Wolf and the Narrator are counterhegemonic devices because they resist dominant eroticized and effeminate stereotypes of female bodies. The plot interweaves Japanese pseudomythology with popular samurai genres and jazz music in order to challenge gendered power dynamics, as well as reimagine narratives about colonialism's relation to Asia. While Rogue Assassin ostensibly relies on a heteronormative incarnation of Japanese bushido masculinity, the characters of the She-Wolf, Narrator, and She-Wolf's Ninja Assistants are embodied by female performers, which in turn destabilize traditionally masculinized roles assigned to characters in *Lone Wolf and Cub* and Mishima's work.

Because She-Wolf is not only able to kill the invading forces of Japan but also murders her own father, Rogue Assassin, she symbolically ends the patriarchal lineage of Japan. Whereas in Mishima's stage play, *Patriotism,* the hypermasculinity of Mishima's persona is magnified to the point that his own body operates as a fetishized object reifying normative readings of Japanese masculinity. *Patriotism* was "inspired by the Army Rebellion of 1936, which Mishima would invest with increasing symbolic importance as his own special brand of patriotism evolved,"[30] and placed the act of ritual disembowelment as a fetishizing of pure Japanese samurai spirit.

In the original *Lone Wolf and Cub,* the central character, Ogami Itto, was personified as a "lone wolf" or *ronin* (wondering masterless samurai) who survives at the outskirts of feudal Japanese society. Itto is a vagabond traveling with his son, Cub, and the protection of his sword. Itto survives in a world where he must dispense justice to rough men, and sleep with a few loose women, in order to protect his male heir and secure the normative functionality of the series. By appropriating these genres and reinscribing them

---

30. Nathan, *Mishima: A Biography,* 175.

into the production, *Deadly She-Wolf* transgresses gender norms and points toward Ho's matriarchal socialist vision by subverting the notion of patrilineality itself. By attempting to create a popular genre that can be politically conscious as well as critical of the culture industry more broadly, this kind of work rebuts historical depictions of an effeminized Asia and Asian Diaspora. *Deadly She-Wolf* challenges an ahistorical reading of colonial encounter, through the diverse bodies and sonic kinesthesia that transverse stage. The minimalist stage of the production also borrowed from the emptiness of the Noh theater, a Japanese performing arts genre that has historically been reserved for male performers.

The eclectic mixture of the creative team also included the transnational critique that Kawahara brought to the collaboration and that fulfilled the sonic kinesthesia of Afro Asian performance. The director, Sonoko Kawahara, spoke to this during interviews about her career as a Japanese female director and her experience collaborating with Ho. Her insight reveals the continual negotiation and tension that exists for centering female performance both globally and in the US.

> In terms of importing some production from the US to Japan, people would be more interested in Western [style]. For example, they would like to have a blues musician or rock and roll. This production should appeal to Japanese people because they haven't seen this yet and they have too much prejudice. They think "Oh, if Asian American made something like Japanese Samurai, it should be a copy of something." Like a second tier or something. That kind of prejudice I can see from Japanese people. But this project is not that. That's why I wanted to direct and I really like this production. It's very original. Among Japanese people, in the *Kozure Okami* world like manga and film are all dominated by male character[s]. There is no room for a female protagonist. This production would probably break expectations of what *Kozure Okami* is about for Japanese people, but I don't think it would affect them in a negative way because this is the modern world. Actually do you know the movie called *Azumi*? Because Fred had this film called *Azumi* in mind and he recommended it me.[31]

Kawahara's statement reveals both a resistance and desire to embrace innovative forms in New York City's Japan Society, where *Deadly She-Wolf* debuted. Challenging predominantly masculinized genres reserved for male practitioners would disrupt a Japanese audience who, given the history of male actors

---

31. Kawahara, Interview with the Author, September 20, 2011.

playing the parts of female characters as seen in *Kabuki Theater*, would anticipate the personification of femininity to be embodied by male performers. The production may also present itself as subversive to US audiences who also anticipate the construction of predominantly masculine samurai characters and motifs exported through the Japanese film industry. Ho's synthesis of *Lone Wolf and Cub* with the female semiotics of *Azumi*, a popular Japanese teenage film about a young ninja girl, raised as a cold-blooded assassin, who must defeat three evil warlords while also battling her own heart, calls attention to the gendered politics of *Deadly She-Wolf*.

Signifiers such as white settlers, African slave trade, Chinese kung fu, and a male samurai hero are complicated by a rereading in which raced and gendered stereotypes are unfulfilled. These expectations are supplanted by antiheroes who call into question the assumed binaries of black–white, good–evil, and East–West. Such is the case in the aforementioned battle between Rogue Assassin and Colonel U. S. A. She-Wolf, whose physical journey ultimately delivers her to a battle with her father, Rogue Assassin, is motivated by a combination of fate and obligation to her retainer, Iyagu. The fact that She-Wolf cuts down her own father, who did not recognize her as legitimate, is yet another direct challenge to the concept of patriarchal lineage that has so often been privileged within Japanese society.

However, Kawahara also revealed how Ho's own sense of paternalism became destabilized during their collaboration. Not only did Ho seem to make certain assumptions about the aesthetics of the production, but also his working process with female collaborators chafed with Kawahara, who had to remind Ho of what collaboration was and how it was important for her to find her own voice within the work.

> Actually, I fought with Fred a lot. Did he mention this? Sonoko, was terrible or something? . . . We fought a lot. We fight each other . . . I think that he says a lot, but I clearly said, no. Probably one thing maybe, American people, you just think Japanese women is more kind or gentle and doesn't say "no" to men, don't you think? . . . I don't know. What's the image of Japanese women in the United States? Don't you think many people think "soft" and "obeying"? . . . That's what I wanted to break! That's what I wanted to break! I'm not sure if it's necessarily the audience's view, but that's what I wanted to break when I display Japanese characters in the piece. But, of course, even Fred as an American; not only Fred, but American people still carry this kind of image of Japanese women character. My personality, when I am doing the direction, I clearly fight back to Fred and I say "No" to Fred and that makes him very uncomfortable. I think he suspected I wasn't that strong—that kind

of personality. I am not interested in what Americans want to see. I want to break that image by presenting the reality of the Japanese female.³²

Kawahara's candor suggests that gender and even transnational politics of *Deadly She-Wolf* move beyond the stage and into the playmaking process. Her critique of Ho as an Asian American male with certain preconceived notions of Japanese cultural norms even suggests a disjuncture between the Japanese diaspora in the US and Asian American sentiments, which have become ingrained through a process of American fetishism and romanticism of the "East." Yet, ironically all of these conundrums emerge in which the "hybridity" of Afro Asia is sliced into yet more complex and nuanced understandings of identity through the uncertain interactions backstage.

While Ho claimed that his matriarchal socialism was an attempt at gender equality, Kawahara's comments reveal a gap between his privilege as a male artist/producer and collaborator, and the gendered power dynamics within the collaborative process. Yet, Ho continued to stand firm with Kawahara as the director for the planned 2013 production of *Deadly She-Wolf* at La Mama in New York. Even as he was dying, Ho made himself vulnerable to Kawahara's criticism, listening, challenging, and following her vision as she took center stage as director.

The production of *Deadly She-Wolf* then becomes a reflection of these microexchanges that are a part of a conversation about the process of playmaking, and the means of production that are manifested through the performance. Kawahara went on to articulate the way in which she perceived the significance of martial arts within *Deadly She-Wolf* being imbued with a certain kind of meaning that is not merely for the purposes of spectacle or entertainment. Rather, *tachimawari* (sword play) within the piece was also a form of creative self-expression.

> I really wanted to direct this play because I think [sic] the subject [of] the Japanese Manga story *Kozure Okami*, but what I think was most meaningful was the fact that Fred want[ed] to use martial arts techniques—like Japanese sword play. Martial arts or these kinds of forms—any form of performance should not be like a circus. It isn't just showing off of the technique. Sometimes I don't appreciate . . . like you know the Chinese super gymnastic performance? Do you know what I mean? . . . Like these British cult talent type of thing where people come on the stage and show off their super technique. I really want[ed] to differ[entiate] the Fred Ho performance from this [sic]

---

32. Kawahara, Interview with the Author, September 20, 2011.

kind of techniques or eye popping entertainment. Because the formality of Japanese sword play is something more than just showing off the technique. So I didn't want this idea for Fred's piece—martial arts on the stage—to be treated just as entertainment or just for show for the audience who likes martial arts. Because I did sword play myself and I am from Japan. I wanted to treat this production more as a philosophy. It is it's own language, not just technique. As a Japanese [person], I think many [W]estern people take some [E]astern culture like martial arts stuff just as technique. So I wanted to convey the formality of this technique or the formality of this style of work. Like something more as a form of expression. Just like any dance or physical movement is a tool of the expression, right? So I wanted to treat this sword play rightly and not superficially. It sounds very arrogant, but since I love this element, I really wanted to direct this to convey something deeper than what you see on the superficial level. I just direct this play as I direct Shakespeare or as I direct Chekhov or any other story. That's my point of view.[33]

For Kawahra, sword play, or *tachimawari,* is the essence of human survival and refinement of years of practice that enables human beings to embody language through the repertoire of performance disciplines. However, in *Deadly She-Wolf,* through the process of sonic kinesthesia, Ho's Afro Asian jazz language turned the training weapon of the *bokken* (wooden sword) into not only a prop but an extension of the performer's body. The sword is wielded as a constant extension of Rogue Assassin and She-Wolf's identities. For Mishima, the body became a locus for the expression of political thought, and as Kawahara suggested, we can also see the body used in ways similar to those of Mishima's *Patriotism,* and as a means of expression.

The same bushido imagery is evoked through the characters of Rogue Assassin and She-Wolf. At the beginning of *Deadly She-Wolf,* the stage is completely dark as the sound of the *koto* (Japanese harp) and *shakuhachi* (wooden Japanese flute), accompanied by percussive tapping, introduces us to the Boy (played by a female actor), who chases after a blood-red plastic ball. The Boy immediately senses something and comes to a halt. Behind her/him sits her/his father, Rogue Assassin, seated in *zazen* with his back to the audience. A red scarf, which symbolizes the blood of the executed, is draped over his body. Ho's baritone sounds off, *dah-dahhhh,* as three members of the ensemble approach, wielding swords. As the first ensemble member attacks, Rogue Assassin draws his *katana* and parries the slash. Up on his feet, he battles the other players and deftly cuts them down. Before Rogue Assassin disposes of

---

33. Kawahara, Interview with the Author, September 20, 2011.

the last player, he sheathes his katana, as if to give his foe one last chance to retreat. But his foe raises his own katana over his head and rushes in, cutting down vertically. Rogue Assassin responds in classic *iaido* form, drawing his katana and slicing through the attacker's midsection. The attacker stumbles, contemplates attacking again, but then immediately falls to his death. Rogue Assassin, now looking in the other direction, twirls the sword in order to flick the blood off it and sheathes the weapon. This very same basic repertoire of drawing and cutting is the foundation of iaido. This form, produced through the body, can be seen in Mishima's archived footage of his martial arts practice. Through the physical actions of Rogue Assassin's choreography, the social imagery of the samurai is evoked, just as Mishima sought to evoke bushido through his own practice and performance. Mishima performed his patriotism through acts such as kendo, iaido, and *seppuku* (ritual suicide) itself. This corollary becomes overtly clear in Mishima's writing, body, and dramatic performance of death. In his essay "Sun and Steel," Mishima reveals, "As I pondered the nature of that 'I,' I was driven to the conclusion that the 'I' in question corresponded precisely with the physical space that I occupied. What I was seeking, in short, was a language of the body."[34] Mishima's body was sculpted by *sun and steel,* and it was through both literature and corpus that he attempted to frame his body as the national symbol. Mishima's ritualized suicide, performed for the Japan Self-Defense Forces in 1970, became the ultimate symbolic act of patriotism, exceeding any previous performance. By disemboweling himself, tearing his entrails open with literal steel, Mishima's body became the living and dying expression *of* sun and steel, melding his body with the blade.

If Mishima's character of the Lieutenant in *Patriotism* is a ghost, a spirit returning home from the shadows of war, then he is not unlike the character of She-Wolf, whom Margraff's narrative uses to flip gendered expectations and places She-Wolf as the antihero whose devotion and sincerity subverts the insincerity of the patriarchal lineage that is crumbling around her. Because Mishima viewed the Japanese condition as being in a quasi-colonial state in its relationship to US imperialism, his performance was subversive and possibly liberating when considered within the racialized and gendered East–West binary. Ho and Margraff's appropriation of Mishima's *Patriotism* and the Japanese bushido spirit is a conundrum that recalls elements of nationalist strategies. However, in the end, *Deadly She-Wolf* smashes the nationalist narrative with the sounds of the Afro Asia Music Ensemble and the choreography of

---

34. Nathan, *Mishima: A Biography,* 5.

female antiheroes as it challenges and reframes the martial arts as nonexclusive strategies.

If the martial arts and the performance of bushido enabled Mishima to find a voice in which to perform a public image of masculinity despite his homosexuality, then *Deadly She-Wolfe* creates a space for the female body to subvert notions of patriarchy through choreography. This is exemplified in the characters of She-Wolf and the boy/girl (who is portrayed by an Asian female actress, Takemi Kitamura), the Narrator, Ninja Assistants, and Kawahara's direction. While battles between Rogue Assassin, Bok Mei Lotus, Colonel U. S. A. (Ulysses Sam Armageddon), and Qaseem the Killing Machine feature a multiethnic cast of predominantly male actors, the guidance of the omnipresent female Narrator pushes us through to an ending that attempts to exemplify Ho's conception of matriarchal socialism through the vengeance of the She-Wolf.

With Bok Mei Lotus and Colonel U. S. A. having been disposed of by Rogue Assassin, the Shogun pleads for Qaseem the Killing Machine to subdue the kaishakunin. Entering the space shirtless, dressed in only flowing white pants and holding Kali sticks, the actor playing Qaseem the Killing Machine is introduced by the Narrator stating, "Now I want just one thing. A decent challenge. To kill the greatest of the great. They promised me this chance to meet you, one on one and I see you are just like me. . . . I say we just go hand to hand. I am beholden to no blood, no law, no nation. I'm burned out on extinction. I fly no flag, but I hit like a plague."[35] Within the multiethnic scheme of the production's cast, Qaseem's body is the representation of Blackness that stands in for the trope of the African Diaspora. Qaseem's performance becomes a metonym for Africa's internal struggle as colonialism wreaks havoc on the continent. In his duel with Rogue Assassin, Qaseem seems like an unrelenting opponent as he battles Rogue Assassin and She-Wolf simultaneously. This, in turn, intensifies his sense of masculinity, as well as the subversive power of She-Wolf when she finally strangles him to death from behind. Rogue Assassin must rely on the antihero, She-Wolf, to deliver the final blow. Qaseem's performance presents a conundrum. On the one hand, his physicality seems hypermasculinized compared to the other male characters, as his washboard abdominal muscles, in conjunction with his pectoral and latissimus flexing, recall Mishima's well-conditioned physique, which he was fond of exhibiting. Thus, Qaseem's hypermasculinity can be seen as homoerotic as well as a hackneyed representation of Black male masculinity.

---

35. Margraff and Ho, "Deadly She-Wolf Assassin at Armageddon."

The defeat of Qaseem sets the stage for a resolution between She-Wolf, Iyagu, and Rogue Assassin. During this resolution, She-Wolf learns that Iyagu is not her father, and that she is actually the bastard daughter of Rogue Assassin. With this, the Boy/Girl who has been in the protection of She-Wolf is reunited with his/her father. This revelation causes She-Wolf to actualize her objective, "execution of the executioner at last."[36] This subsequent killing of the executioner echoes Mishima's ritualized decapitation at the hands of one of his own followers. In the final choreography between She-Wolf and Rogue Assassin, both utilize the extension of the sword as an expression of the dramatic tension that has been building between father and daughter. Recalling Kawahara's desire for the movement of the swordplay to embody her philosophy of the production, the final sequence of the choreography contains a pause during which She-Wolf and Rogue Assassin stand diametrically opposed on a diagonal to the front line of the proscenium stage. Who will win, father or daughter? This pause builds a tension between the two actors' bodies. As the Boy/Girl watches, the tension is released as She-Wolf and Rogue Assassin charge at each other with swords drawn. The linearity of their paths of motion is drawn as they crisscross on a diagonal, and She-Wolf's sword slices Rogue Assassin from the neck into the eye. Her sword cuts through and out extending the amplification of the movement as Rogue Assassin's energy is diminished, and his dead body slumps to the stage.

The narrative concludes as the Boy/Girl grabs his/her dead father's sword and prepares to thrust it into She-Wolf's abdomen. However, too much has passed between them, and rather than fight, She-Wolf offers her katana to the Boy/Girl, as the Narrator suggests the following:

> (*As She-Wolf turning to the Boy, the only one left:*)
> She-Wolf: In the silhouettes of my inferno, distilled upon my soul . . . You were both there . . . preying on the fangs of the corrupt . . . that threaten the survival of the pack. I couldn't . . . fight you on my own. Perhaps I've come to love you as your . . . father will love you always. Without vengeance, without doubt . . .[37]

The Boy/Girl receives She-Wolf's sword and unsheathes it. Reminiscent of Mishima's iaido practice, the Boy/Girl sits in *seiza* as he grips the sword, grasping its meaning just as the audience grasps the meaning of the myth that has unfolded. Standing behind, the Narrator, personifying She-Wolf, states:

---

36. Margraff and Ho, "Deadly She-Wolf Assassin at Armageddon."
37. Margraff and Ho, "Deadly She-Wolf Assassin at Armageddon."

Pick up the sword to defeat the sword. But when the sword has been defeated, you must set it down. Still knowing how to use it. How to trust. To save the one with no blood on his hands. Who had a father, thereby everything . . . Should hold onto that . . .[38]

In the penultimate moment, through this very simple bit of physical action, the Boy/Girl actualizes the fulfillment of Rogue Assassin's legacy and She-Wolf's training, as he/she resheathes the katana. Fred Ho's baritone saxophone plays an ominous downward scale that is followed by a rush of cymbals and then the high-pitched sound of the shakuhachi. The Afro Asian hybridity of this musical cue closes the chapter of this violent fable, while leaving the possibility for other incarnations in the future.

The Sweet Science Suite

In 2011, Ho was awarded a Guggenheim Fellowship to develop a new performance piece for the museum's Works and Process program. The *Sweet Science Suite: A Scientific Soul Session Honoring Muhammad Ali*, was Ho's last performance. A collaboration with choreographer Christal Brown, the piece was intended as both an homage to "Muhammad Ali's indomitable spirit"[39] and another exploration into Fred Ho's Afro Asian martial arts jazz theatrical performances. To cope with the woes of his fight with cancer, Ho watched Ali's documentaries and old fight films. He encapsulated his vision of the piece during the first Q&A held on the stage at the museum's Peter B. Lewis Theater between *Movements 2* and *1* (*Movement 1* followed *Movement 2*; see explanation below) with moderator Valerie Gladstone. "I sat down and I decided that I was going to write an homage to Ali, his spirit, but do it in a transgressive kind of way. Something that would evoke the period of the '60s and '70s, particularly the soundtracks of the black exploitation and yellow exploitation films, but with a Sun Ra-nian futuristic bent to it."[40] The *Sweet Science Suite* served as a transhistorical connection between Ali and Ho's former memberships in the Nation of Islam as well as Ali's transformation from Cassius Clay to a political figure outside of the ring.[41]

---

38. Margraff and Ho, "Deadly She-Wolf Assassin at Armageddon."
39. Ho, Interview with Valerie Gladstone. New York, November 13, 2011.
40. Ho, Interview with Valerie Gladstone. New York, November 13, 2011.
41. Ho joined the NOI and took the name Fred 3X.

In 1964, Clay unveiled an unorthodox and graceful fighting style when he scored a TKO (technical knock-out) against Sonny Liston to win the heavyweight championship. Surrounded by more than four hundred reporters from around the world during the weigh-in, Clay repeatedly echoed his famous phrase: "Float like a butterfly sting like a bee! Hey, rumble, young man, rumble!" Clay's prefight loquaciousness manifested itself in the ring as he slipped around and in between the more truculent and hard-hitting Liston. Clay sent stinging jabs to Liston's head and flying body blows to his collapsing abdomen over six rounds before Liston failed to answer the bell for the seventh round. One year later, after changing his name to Muhammad Ali, he would display a similar kind of elusive, graceful movement when he defended his title against Liston, knocking him to the canvas with what seemed to be a phantom counterpunch to a Liston jab that Ali simply sidestepped.

When Ali refused to be inducted into the US Army in 1967, he was stripped of his title, barred from the boxing ring, and threatened with jail time and a $10,000 fine. In 1971, the Supreme Court reversed Ali's conviction, but nearly four of his best fighting years were lost. However, as the 1996 documentary *When We Were Kings* demonstrates, Ali was determined to regain his heavyweight title. He would ultimately do this by beating the undefeated heavyweight champion, George Foreman.

The Foreman bout, dubbed the "Rumble in the Jungle," was staged in Zaire on October 30, 1974. The event had implications that reached far beyond the realm of sport. It became something more than boxing; it was about competing ideals of Black masculinity within the dialectic of struggle. Foreman represented an agenda of assimilating into American capitalism, whereas Ali represented the Pan-Africanist campaign, which he imbued with the NOI's performance of discipline and Black cultural nationalism.

Rather than fight Foreman punch for punch, Ali's guerilla tactic, referred to as "rope-a-dope," recalled the strategies of the Vietcong, who could not match the US military's firepower. The asymmetric distribution of power necessitated that the Vietcong exhaust their enemy through hit-and-run techniques, or to use a boxing term, stick-and-move, in which the faster and more agile fighter keeps moving away from a larger flat-footed opponent.

By throwing a series of right-hand leads at the beginning of the bout, 32-year-old Ali confused and enraged the younger, stronger 24-year-old Foreman. Ali convinced Foreman that he was going to dance, as he had often done in the past, encouraging the crowd in Zaire to cheer "Ali, bomaye" (Ali, kill him). However, because of Ali's long absence from the ring, and subsequent decline in athletic ability, he could not beat Foreman by trading blows.

Instead, Ali retreated to the ropes, leaning against them allowing his body to absorb Foreman's power until the fifth round of the fight. By the seventh round, Foreman had run out of gas, and with 12 seconds left in the eighth round, Ali knocked Foreman out with a left jab and a right cross.

By placing the bout in Zaire, formerly the Belgian Congo, the Pan-African and Asian liberation struggles embodied at the Bandung Conference were once again made visible to a broader global audience. The "Rumble in the Jungle" was in fact a form of racial kinesthesia that attempted to hail and summon a political solidarity between the struggles of Blacks in the United States and the decolonizing struggles of Black Africa. As film director Spike Lee suggests at the beginning of *When We Were Kings*: "For these two African Americans to come home was of great significance. Because of Hollywood and TV a lot of us had been taught to hate Africa. There was a time when if you called a Black person an African they would be ready to fight."[42] Lee's statement shows the change in perspective wrought by the liberation struggles of the 1960s, a perspective that Ho transliterated as the music and choreography of his *Movements 1* and *3*.

While Ho created a total of six movements, three different pieces comprised the version of *Sweet Science Suite* that I experienced on November 13, 2011, at the Guggenheim Works and Process presentation: *Movement 2: Float Like a Butterfly, Sting Like an Afro Asian Bumblebee*; *Movement 1: Shake Up the World*; *Movement 3: No Vietnamese Ever Called Me Nigger! Movement 1* began with a brief introduction by Works and Process producer Mary Sharp Cronson. The lights dimmed and the buzzing sound of Ho's baritone sax performing a variation of Nikolai Rimsky-Korsakov's "Flight of the Bumblebee" (1933) in 5/4 time opened the piece.

In keeping with his cancer warrior ethos, Ho performed his baritone in spite of his illness. He accompanied the all–African American dance ensemble, which consisted of six men and one woman, Toni Renee Johnson, who also served as dance director for the piece.[43] The dancers' bodies were draped in kente- and dashiki-style clothing during Ho's solo, *Float Like a Butterfly*, which was inspired by Billy May's "Green Hornet" theme (1966) and the Rimsky-Korsakov interlude.[44] The solo was backed by the Green Monster Big

---

42. Gast, *When We Were Kings* (1996).

43. In addition to Johnson (rehearsal director), the dancers were Marcus Braggs, Dante Brown, Edwardo Brito, Roderick Callawa, Gilbert Reyes, and Ricarrdo Valentine.

44. For a complete description of the event's programming, see the Guggenheim archive at https://beta.worldcat.org/archivegrid/collection/data/794928204. The page refers to the video of the event (see Cronson et al., 2011).

Band conducted by Whitney George. Half of the band was divided between house left and right of the audience, with the other half in the pit.

Sweet Science Suite historicized, problematized, and in some cases even mythologized Afro Asia as a form of coalitional politics. The production and subsequent question-and-answer session explored Ali's refusal to participate in the Vietnam War, his conviction for draft evasion, the subsequent loss of his title, his impoverishment, and his eventual comeback against George Foreman. The production was counternarrative choreography, with permutations inside and outside the ring mirroring Ali's graceful and at times unorthodox tactics. One of those tactics was to develop a cult of personality, which he used to contest domestic racism and global imperialism. The collaboration between Ho and Christal Brown, whose father was a Vietnam veteran, was also a vehicle through which to make visible the body politics of choreography. Ho and Brown used modern dance, jazz music, and boxing—"the sweet science"—to illustrate the Black experience in the Vietnam War through Brown's memories of her father.

Movement 2 set the stage for the metaphorical death of Cassius Clay, the story of Muhammad Ali's conversion to the NOI, and Ali's comeback. I was able to feel the sonic kinesthetics of music, see the live choreography of flesh, hear and participate in the whistles and the "yeaaahs" that summoned and acknowledged the audience's appreciation of the choreography and its seven dancers, as well as the twenty musicians in the Green Monster Big Band. Each movement of the dancers seemed to be a celebratory response and affirmation of the young Cassius Clay. His identity was captured by the interplay between ensemble members as they sparred amongst each other—shadow boxing, bobbing and weaving like Clay's graceful dancing in the ring in his first Liston fight.

The lightness and nimbleness of Clay's body came alive through the dancers onstage as each member of the ensemble alternated between the structured boxer's stance and the choreographed pirouettes and jetés of their sometimes balletic solos. Ho and the Green Monster Big Band's constant refrain of the *Green Hornet* theme underscored the movement. Edward Brito, a dancer with boxing experience, leapt through the air, his feet, abdomen, and head parallel to the ground for what seemed almost a meter, until his fingertips finally reached the stage again, as he landed in a controlled roll. The ensemble then picked him up and hoisted him above their heads before placing him back down on his feet. Then they retreated offstage in a series of choreographed steps: they folded their arms, took one step back upstage right, made a Black Power salute with their fists in the air, pointed, took one step back upstage right, and repeated the sequence again until they had completely exited offstage.

Their retreat segued into one of two dance solos by Toni Renee Johnson as she continued to weave the story of the transformation of Cassius Clay into Muhammad Ali as a metaphorical search for a Black American identity. The sartorial presentation of Johnson was vastly different between her first and second solos.

In the first solo, Johnson wore a black-and-white striped dress that was split up the front and connected by small metal chains, revealing her abdomen. The solo ended with a raised open palm to the audience, demanding that we "talk to the hand"—she was to be taken seriously. In Johnson's second solo, she appeared in an all-black *khimar* (a long headscarf worn by Muslim women, typically gathered or fastened under the chin and covering the body to variable lengths. The change illustrated the shift in political consciousness from 1966 to 1967—from Negro to Black, from Clay to Ali, and from Civil Rights to Black Power.[45]

One of Ho's sax solos provided the music for Johnson's second dance. As he played, Ho leaned back, recalling Ali's submissive posture on the ropes as he received punishing blows from Foreman. Ho's entire body seemed as if he was pulling the weight of his feet into his lungs and raising his baritone to the highest altissimo possible. This in turn elicited a "yoooo" response from a spectator as Ho's voice took his audience to the edge of sound with a piercing pop of the saxophone's reed, and then, ever so gently, led us back down to the soulful bottom of the instrument's lower register. At this point the dancers paused in their movement, faced the audience, and simply sat down on the floor. When Ho hit these octaves within the piece, the sound became an interlocution between saxophone, dancing body, and spectator.

Movement 1 followed *Movement 2* and sharpened the image of the transformative experience that Ho was attempting to capture. At the top of *Movement 1* the lights came up on two dancers onstage revealing their black-and-white clothing: black suit trousers, white shirt, and black tie. The dancer downstage right stood still, an erect spine proclaiming pride. This erectness was contrasted by the fluid movement of the upstage dancer, whose body pulsed back and forth from all fours on hands and knees to standing. The difference between stillness and movement staged a tension among the ensemble that correlated to the mounting tension within the Black community. The Black intelligentsia of the 1950s and '60s—the dancers in black pants and ties—were juxtaposed with the more proletarian dress code of the other dancers in tank tops and casual khakis. In turn, *Movement 1* signified the discord within

---

45. Stokely Carmichael gave his "Black Power" speech in Greenwood, Mississippi, on October 20, 1966.

FIGURE 4.5. Toni Renee Johnson, in a modernist looking dress, looks back at the audience, bringing her first solo to a close

FIGURE 4.6. Johnson, dressed in a *khimar*, appears alongside Ho in her second solo of *Movement 2* in *Sweet Science Suite: A Scientific Soul Session Honoring Muhammad Ali* at the Guggenheim Museum's Peter B. Lewis Theater on November 13, 2011

the Black community about how to deal with US social-economic inequity. *Movement 1* employed tableaus in which the dancers were positioned in contrapuntal alignment to each other—tableaus that were more synchronized into specific poses and gestures than the nonspecific free flow of *Movement 2*. Members of the dance ensemble squared.

The intelligentsia could have been the NOI itself, but the NOI was just one of many groups within the Black liberation movement and representative of the various approaches in the struggle for social justice. Like Ali, radicals such as the Black Panther Party's Huey P. Newton and Radical Action Movement's Robert F. Williams led transnational Afro Asian movements that sponsored meetings, letter-writing campaigns, underground newspapers, and armed self-defense education. Thus, the stylistic transition of the early 1960s, as witnessed in the choreography of *Movement 1*, paralleled the uncertain and perhaps multifarious transition from Civil Rights to Black Power. This transition was inscribed in the choreography as the dancer wearing the aforementioned two-toned suit finally performed the erect posture of the Black Power salute, a gesture that accompanied the sonic kinetics of the alto saxophone.

After the performance, I interviewed dancer Ricarrdo Valentine. I asked about Brown's directing during the rehearsal process: How did Brown engage the Black Power movement? I wanted to know how much Brown emphasized the actual movement as a manifestation of political action and what kind of research was involved. Valentine responded:

> I found myself wanting to do my own research about the Black people coming up in the movement back in the day. I would read books on different leaders like Marcus Garvey. I would watch a lot of documentaries just to really understand what was going on back in the '60s. I had to really personalize it and just use it in my movement. When it was time to do the fist—especially one section when we create the portrait of the two guys who went to the Olympics, the two Black men, they hold up their fists—we used that in our choreography. I think that picture was very important. They didn't have any shoes on. It was Black Power in the air. They felt confident in who they were as young men at that time. I think a lot of the ways that they carried themselves back in the day, very confident, and it's something that you don't see now in my opinion.[46]

---

46. Richard Valentine, Interview with the Author, November 13, 2011.

FIGURE 4.7. Roderick Callaway stands with fist raised high after having knocked out the others who are on the ground in *Sweet Science Suite: A Scientific Soul Session Honoring Muhammad Ali* at the Guggenheim Museum's Peter B. Lewis Theater on November 13, 2011

The *Sweet Science Suite* attempted to recall connections between global political movements and Ali as a "choreography of empathy"[47] and solidarity. The image of Tommie Smith and John Carlos, US sprinters at the 1968 Olympics in Mexico City, with bowed heads and raised fists in protest against racism in the United States, connected with people around the world who were struggling against oppression.[48] As the dancer struck the Black Power pose, the other ensemble members immediately collapsed to the ground: they were literally knocked over by the force of the gesture. The Black Power salute was a recursive thematic gesture anticipating the climax of *Movement 1* in which one of the Black Power dancers dressed in a shirt and tie threw a flurry of punches aimed toward the other ensemble member, also in a shirt and tie, who reacted as if being knocked out. The dancer who'd thrown the flurry of punches then

---

47. Foster, *Choreographing Empathy: Kinesthesia in Performance*, 2.
48. Mexico City hosted the 1968 Olympic Games amid serious civil uprisings. Ten days before the Games were scheduled to open, scores of university students were killed by army troops, mirroring both the resistance and suppression of aggrieved people everywhere.

delivered a knockout blow to the audience, bringing *Movement 1* to a close and the audience to its feet.

The phrase, "No Vietnamese Ever Called Me Nigger," is popularly associated with Ali because of his stance against American involvement in Vietnam, but the phrase was actually first used by Stokely Carmichael.[49] While the slogan signifies the converging struggles of those who opposed the Vietnam War and those fighting racism, it also raises the visibility of the large numbers of the Black community who fought in Vietnam. This legacy was embodied in Christal Brown's choreography. During the second Q&A, Gladstone asked Brown about her movements:

> I think that artists are a lot like vessels. You pour a lot of things in them and you can mix a lot of things together. What happened here was that everything that was in me, just kind of poured out. I started with *Movement 3* which is what you'll see next and I started with *Movement 3* in terms of how I could relate to it. *Movement 3* is "No Vietnamese Ever Called Me Nigger." My father lost his legs in Vietnam. I was really pulled to the music because it had a melancholy type of feel to it. The soloist that you'll see, Dante Brown, I was fortunate enough to be in a room with him where he didn't ask me a lot of questions. I would just do something and he would do it too.[50]

Movement 3 exists for Brown as a process of expressing how the Vietnam experience affected her and her family. Her father's experience prompted Brown as a researcher and artist to embody his loss of legs. She went on to reveal how she internalized her father's experience and grafted it onto male bodies during the rehearsal process. "I should also say that when Fred asked me to do this project, it's a huge leap for me because my company is all women. So working with men, I had to bring my own level of bravado to the table. So having Dante there as a body to help me figure out what happens on a man's body was really important for the entry into the process."[51]

The grafting of Christal Brown's experience onto Dante Brown's body (no relation to Christal) vis-à-vis the choreography was an act of imagination and

---

49. Stokely Carmichael, "Hanoi in English to American Servicemen in South Vietnam." aavw.org, October 29, 1967. Accessed September 15, 2015, https://www.aavw.org/protest/carmichael_carmichael_abstract26.html.

50. Brown, Interview with Valerie Gladstone, New York, November 13, 2011. For a complete description of the event's programming, see the Guggenheim archive at https://beta.worldcat.org/archivegrid/collection/data/794928204.

51. Brown, Interview with Valerie Gladstone, New York, November 13, 2011. For a complete description of the event's programming, see the Guggenheim archive at https://beta.worldcat.org/archivegrid/collection/data/794928204.

interconnection[52] that enabled Brown to trace the echoes of her father's experiences in Vietnam and bring them into the present in relation to the collective experience of Afro Asian performance. When reconsidered in this context, the legacy of Black masculinity in Vietnam is reinscribed into the present as the past is brought forward through the Black female body.

The traces of events and memories grafted onto Dante Brown's body were visible during the opening moments of *Movement 3*. Brown emerged into a blue spotlight as a tenor sax duet without mouthpieces created a sound that resembled a Japanese shakuhachi flute. It was ghostly in spirit, with a melancholy, almost bluesy feel. Dante Brown's body seemed to float on the stage as he moved in slow motion, performing a series of gliding turns, his arms extended and rotating. The stage lent itself to a ghostly past that was enhanced by a moaning sound created by the bassist sliding his fingers along the neck of the bass.[53]

This mapping of Dante Brown's body with past experiences became most vivid when Brown was stripped to his briefs by other members of the ensemble wearing black ski masks and paramilitary fatigues. Dante Brown's nearly naked body began to move to the new repertoire that the guerillas taught him. The dancers then proceeded to school the almost naked Dante Brown in the lessons and tactics of guerrilla warfare. His body was symbolically resurrected as a focal point of transformation, simultaneously actualizing the transformation of his physical body changing from a fighter in military fatigues into a political spokesman in a dark suit.

Movement 3 combined guerilla representations, US military, and NOI marching disciplines, putting the liberation struggle of US Blacks in conversation with Blacks who fought in Vietnam. It climaxed with a tableau of the six dancers in black suits (Figure 4.8). Having done a quick-change offstage during Dante Brown's solo, the other dancers, now dressed in the NOI's signature bowtie and dark suit, point at the audience, almost as if speaking back to the witnesses of the event, asking: "What is your response?" It was their "final call," beckoning to the audience as did the newspaper of the NOI, *The Final Call*.[54] In recalling Christal Brown's father's experience in Vietnam, the violence enacted upon his body, and his loss of mobility, pain was transformed into power through the choreography of the dancing body.

---

52. Taylor, *The Archive and the Repertoire: Performing Cultural Memory in the Americas*, 82.

53. At one point, I looked into the pit because I was certain that the sound was a person humming, but there was no vocalist. I realized after several seconds that it was the upright bass creating this human-like sound.

54. The precursor of *The Final Call* was *Muhammad Speaks*.

FIGURE 4.8. The ensemble has transitioned into suits resembling the style of the Nation of Islam in *Sweet Science Suite: A Scientific Soul Session Honoring Muhammad Ali* at the Guggenheim Museum's Peter B. Lewis Theater on November 13, 2011

What Remains: An Afro Asian Futurism[55]

At the end of his life, Ho committed himself to a major push to free political activist Russell "Maroon" Shoatz,[56] advancing ecosocialism, and building upon his idea of matriarchal socialism through a new organization he helped develop called Scientific Soul Sessions (SSS). A refrain on Afro Asian futurism as alternative temporal and spacial maps provided by a perception of past and future affective worlds, the SSS represented Ho's final transformation on his lifelong journey. The SSS was an intergenerational collective of writers, artists, and activists who were committed to spirituality as an essential element in the struggle for liberation with the understanding that the struggle for liberation is "scientific" because it seeks answers and solutions. The SSS had

---

55. Price, "Remembering Fred Ho: The Legacy of Afro Asian Futurism."

56. Shoatz was incarcerated for forty years at the Pennsylvania State Correctional Institution at Graterford; he was held in solitary confinement for twenty-two years. While Shoatz remains incarcerated, the attention brought to Shoatz's case by the Scientific Soul Sessions (SSS) helped bring about his release from solitary confinement on February 22, 2014.

"soul" because it believed in moving beyond limits, reaching out to people, natural creatures, and to the cosmos, imagining and doing the impossible. Many of the members active in the SSS were younger musicians—such as composer, singer, and writer Marie Incontrera, and Ben Barson, Ho's baritone protégé—who performed in the Afro Asian Music Ensemble and jazz martial arts performances. Like the Black Panther Party's Ten-Point Program,[57] the SSS mission revolved around eleven points that aimed to prefigure a society free of imperialism, colonization, racism, heteropatriarchy and capitalist exploitation.[58]

However, unlike the Black Panther Party, which emphasized masculinist conceptions of leadership and organizing, the Scientific Soul Sessions was predicated on being led by women toward a future in which the social construct of gender was eliminated and humanity was re-socialized, in which the values of caring, nurturance, creativity, compassion and collectivity dominate. After Ho's death, the now defunct SSS committed to performing his musical works dedicated to matriarchal socialism, ecosocialism, and developing a queer subjectivity. Ho's songs, such as "Yes, Means Yes. No, Means No. Whatever She Wears, and Wherever She Goes," were the theme for live performance events such as the *Year of the Queer! & Sun Ra Celebration*. The event was held at Joe's Pub on January 19, 2015, performed by the Eco-Music Big Band, and led by Marie Incontrera, who acted as composer, conductor, and bandleader, and whose work spans queer opera, political big band, and music for the oppressed. Through her writing, Incontrera explored and continues to explore a queer blues epistemology launched by sonic kinesthesia. Ho's aggregate performances, including *Voice of the Dragon* and *Sweet Science Suite*, were more than mere performances. They were ways of organizing communities through performance in order to rehearse for a posthumous political mobilization into the future.

Ho's sonic kinesthesia placed into conversation a multiplicity of transhistorical connections around struggles for racial, gender, and class justice, which were embedded in his political activism, live performance, recorded music, and writing. In many ways, Ho's work was a reiteration of the writings of both Fanon and Baraka and their efforts for liberation from the varied effects of white settler colonialism. The archive and cultural imprint that Ho developed through his collaborations with many artists and scholars left behind a model

---

57. In October 1966, Huey P. Newton and Bobby Seale created the Black Panther Party's Ten-Point Program, published in all of the Party's newspapers and in Newton's book, *Revolutionary Suicide*, 122–24.

58. For more of a description on Scientific Soul Sessions see Price "Remembering Fred Ho: The Legacy of Afro Asian Futurism."

for forging a pathway forward, away from self-destruction. His critique of capitalism's effect on a sustainable environment has proven accurate, anticipating the very global crisis that we find ourselves in as a species in 2016. "Capitalism . . . is the cancer for Planet Earth; and cancer . . . is the exponentially increasing environmental and social toxicity of capitalism assaulting the individual person."[59] At this moment, the cancerous effects of capitalism threaten a sustainable relationship between human beings and their environment, and as a result, scholars, activists, and artists continue to engage Ho's work in their classrooms, theaters, texts, on their streets, and in the sonicscapes that continue to embody his spirit.

---

59. Ho, *Diary of a Radical Cancer Warrior: Fighting Cancer and Capitalism at the Cellular Level*, xl.

CHAPTER 5

Here Be Dragons

The Odyssey Toward Liberation

> Sing in me, Muse, and through me tell the story
> Tell me, Muse, of the man of many ways,
> the wanderer, who was driven
> far journeys, after he had sacked Troy's sacred citadel.
> Many were they whose cities he saw,
> whose minds he learned of,
> many the pains he suffered in his spirit on the wide sea,
> struggling for his own life and the homecoming of his companions.
> —Homer[1]

Moving Bodies Creating Movements

Movement is breath. Breath is life. Policing in America suffocates. To be unable to breathe is to be unable able to live. The carceral system is a method of restricting life through the restriction of movement, and the prison regime of the US incarcerates more people than any other country in the world. Black and Latinx people are disproportionately incarcerated by American policing and the prison system.[2] These facts should be no surprise of course. America's prison regime is a continuum of the slave-catching system of the American colonies that began in 1619[3] that sought to restrict the movement, escape,

---

1. As stated by the Ensemble for the 2012 production of The Odyssey Project. For this particular adaptation, we used Richmond Lattimore's 1967 translation of *The Odyssey*.

2. For a recent update on facts and figures for rates of incarceration by race, ethnicity, and gender, see the Pew Research Center's updated report for May 6, 2020, which shows that Black imprisonment rate in the US has fallen by a third since 2006, https://www.pewresearch.org/fact-tank/2020/05/06/share-of-black-white-hispanic-americans-in-prison-2018-vs-2006/.

3. With the arrival of the first documented Africans to the colonies that would become North America, slave owners in the North and the South were eager to protect their investment and employed slave catchers to capture those who sought to manumission themselves or others out of bondage.

FIGURE 5.1. A member of the ensemble in the role of Odysseus holds the fans that he used to defeat the Suitors

migration, and freedom of the colonies', and subsequently America's, most valuable asset that it ever possessed: the slave.

Marauding groups of slave catchers in conjunction with the watchful eyes of everyday citizens were the precursors to sheriffs and constables, which then evolved into the modern-day police apparatus. As Michelle Alexander suggests, the New Jim Crow or mass incarceration is a caste system—an entire collection of institutions and practices that is "a gateway into a much larger system of racial stigmatization and permanent marginalization."[4] Those who work with incarcerated communities know the challenges, from the most interpersonal interactions to the public policy struggle to end Jim Crow policing and mass incarceration through legislation. Public policy change is too late when you cannot breathe. What is it then that can offer one their breath? If the prison restricts movement, police choke the breath out of people, and the entire criminal justice system asphyxiates Black people, causing as Frantz Fanon suggested, *espanto*, terror, then how can we then resuscitate and make

---

4. Alexander, *The New Jim Crow: Mass Incarceration in the Age of Colorblindness*, 12.

whole again the marginalized and terrorized? It is no surprise that the words I CAN'T BREATHE have become a rallying call for the Black Lives Matter movement. How then can this system of locking people into the stillness of captivity be addressed? How can people who have been dismissed to the vortices of violence restore themselves and be made whole again?

As I suggested in previous chapters, the stories of the "dragons" in this chapter are the stories of the Third World struggles, borrowings, and reinventions of self. The martial arts rehearsals and performances are acts, gestures, and routines, "restorative acts" and "redemption songs" of those who have been struggling under foot, often using their body as if it is the only cultural capital that they had through a process of what I call restorative kinesthesia. The dragons of this chapter were and are incarcerated youth, boys ages thirteen to eighteen, who are considered "wards of the court." They are in a liminal position between going to juvenile hall and going home. The restoration of damaged youth is a healing arts platform that was created by Professor Michael Morgan in the summer of 2011 called The Odyssey Project (TOP), which is a course that partners University of California, Santa Barbara students with incarcerated youth, using Homer's epic poem, *The Odyssey*. Offered as a class called "The People's Voice" through the Department of Theater and Dance, The Odyssey Project began collaborating with the Santa Barbara Department of Youth Probation's Los Prietos Boys Camp (LPBC). Over the course of a six-week class/rehearsal process, the dragons learn acting, writing and spoken word exercises, mask making, choreography, mime, and of course, martial arts. Yet, these dragons also struggle to emerge into and articulate their own raced and gendered identity, using their bodies and movement to liberate themselves from the impingements of the carceral system. While not a panacea, my use of the term restorative kinesthesia borrows from both restorative justice and Schechner's seminal concept of performance as "restored behaviors." However, restorative kinesthesia suggests how martial arts practice afforded the opportunity for the youth involved in TOP to find their breath and reclaim their voice through kinetics of aikido-based movement, and how collectively the repertoire became a vocabulary for the choreography of Odysseus's conflicts within the diegetic experience of the ensemble. Much in the vein of the Black Panther Party's martial arts programs or Fred Ho's Afro Asian radical performances, restorative kinesthesia involves mobilizing, organizing, and politicizing to explore and create a context articulating the political and historical conditions in which the youth of today move, write, rap, and perform.

Writing on race, sexuality, and masculinity, the poet, essayist, novelist, and dramatist James Baldwin responded to the struggle of the Black Dragon (the

Third World peoples of the Americas) in his essay, *Here Be Dragons*, as not only a warning but an act of resistance and transformation.

> Ancient maps of the world—when the world was flat—inform us, concerning that void where America was waiting to be discovered, HERE BE DRAGONS. Dragons may not have been here then, but they are certainly here now, breathing fire, belching smoke; or, to be less literary and biblical about it, attempting to intimidate the mores, morals, and morality of this particular and peculiar time and place. Nor, since this country is the issue of the entire globe and is also the most powerful nation currently to be found on it, are we speaking only of this time and place. And it can be said that the monumental struggles being waged in our time and not only in this place resemble, in awesome ways, the ancient struggle between those who insisted that the world was flat and those who apprehended that it was round.

As Baldwin's passage suggests, European explorers thought of the "dark continent" of Africa and the geography of the "New World" as laden with serpents, uncivilized and primitive beings, as well as noble savages to be conquered, placed in bondage, and slaughtered when necessary. But Baldwin so cunningly anticipated the response to colonialism through his title: HERE BE DRAGONS. Furthermore, it is my contention that as Baldwin suggested, the Black and Brown dragons who participate in The Odyssey Project *breathe fire* and *belch smoke* through their poetry and through movement and choreography as they dance with antiquity and restore Homer's poetry with their own words and rhythms in order to challenge the "mores, morals, and morality of this particular and peculiar time and place."[5]

I was fortunate enough to become involved with TOP during its inaugural year when I was a graduate student at UCSB. As I suggested in the preface, I began training aikido as an adolescent (the same time I began doing theater) and had always yearned for the opportunity to integrate the two disciplines. When Professor Morgan approached me about developing an outreach platform for incarcerated youth, I realized that my own experiences with movement practices such as aikido and theater had finally found a convergence through my research on Afro Asian performance. My work with Fred Ho's Afro Asian jazz martial arts performances provided a template and the encouragement to experiment with integrating aikido-based movement practices with the other theater techniques that were introduced to the ensemble throughout the six-week course. The Los Angeles–based artists who drove up

---

5. Baldwin, *Price of the Ticket* (1985).

to Santa Barbara were choreographers and DJs whose work was rooted in the hip-hop tradition, and yet our movement practices seemed to melt together in true interdisciplinary fashion. Sometimes I would warm up the ensemble before introducing a particular technique or concept that I wanted to focus on, but on the days when the ensemble had engaged in dance, the endorphins were already moving and the warm-ups for aiki movement shifted seamlessly from dance to aiki movement. When time permitted I danced with the ensemble to warm up and feel the energy of the group prior to taking out the mats for the martial arts component of the rehearsal process.

Like the Black Panther Party's Oakland Community School's martial arts program, TOP's martial arts sought to organize, mobilize, and even politicize the youth who struggled to find their voice and, like the protagonist/antagonist, Odysseus, find their way back home. Under the broader rubric of Afro Asian performance, the martial arts in TOP attempted to address both individual and community in order to make them whole.

Aside from the daily practice of health and physical fitness, many martial arts bear healing elements. In jujitsu, aikido, karate, and especially judo, learning to revive or resuscitate an injured practitioner is part of the requirement for progression. In Japanese jujitsu, judo, and aikido, the techniques that emphasize *osae-waza* (pinning), *shime-waza* (choking), *nage waza* (throwing), and *kansetsu-waza* (joint breaking or manipulation) may result in a practitioner/opponent losing consciousness or dislocating a bone. A *judoka* is sometimes choked into unconsciousness,[6] and in aikido, joint displacement or lacerations can also occur. In response, these arts developed the practice *kappo* (resuscitation techniques), which when applied promptly mitigates the injury. While kappo is part of the catalogue of judo techniques, it was actually developed through Japanese jujitsu during the eighteenth century alongside *sappo*, the art of attacking the body's vital points, and both were treated as secret arts.[7] To introduce martial arts to marginalized youth who have been incarcerated is to breathe fresh air into their lives and is a form of resuscitation—or restoration. Like kappo, I think of the term restorative kinesthesia as not dissimilar from work around concepts of "restorative justice"[8] in commu-

---

6. Kanō, *Kodokan Judo*, 252.

7. Kanō, *Kodokan Judo*, 252.

8. While restorative justice is a concept that is evolving and becoming more popular amongst prosecutors, criminal justice officials, and the public generally as a response to individual crimes, I am invoking the term as one that starts with restoring communities that have already suffered transgressions at the hands of larger metastructures (i.e., Native American genocide and the reservation system, the African Slave Trade, US chattel slavery, Jim Crow, and the subsequent racial/gender inequality). Hence, to engage in restorative justice to restore whole communities economically, environmentally, and politically requires first acknowledg-

nities. It helps to address grievances through dialogue and compassion instead of punishment. This notion recalls June Jordan's dialogical work[9] and the subsequent restorative justice pedagogy that emerged as practiced at the June Jordan School for Equity. To create such a learning environment necessitates building a community from the ground up wherein participants are required to reflect upon their actions as both meditation and transformation to create new acts that seek out fairness for themselves and the community. This chapter is committed to theorizing how through a conjunction of hip-hop, spoken word theater, and martial arts gestures and routines, the participants involved in TOP, especially the adolescents who are have been deemed by the courts to perform the role of the incarcerated in their everyday life, are able to create a sense of agency through restorative kinesthesia.

A Conjunctive Formation

TOP drew on martial arts principles, in particular those found in aikido,[10] as a way to narrate moments of conflict and celebration by harnessing, focusing, and choreographing the kinetic energy of LPBC and UCSB members into constructive moments of encounter throughout the rehearsal period and the final performance. Seemingly disconnected communities of prisoners and students were simultaneously embroiled in processes of rehabilitation and education. As a theater and martial arts practitioner and a doctoral student in theater studies writing about performance disciplines like martial arts, jazz, and dance, I benefited from the opportunities TOP provided me to meld scholarship and practice by creating the martial arts choreography for the final confrontation between Odysseus and the Suitors.

My work with TOP became an exploration into the ways in which performance practices (martial arts, dance, graffiti, and hip-hop poetry) can work in conjunction to be a cathartic and therapeutic tool to awaken agency and subjectivity in young people. Many youths in the prison system are imprisoned not just by the penal institutions but also by the institutions' disciplinary practices. Disciplinary practices also occur in a different form and with a different valence in the state university. Programs such as TOP, Unusual Suspects in Los

---

ing such transgressions and then developing communities from the ground up so that they can sustain the challenges and pressures they face when confronted with exploitative capitalist structures.

9. Jordan, "Report from the Bahamas, 1982."

10. Aikido is a Japanese embodied discipline, literally translated as "the way of joining." I have been studying this art form for twenty years, including three years in Japan.

Angeles, Rhodessa Jones's Cultural Odyssey,[11] and my subsequent work with prison activist Bryonn Bain offer models through which to make interventions with populations who have had contact with the criminal justice system. These models also demonstrate that a radical reconsideration of how we conceptualize pedagogy through performance can fundamentally alter what are perceived as legitimate forms of knowledge production and identity formation by traditional armchair scholars and policy officials. However, I would argue that TOP is unique in that it attempts to restore a sense of the commons by actively bringing marginalized, in this case criminalized, youth into a public university, while simultaneously redirecting the state's attention away from a mode of *discipline and punish* to a mode of *perform and liberate*.[12]

The collaboration between UCSB and LPBC, however, did produce and reveal power dynamics that were not free of tension. There were moments in which the necessity of rehearsal time and focus came into conflict with the desire to enforce rules and regulations by probationary staff. UCSB was initially concerned with the image of the university and the presence of incarcerated individuals on campus. I questioned whether our impact would matter or if we were simply replicating empty rhetoric around art and social justice. Others suggested that, because Homer's *Odyssey* is a key text in the canon of European literature, we were reifying a form of Eurocentrism. When discussing these issues with Morgan, I would often refer to ethnographers such as Dwight Conquergood and Joyce King, whose work reminds us that the overriding goal of critical ethnography is to "free individuals from sources of domination and repression."[13] We sought in this project a similar liberation from the repression of Western forms through a direct engagement with the heart of the Western canon. This critical approach also requires that ethnographers work within communities and as part of the community, learning and co-performing, and constructing knowledge and identity from the "ground level, in the thick of things."[14] Within the context of the rehearsal, class, and performance, TOP attempted to create a level playing field, in which all members of the cast were students who recognized the importance of supporting one another throughout the duration of the process.

---

11. See Courtney Elkin Mohler's essay "How to Turn 'a bunch of gangbangin' criminals into big kids having fun'"; and Rhodessa Jones at http://www.culturalodyssey.org/v2/aboutus/rhodessa_bio.html.

12. The analysis in this article is based on the rehearsals and production in 2012, which is partly captured in a documentary film for which I served as associate producer. The video can be viewed at https://www.vimeo.com/59348805.

13. King, "Critical and Qualitative Research in Teacher Education: A Blues Epistemology for Cultural Well-Being and a Reason for Knowing," 1119.

14. Conquergood. "Performance Studies: Interventions and Radical Research," 146.

I observed numerous times how Morgan successfully decentered himself in order to let individual voices be heard and let the ensemble collaborate as a collective. He has gone to extreme efforts to use TOP as a platform through which to engage the university more closely with parts of the Santa Barbara community that do not wield the same socioeconomic mobility as that of the university's student body and faculty. He has engaged LPBC members in their homes, local youth centers, schools, and through public officials, and has successfully pipelined some former LPBC members into junior college. Like Derek Walcott's 1993 Caribbean *The Odyssey: A Stage Version*,[15] TOP creolized Homer's epic poem through a third-person narrator so that each member of the ensemble had an opportunity to embody the heroic elements of the story and become a hero. The concept of embodying the heroic element of the story was a recurrent theme throughout the rehearsal process, as it was, perhaps, what these adolescents needed to see themselves as most—heroes rather than criminals—and this concept was actualized through the martial arts choreography when Odysseus confronted the Suitors.

The choreography and aikido-based exercises that I introduced during the rehearsal process offered a vehicle through which the ensemble was able to explore movement as a form of storytelling, discipline, relaxation, concentration, and conflict resolution. Because the final performance took place at a professional venue that was neither LPBC nor UCSB and included a postperformance discussion with the audience and cast, the final performance was an opportunity to transgress racial, social, and economic borders, allowing the cast to glimpse, if only for a moment, a world of opportunities beyond the walls of carceral systems, be they the school or the prison. I write this chapter as a way of broadening the discussion about incarceration and hopefully of inspiring and encouraging others to think critically and creatively about making attempts toward liberation through performance.

Troubling LPBC and the Mission of Santa Barbara

The County of Santa Barbara Probation Department was developed between 1906 and 1909, and LPBC was established in the summer of 1944. It was conceived of as a facility to which the "Juvenile Courts of both Santa Barbara County and Ventura County could commit boys who needed to be removed from the community, but whose records were not serious enough to justify

---

15. Walcott, *The Odyssey: A Stage Version*.

committing them to the California State Youth Authority."[16] Currently, LPBC is located on seventeen acres in the Los Padres National Forest. The facility serves as both a school and a detention center for young men between ages thirteen and eighteen. Once an individual turns eighteen the juvenile probation office must release them unless they have committed an infraction that sends them to adult prison. "Discipline, respect and responsibility are the motto of the facility" (County of Santa Barbara, LPBC). The program also embraces a zero-gang tolerance philosophy and strives to provide prosocial training opportunities and life experiences that help to broaden a boy's worldview and attitude.[17] The emphasis on a zero-gang tolerance philosophy is a response to the current perceived threat of a rising gang problem.[18] Cities within Santa Barbara County like Lompoc, a community from which many of the boys in LPBC come, have responded by implementing gang injunctions. These injunctions are similar to the concept of Joseph Roach's "bodies of law . . . a cultural system dedicated to the production of certain kinds of behaviors and the regulation or proscription of others."[19] The law operates as a function of a type of performance, in which "regulatory acts and ordinances produce a routine of words and gestures to fit the myriad of protocols and customs remembered within the law or evoked by it."[20] Designed to control populations by limiting their access to the commons and regulating the physical spaces into which bodies can enter, the injunctions are part of a longer historical trajectory of the Mission of Santa Barbara, established in 1786.[21]

However, the Mission of Santa Barbara, as part of the colonial mission writ large, performed an additional function of affecting memory, in which certain incidents and historical facts are erased and forgotten. As Roach suggests, "Selective memory requires public enactment of forgetting, either to blur the obvious discontinuities, misalliances, and ruptures or, more desperately, to exaggerate them in order to mystify a previous Golden Age, now

---

16. Technically considered "wards of the court," the sentences of these young adults range from 120 to 180 days. Wards have the possibility of being released back into the community either under their own recognizance or else on some form of probation.

17. An introduction to LPBC can be accessed at http://www.countyofsb.org/probation/default.aspx?id=1062. Neither this site nor the County of Santa Barbara probation department report by ethnicity or gender.

18. According to the "Executive Summary" in the January 2012 "South Coast Task Force on Youth Gangs Annual Report," there were approximately 32,655 youths ages 5–19 years living in Santa Barbara County. Of this number, law enforcement officials estimate that there are approximately eleven youth gangs, with 186 youths involved in gangs in the South Coast. However, these reports fully ignore ethnicity and gender.

19. Roach, *Cities of the Dead: Circum-Atlantic Performance*, 55.

20. Roach, *Cities of the Dead: Circum-Atlantic Performance*, 56.

21. For more on the Mission of Santa Barbara, see https://www.missionscalifornia.com.

lapsed."²² Like the amnesia that accompanies discussions of chattel slavery, memories torture themselves into forgetting the past genocide of indigenous groups, such as the peoples of the coastal area of Santa Barbara known as the Chumash and the Samala who lived in the Santa Ynez Valley where LPBC is located.²³

The actual location of Los Prietos is haunted by both its geography and its discursive function for marking Blackness (indigenous or African) as Other. Literally translated from Spanish, the ancillary meaning of the word *prieto* means dark or blackish. While Erwin Gudde's *California Place Names* suggests that "the descriptive adjective, meaning 'dark,' 'blackish,' was repeatedly used in Spanish times and is preserved in the names of several mountains."²⁴ It is also believed that this term was used as an adjective for the Samala people who originally inhabited the region. In the racial coding that describes one's social relationship in Spanish, certain words may be used in exchange for others; for example, "the term *trigueno* was chosen over negro, *prieto* over *moreno*."²⁵

In the transformation from the Catholic Church's colonial mission to the secular imagined community (nation) of the United States and the state of California, the indigenous population is substituted through surrogation, a process through which "culture reproduces and recreates itself,"²⁶ for the Chicanas/os and African Americans who fill the void and are marked as "Los Prietos." As scholars like Michelle Alexander and Victor Rios have demonstrated, "The primary way by which racialized populations are regulated is through punitive social control, which in turn establishes social control as a race-creating system."²⁷ The prison regime and the school-to-prison pipeline have placed black and Latino bodies disproportionately in the crosshairs of the state and "the war on drugs," in turn leading to a racialized caste system that Alexander posits as "the new Jim Crow." The school-to-prison pipeline both maintains the twenty-first-century Jim Crow system through the panoptic scope of the prison regime and maintains whiteness as an extension of colonialism and the normative mode of the university. In contrast to the predominantly white campus of UCSB,²⁸ of the seven young men from Los

---

22. Roach, *Cities of the Dead: Circum-Atlantic Performance*, 3.
23. For more on the history of the Chumash and the Samala, see http://algoxy.com/stolen-land/ and http://www.chumashlanguage.com/, respectively.
24. Gudde, *California Place Names: A Geographical Dictionary*, 257.
25. Dominguez, *White by Definition: Social Classification in Creole Louisiana*, 275.
26. Roach, *Cities of the Dead: Circum-Atlantic Performance*, 2.
27. Rios, *Punished: Policing the Lives of Black and Latino Boys*, 30, 31.
28. Statistics for UCSB admissions are available at http://admissions.sa.ucsb.edu/quick-facts.asp.

Prietos, two were Caucasian, one was African American, and the other four identified as Black or Latino.[29] When the young men would make the twenty-two-mile trip to the UCSB campus four times a week for rehearsal, they were in effect contesting the university as a white space, a fact of which Morgan and I were acutely aware, being two of the few African American men on campus. Ironically, of the six UCSB students in the company, all but one came from departments other than the Department of Theater and Dance. This open-campus and interdisciplinary system of casting created a more diverse ethnic mixture of UCSB student participation, which, despite the homogeneity of the overall student body, included two Asians, two Latinas/os, and two Caucasians. Unlike the all-male LPBC cast members, the UCSB contingent consisted of three men and three women. As an intervention tool, TOP collapsed personal experience into a convergence of embodied theory, practice, and pedagogy in order to contest normative modes of epistemology and ontology.

Pedagogy and Discipline as Acts of Recovery

My interest in working with the ensemble using martial arts principles early in the rehearsal process emerged out of my experiences as an actor and martial arts practitioner. Placing emphasis on exercises to develop relaxation and concentration through corporeal discipline is essential in preparation for movement and attuning one's embodiment through proprioceptive awareness.[30] As Shaun Gallagher writes, "Movement and the registration of that movement in a developing proprioceptive system (that is, a system that registers its own self-movement) contributes to the self-organizing development of neuronal structures responsible not only for motor action, but for the way we come to be conscious of ourselves, to communicate with others, and to live in the surrounding world."[31] However, martial arts is also a strategy for cultivating a sensitivity of one's relationship to a community, which may further foster understandings of subjectivity that transcend beyond the immediate performance environment, such as rehearsal or studio space.

By cultivating the physical body and the body of the community, TOP attempts to disrupt Foucauldian notions of discipline as punishment by reani-

---

29. My observations of the population at LPBC were consistent with the demographics of the seven young participants, as well as with the averages of disproportionate prison populations presented by Alexander and Rios.

30. Proprioception is the ability to locate the different body parts without consciously having to think about it.

31. Gallagher, *How the Body Shapes the Mind*, 1.

mating the body as a knowing subject through an act of recovery—as a way of reclaiming the voice, which hopefully chafes against the regimented and, at times, oppressive disciplining of the state apparatus. Each ensemble member brought a vitality and vibrancy that was both creative and destructive, and the martial arts exercises became a conduit for harnessing the focus of an "unruly body,"[32] preparing the performers to engage in other forms of public presentation and understanding the Other through socio-somatic praxis. Similar to dance, a martial art like aikido is a practice in which the tactile experience of skin touching skin allows for both an exchange of embodied knowledge and a reconsideration of identity as the body becomes accustomed to engaging with the Other physically in a noncombative and cooperative construction of knowledge.

Martial arts in TOP represents a synthesis of the kind of polemic work of Fred Ho,[33] as well as that of theater scholar–practitioners like Phillip Zarrilli and Eugenio Barba, who have approached the interconnection of the actor's body and martial arts disciplines as a form of theater and performance anthropology. Performance disciplines offered in TOP operate as both cognitive exercises over the material body and as specific cultural ideas about movement. Barba's theory of "dilating the body," in which the "body is above all a glowing body, in the scientific sense of the term: the particles that make up daily behavior have been excited and produce more energy, they have undergone an increment of motion, they move further apart, attract and oppose each other with more force, in a restricted or expanded space."[34] As a form of opening and preparing the body for physical expression, this concept of the dilated body becomes even more palpable when considered in conjunction with the stymieing effects of violence experienced in the home, the street, the school, or within carceral space. Opening up to the other members of the ensemble or an audience also means becoming visible, which creates a sense of exposure. Using martial arts movement can be a vehicle through which to harness and focus the attention of those who are most vulnerable and afraid to open up, oftentimes because they have been wounded (including experiencing physical abuse) in the past. Thus, performance disciplines offer confidence and prepare the body for the stress of being vulnerable and exposed when

---

32. Sadick, "Rap's Unruly Body: The Postmodern Performance of Black Male Identity on the American Stage."

33. Fred Ho is a Chinese American baritone-saxophone player, writer, and political activist who has produced numerous Afro Asian jazz/martial arts operettas.

34. Barba and Savarese, *A Dictionary of Theatre Anthropology: The Secret Art of the Performer*, 52, 53.

on the stage and in daily interactions. This kind of training and preparation requires an acute attention to one's breathing, posture, and kinetic energy.

Maintaining all of these key elements of embodiment (breath, posture, and kinesthetic awareness) under duress while simultaneously remaining relaxed and focused presents a psychophysical challenge for the actor. I introduced embodied aikido[35] exercises like *irimi tenkan*[36] and basic body mechanics found in *ukemi*[37] during rehearsal. I attempted to address the psycho-physical challenge by bringing the ensemble, those involved in the martial arts choreography in particular, to a point of dilation, where the body attempts to achieve a "state of awareness in which it is poised to act on the edge of a breath and able to ride an impulse through the breath/action/thought."[38] During moments of unpredictable violent encounter, the body can become flooded with adrenaline and endorphins, constricting the breath and elevating the pulse, whereby the ability to react and maintain control over bodily actions is impaired. Conversely, the rush of adrenaline and endorphins within a physical confrontation can create a state of euphoria. In an interview featured in the TOP documentary film, an LPBC member, Alan, states: "My family . . . like, my mom's side of the family and my dad's side of the family, they're both kind of gang-related, so they have a lot of violence in them. I was mad at everything. I got into that one fight, and when I got into that one fight, it was like taking that first hit from the drug. It relieved me. All of my problems just went away."[39] As Alan's experience with street fighting suggests, violence acts as a kind of euphoric rush. It is this psychophysical impulse and kinesthetic energy that musicians like the aforementioned Fred Ho cultivated through "kung fu breathing" when extending the boundaries of playing the baritone saxophone.[40] Furthermore, as chen taijiquan practitioner and teacher Stephan Berwick suggests in the 2013 documentary film *Urban Dragons: Black and*

---

35. These aikido-based principles are exercises and principles that I borrow and appropriate from my aikido-training experience.

36. *Irimi* is derived from the commonly used verb *ireru*, which means "to enter"; *tenkan* connotes "changing" in a manner that is circular or turning. When placed together, irimi tenkan translates either as "to enter and turn" or "to step in and turn."

37. *Ukemi* is a Japanese term that connotes the art of falling down safely in order to preserve the integrity of the body.

38. McAllister-Viel, "(Re)considering the Role of Breath in Training Actors' Voices: Insights from Dahnjeon Breathing and the Phenomenon of Breath," 172.

39. There are currently two different version of The Odyssey Project documentary film. The quote from Alan can be found in the version directed by Mark Manning, https://vimeo.com/59348805. A shorter version of the film, which is a prelude to the feature film, can be found at The Odyssey Project website, http://odysseyprojectfilm.com/.

40. I conducted extensive interviews and research on Ho and his work. Kung fu breathing represents part of his approach to creating music as a transformative liberatory practice.

Latino Masters of Chinese Martial Arts: "Chinese martial arts have a very clear cut sense of family and that family structure can supplant that structure that young people are finding in gangs. . . . It can appeal to different groups who need to find ways to not only protect themselves, but to find pride within themselves within the groups that they are a part of."[41] Following Berwick's lead, we can see how intercultural appropriations through performance disciplines offer possibilities for practitioners and communities to embody alternative identities.

Practitioner-scholars like Ho, M. T. Kato, D. S. Farrer, and John Whalen-Bridge have demonstrated how the connections between "martial arts discourses"[42] and popular expressive practices like graffiti, rap, and break dancing have resonated with marginalized youth as epistemologies and modes of identity formation. Unlike traditional forms of writing, in the United States, these vernacular forms of knowledge production ignited the evolution of hip-hop aesthetics starting in the late 1960s and early '70s, coinciding with the popularization of the kung fu cultural revolution in cinema.[43] Martial arts, along with graffiti and break dancing, became a part of America's city landscapes against the backdrop of broken writing on broken walls, breaking racialized borders through soundscapes and visual inscriptions. Yet, these very practices of cultural expression have been denigrated by law enforcement agencies, subsequently reenforcing normative codes to maintain hegemonic regimes and discourses of power. The temporal regulating of bodies as a system of population control allows the state, through the prison regime, to punish such vernacular practices. These codes recall Roach's bodies of law, which are also aimed at training certain populations to perform in order to become "consumer citizens"[44]—good consumers—or otherwise face criminalization. In TOP, these vernacular ways of knowing, being, and doing are embraced not only as a form of self-expression, but as a "blues epistemology,"[45] which contests the dominant forms of knowledge production that the current "teach to the test" model cannot support.

When working on creating choreography for the fight scene between Odysseus and the Suitors, it was extremely important to build trust over the six-week rehearsal period. Because each of the Suitors was attacking Odys-

---

41. Hunter, *Urban Dragons: Black and Latino Masters of Chinese Martial Arts* (2013).

42. Farrer and Whalen-Bridge, *Martial Arts as Embodied Knowledge: Asian Traditions in a Transnational World*, 2.

43. Kato, *From Kung Fu to Hip Hop: Globalization, Revolution, and Popular Culture*, 179.

44. Lipsitz, *Possessive Investment in Whiteness: How White People Profit from Identity Politics*.

45. Woods, *Development Arrested: Race, Power, and the Blues in the Mississippi Delta*.

seus with weapons at different speeds, different heights, and different lines of attack, proper attention had to be paid to the way each body moved through space. The goal was to build an awareness of one's own physical abilities and limitations, while simultaneously increasing an appreciation for others within their immediate environment and beyond. We built the choreography through collaboration and discussion rather than the regimentation that the boys are so accustomed to when receiving orders in the camp. Like the military, in the camp, the boys respond to the probation officers (POs) with "Yes, sir" and "No, sir," and observe militaristic codes and gestures, such as saluting, marching, and standing at attention with hands at their sides or standing at ease with their arms interlocked in the small of the back. In contrast to this form of regimentation and stiffness of the skeletal frame, at no point did I want them to develop the choreography through a rote memorized form, or kata. Rather, I introduced the *jo* (a cylindrical piece of solid white oak used in aikido) as both potential tool and weapon, suggesting that it was up to them to decide how they would use and move with it. That discovery had to be made within their own bodies and through their own choices. I encouraged the Suitors to think of the movement of the *jo* as a metaphor for their own intentions and how, like Odysseus, we are all presented with choices and possess both creative and destructive energy. Thus, the aikido-based movement and choreography, in conjunction with dance, mask-making, and construction of the actual script, were vehicles through which company members could recover their voices and own the stories of their own odysseys. The exercises for building vehicles of creative expression became moments through which performers could assert agency and control over their situation, even when they were feeling tired or noncompliant under the watchful gaze of the state.

At times, martial arts training also presented a challenge to the LPBC boys, some of whom wanted the simulated violence that we were learning to resemble that found in video games or the violence they had experienced in their own lives. This process benefited from the fact that a UCSB alumnus from the department who had been involved in the previous incarnation of the project served as a role model for the LPBC ensemble members who were involved in the fight scene. The rehearsal process also created the opportunity to have discussions and moments of insight about how we might use our bodies in different ways that were not destructive or harmful, despite the fact that we were dealing with inherently violent material within the world of the play. In the simplest terms, we had to "give in to get our way" and recognize that we were there to tell a collective story. In order to do this, I used aikido-based principles that enabled us to construct a base of agreed upon vocabulary and repertoire. Morgan observed that the movement exercises assisted in focusing the energy of the ensemble members, and we, in turn, began to integrate these exercises amongst the entire cast. Because we were unsure of the physical limitations and abilities of UCSB and LPBC members, we started the group exercises slowly and gradually progressed to more taxing movement skills.

By introducing physical training as group exercise, we had the opportunity to observe each participant without "auditioning" them for the actual scene. The choreography required each of the Suitors to be neutralized by Odysseus's energy as they attacked. To make this neutralization visible, the ensemble members involved in the choreography would attack, fall down, roll, recover, and attack again before being finally frozen and meeting their demise. One of the most important exercises was getting the ensemble comfortable with falling down and rolling on concrete. While the standard forward roll taught in aikido was acceptable, the roll can often be painful on the joints, particularly the shoulder, when performed on a hard surface. The Suitors were also attacking using the *jo* and would have to roll and recover with the prop in order to attack again. Thus, we turned the angle of the roll from a direct linear, 180-degree roll to more of a forty-five, so that body would meet the ground at a horizontal angle, thereby smoothing out the impact. For Jay, who suggested that his shoulder was beginning to bother him from a previous injury, we allowed the energy from Odysseus's parry to turn the axis of his body so that he would meet the ground with his gluteus maximus muscles first and then rotate into the roll and recover.

Perhaps the contradiction between martial arts as acts of restorative kinesthesia were best embodied in the tension between the LPBC boys learning and practicing a martial arts repertoire, while simultaneously being surveilled by the watchful eyes of POs, some of whom admittedly have martial arts experience in their backgrounds. The POs are sworn peace officers of the state of California and sanctioned to carry out the duties of any local law enforcement official. They were equipped with walkie-talkies, handcuffs, mace, and batons, and we could not help being cognizant of their authority. The POs closely monitored, recorded, and reported the daily behavior of the LPBC boys to the Los Prietos officials. I emphasized to the LPBC performers the importance of maintaining their focus and safety at all times, especially since we were using wooden oak sticks in such close proximity.

In contrast to the *jo* carried by the Suitors, Odysseus used two folding fans (Figure 5.1) as a way of defending himself from the Suitors' assaults. While in Richmond Lattimore's translation of *The Odyssey* (1967) Odysseus uses a bronze spear to defeat the Suitors, Morgan and I wanted to present the idea that Odysseus is able to transcend the kind of gratuitous violence that he had been exposed to and had himself enacted during the Trojan War and his epic journey home. The use of the fans provided dynamic visual and sound effects but also offered the suggestion that Odysseus's energy harmonizes the aggressive violence of the Suitors. The fans, used both in Japanese and Chinese martial arts practices, offered another layered and hybrid part of the semiotics of the choreography. The fan can be seen in many chen taijiquan and kung fu forms and practices, but I drew on my own experiences and understanding of the fan as an extension of the body and alternative to the sword, thus diminishing the overall sense of violence, while still remaining martial. The movement and choreography within the scene was predicated on spontaneous and organic movement between each Suitor's attack with the *jo* and Odysseus's response in the moment. This call-and-response relationship allowed Chase, who played the role of Odysseus in this particular scene, to improvise during rehearsal and find his own kinetic response to each particular thrust and strike from the *jo* of the Suitors, who had fanned out and surrounded him in a circle. The ensemble members were thus forced to listen to one another's bodies as each thrust and parry with the *jo* operated as a dialectic between the Suitors and Chase. One by one, each attacked and Chase responded effectively, allowing their energy to continue past him as he entered and turned based on the irimi tenkan principles we worked on throughout rehearsal. After each performer had passed and Chase had addressed the intention of his attack, Odysseus froze him in his place by sending his energy out to the periphery of the circle, where each of the Suitors prepared to attack again. Odysseus then flipped open the fans, one in each hand, which forced the Suitors' bodies to stiffen as if struck by a thunderbolt from Zeus. Odysseus then closed the fans, folded his arms, and dropped his head, causing the Suitors to drop their weapons simultaneously and retreat to the underworld (Figure 5.1). With this scene, TOP attempted to speak to the conflict and violence that many of the LPBC boys have experienced in their lives. Rather than cutting or stabbing the Suitors with a sword, Chase's movement sought to harmonize with the Suitors' aggression. The closing of the fans brought a resolution to the conflict within the immediate moment of the play but also sought to ground the participants within a different understanding of how conflict might be resolved through restorative kinesthesia.

    Creative corporeal discipline embodied within the martial arts of the scene between Odysseus and the Suitors also provided a symbolic sense of closure for the journey that had begun six weeks prior for both UCSB students and LPBC members. During the rehearsal period for the 2014 iteration of TOP, we were able to utilize gymnastics mats. This provided an opportunity to spend more time exploring different forms of ukemi and incorporate aikido-based exercises more deeply into the rehearsal process. During this period, I structured the rehearsal process similar to an introductory aikido workshop. All of the ensemble members learned how to perform forward rolls across the mat, perform side falls, and back rolls. Interestingly, the ensemble members who were not involved in the fight choreography expressed enthusiasm for learning more aikido generally. The basics of aikido movement are a total body workout and integrate the majority of the major muscle groups throughout the body as well as core abdominal, hip, and gluteus muscles. These are the muscles often targeted in core strength conditioning and are required for sustaining the breath and voice on stage during live performance.

In addition to the physical conditioning, doing these exercises prepared the ensemble to more fully explore their relationships to each other. While time was limited, I was able to further inculcate the cultural performative aesthetics of aikido and introduced the etiquette of asking permission from your partner to practice with you and to thank your partner after training with you before moving onto the next training partner. Again, we explored the principles of irimi-tenkan, but in 2014 we used irimi-tenkan to prepare for fight choreography as well as explore the embodied process of blending with an aggressor's energy in order to redirect that energy into *waza* (technique). By having *uke* (the individual who is attacking and hence being thrown) attack with a *yokomenuchi* (strike to the side of the head), *nage* (the individual who is receiving the attack and hence executing the technique) steps in and turns and then redirects uke's energy. From there any number of techniques can unfold, such as *kotegaeishi* (wrist turn), which when executed with speed and precision can cause discomfort if not injury if uke resists the technique. Again, ukemi is not only a form of learning the technique but also way of preserving one's body from injury. However, aside from the technique, the essence of irimi-tenkan can be used as a metaphor for how to actually engage conflict or certain challenges with which we (all of us) are confronted in our daily lives. Yet, in order to study conflict, we need to use an agreed upon vocabulary of movements (acts, gestures, and routines) that a community comes to learn, acknowledge, and accept. Using irimi-tenkan, uke and nage each step forward, pivot, and then turn as the front foot then slides back. They are mirroring each other, modeling each other's behavior, studying the other body in front of them, and hence studying themselves. They are of course also learning a key component of any martial art: to know thyself—a lesson that one could argue is at the heart of Homer's epic poem.

Within the symbolic order of the narrative, the conflict between the Suitors and Odysseus is also the penultimate event before Odysseus can finally bring peace to his house and reunite with his wife, Penelope. To mark this transition within the story, Chase briefly performed a ritual similar to that by a Chumash elder at the beginning of the play. Chase cleansed the stage with sagebrush and an eagle's feather, an act that served to clear the negative energy of the Suitors, who had retired to the underworld at the end of the fight scene. This cleansing ritual also prepared the space for the reunification of Odysseus and Penelope. For the audience, the ritual reiterated the fact that the action of the performance witnessed onstage had transpired on hallowed ground.

Like Ho's radical sonic kinesthesia, TOP attempted to stage a heroic neo-myth by synthesizing performance strategies as varied as martial arts, hip-hop dance and poetry, and indigenous ritual practice. Because of the disciplining and liberatory potential of martial arts, UCSB and LPBC were united throughout the rehearsal process and final performance, enabling them to explore a range of international and transcultural shared bodily knowledge. The discipline displayed among the UCSB students and the boys from Los Prietos sought to upend and resist preconceived assumptions that these groups held about each other, as well as about themselves. UCSB students admitted during interviews for the film that they, in fact, felt initially concerned knowing that some of the boys had been involved in acts of violence resulting in their incarceration. The students also admitted that working on TOP forced them to think about what theater is and what it does for its participants; they were also forced to confront their own uncertainties regarding how they felt about incarceration. At the same time, from my observation, LPBC members discovered how open and receptive the UCSB students were to their concerns. The members admitted to being inspired by the students and realizing that the university experience was one that they also could achieve. Interacting through performance disciplines afforded TOP's participants an opportunity to reconsider their own subjectivity, as well as the identity of the Other, by embodying the characters in the world of the play and sharing their odyssey with the public.

POST
===

A Virtual Kinesthesia

As I have argued throughout this project, one way that historically marginalized people achieved new forms of cultural capital within the violent and stagnating impingements of racial regimes was by moving and engaging movement practices. *Black Dragon* has attempted to demonstrate how mobility functioned as a form of liberation from the rancid assaults of white supremacy. By obtaining "mastery" of the acts, gestures, and routines that were part of Asian martial performative traditions, African American men engaged in what Mauss referred to as the "Techniques of the Body" or what Noland articulated as "organizations of kinetic energy,"[1] that served to refigure their own subjectivity. While neither the practice, consumption, or representation of martial arts could make one invincible, the kinetic possibilities of martial arts provided a feeling of invincibility or an affective bodily capacity, efficacy, and agency that could be summed up as a sense of courage to take on any challenge no matter how daunting or suicidal. Though my use of the term *racial kinesthesia* functioned as a broad social-somatic concept through which to understand the unique acts, gestures, and routines associated with martial arts, I have also extended the term to apply to broader forms of movement, such as migration, as well as those objects that signify movement, such as clothing, weapons, emblems, and linguistic utterances, that made up Afro

---

1. Noland, *Agency and Embodiment: Performing Gestures/Producing Culture*, 22.

Asian performance and the martial arts imagination. Thus, each chapter of this book examined a variation on kinesthesia and also considered the specific social political conditions under which Afro Asian performance emerged.

Transcultural kinesthesia tended to the lived experiences of martial arts practitioners such as Ron Van Clief, Moses Powell, Steve Muhammad (formerly Steve Sanders), and Donnie Williams who improvised to create new and at times unorthodox communities and systems of knowledge practices born out of movements for social economic mobility and survival. In contrast, *communal kinesthesia* suggested the way in which the Black Panther Party for Self-Defense utilized martial arts as a pedagogical platform to politicize, organize, and mobilize within the Oakland Community School. Led by Party member Steve McCutchen, the martial arts program at the OCS/OCLC existed from 1974 to early 1979 and took inspiration from the Eastern political philosophy of Mao Tse-Tung and Kim Il Sun. The term *mediated kinesthesia* articulated the relationship between performance, power, identity, and movement in martial arts media and popular culture. Here, mediated kinesthesia included martial arts choreography as well as the intersubjective relationships that comprised the diegesis of martial arts media. Mediated kinesthesia identified the ways in which the kinetics of the movement image also impacted and inspired the fan culture that consumed movement images and in turn reshaped the possibility of youths who made themselves through a martial arts mythology that offered an imaginative terrain of Afro Asian performance. My discussion on *sonic kinesthesia* centered on how movement became embodied through the radical sounds of Chinese American saxophonist Fred Ho, who formulated his own Asian American consciousness in conjunction with the martial arts through his live Afro Asian jazz martial arts theatrical performances. Lastly, *restorative kinesthesia* described the way in which movement arts have been deployed to hasten restorative justice performance projects with incarcerated youth and university students. In the case of The Odyssey Project, martial arts concepts were introduced as a vocabulary for performance movement and a process for building confidence as well as interrogating conflict within the lives of the participants and the narrative of Homer's restored poem.

While my use of the term racial kinesthesia has focused on the performance of Black masculinity and martial arts, I believe there are broader implications for the study of movement, race, and gender, especially within the realms of new media and online platforms. What happens when our feelings about movement and motion become embodied in online avatars and augmented or virtual reality spaces? While the entertainment economy of live sports continues to grow as new emerging markets open in Asia with partnerships between China and the National Basketball League, for example, conflicts over capital and bodies are inevitable. Yet, the racial kinesthesia of live sports is also set to be potentially eclipsed by the proliferation of mediated kinesthesia in E-Sports and online gaming. In this cyber reality, new identities are once again reimagined within the digital domain. While virtual reality entertainment, let alone gaming, is still very much in its infancy, the imaginary possibilities for digital cultural practices such as martial arts become unpredictable. If and when the human synaptic connection between the virtual and the nonvirtual collapse, what might that world feel like?

Perhaps the Netflix series *Black Mirror* offers a potential glimpse into what *virtual kinesthesia* might look and feel like without foreclosing the entangling possibilities of new understandings of race and sexuality. In the *Black Mirror* episode titled *Striking Vipers,* two old friends Danny (Anthony Mackie) and Karl (Yaha Abdul-Mateen II) are reunited when Karl shows up at Danny's thirty-eighth birthday party. Danny, now married with children, has slipped into the routine of suburban and corporate life, while Karl, a music artist, still roams the urban landscape in search of romance from women ten years his junior. As a birthday gift, Karl offers Danny the virtual reality version of the video game that they used to play as twenty-year-old roommates called *Striking Vipers*. A fictitious version of the martial arts video games *Mortal Combat* and *Streetfighter,* the upgraded version called *Striking Vipers X* uses a "virtual add-on" that drops the user into a new kind of virtual experience wherein the "game emulates all physical sensations."

However, in the virtual world of *Striking Vipers X,* Danny and Karl appear not as two Black men in the urban landscape in which they live their daily lives in the flesh, but rather as Asian martial arts avatars. Danny embodies the character of Lance (Ludi Lin) an Asian twenty-year-old with well-defined muscles, a cyber punk mohawk, and a gi with flames embroidered on the sides. Whereas Karl appears as Roxette (Pom Klementieff), who dons combat boots to match her tight miniskirt with fishnet stockings and a bright blonde cyber punk bob haircut. Both characters immediately evoke visual aesthetics of cosplay and anime. When Lance and Roxette meet for first time, Roxette quickly gains the upper hand on Lance, using a series of kicks, punches, leg sweeps, and body slams to pummel Lance into the ground as the two spar to what sounds like electronica video songs. However, when Roxette and Lance lock-up and begin grappling on the ground, their playful sparring session quickly becomes heated with passionate kissing until Lance, as Danny, realizes that he is kissing the virtual avatar of his friend Karl. Both characters immediately demand to "Exit Game" and return to the material world. Yet, Danny and Karl keep coming back to the online virtual world of *Striking Vipers X,* each time facing off as Lance and Roxette and as if they are two "bros" about to physically fight before running into each other's arms for another sexual encounter.

Striking Vipers X is an Afro Asian futuristic cyber punk erotica in which the love and perhaps even unstated sexual attraction between two Black men becomes actualized by the digital skin manifested in the virtual kinesthesia of the digital domain. The show calls our attention to the blurring between desire to feel with this new skin and perhaps the lack and wanting that cannot be achieved within the lived experiences of Danny and Karl. Despite Danny's love for his wife, Theo, who desperately wants to get pregnant with their second child, he becomes captivated by the feelings and sensations of moving in the virtual world with Karl.

When Lance asks Roxette how does it feel being in a woman's body, Roxette describes the experience as one of movement. "It's different. Like the physical feeling of it is more sort of satisfying. I can't really explain it. One's like a guitar solo the other's a whole fucking orchestra. The tune's basically the same . . . different tempos though."[2] In the virtual world of the game *Striking Vipers X,* kinesthesia becomes a new way of accessing feelings and sensations of the body. For Danny and Karl, and perhaps for all of us, the exploration of feelings that are confined to our corporeal kinetics of the nonvirtual world are foreclosed. Movement is the conduit through which a body becomes real, actualized, felt, experienced, and understood. Just as Van Clief or Jim Kelly wanted to transform themselves into heroes through the martial arts movement practice, *Striking Vipers* teeters on an Afro Asian performative futurism that is not quite here, but yet has always been close enough to feel.

---

2. Harris, "Striking Vipers" (2019).

BIBLIOGRAPHY

Abbott, Randy. *San Nukas*. New York: Black Horizon Films, 1969.

Abdul-Jabbar, Kareem, and Raymond Obstfeld. *Becoming Kareem: Growing Up on and Off the Court,* New York: Little, Brown Books for Young Readers, 2017.

Ahn, Jeong D., Suk ho Hong, and Yeong K. Park. "The Historical and Cultural Identity of Taekwondo as a Traditional Korean Martial Art." *International Journal of the History of Sport* 26.11 (2009): 1716–34.

Alexander, Jacqui. "Groundings on *Rasanblaj* with M. Jacqui Alexander." https://hemisphericinstitute.org/en/emisferica-121-caribbean-rasanblaj/12-1-essays/e-121-essay-alexander-interview-with-gina.html.

Alexander, Michelle. *The New Jim Crow: Mass Incarceration in the Age of Colorblindness*. New York: New Press, 2010.

Asai, Miyo Susan. "Cultural Politics: The African American Connection in Asian American Jazz-based Music." *Asian Music: Journal of the Society for Asian Music* 36.1 (2005): 87–108.

Austin, J. L. *How to Do Things with Words*. Cambridge, MA: Harvard University Press, 1962.

Aziz, Maryam. "Our Fist is Black: Martial Arts, Black Arts, and Black Power in the 1960s and 1970s." *Kung Fu Tea*. https://chinesemartialstudies.com.

Baldwin, James. "Here Be Dragons." In *The Price of the Ticket,* 196–210. New York: St. Martin's/Marek, 1985.

Barba, Eugenio, and Nicola Savarese. *A Dictionary of Theatre Anthropology: The Secret Art of the Performer*. New York: Routledge, 2006.

Black Belt. September 1969.

Brown, Christal. Interview with Valerie Gladstone. New York, November 13, 2011.

Brown, Nell Porter. "Chords of a Revolution: A Jazz Musician Thrives in Brooklyn." *Harvard Magazine*, May–June, 2005.

Burr, Martha, and Mei-Juin Chen. *The Black Kung Fu Experience: Lotus Films International*. Produced by Martha Burr and Mei-Juin Chen. Arlington, VA: PBS, 2013.

Butler, Judith. *Gender Trouble: Feminism and the Subversion of Identity*, New York and London: Routledge, 2015.

———. "Performative Acts and Gender Constitution: An Essay in Phenomenology and Feminist Theory," *Theatre Journal* 40.4 (December 1988): 519–31.

Calmore, John O. "Reasonable and Unreasonable Suspects: The Cultural Construction of the Anonymous Black Man in Public Space (Here Be Dragons)." In *Progressive Black Masculinities*, edited by Mutua D. Athena, chapter 8, pages 137–54. New York: Routledge, 2006.

Certeau, Michel. *The Practice of Everyday Life: Vol. 1*. Berkeley: University of California Press, 1984.

Chambers-Letson, Joshua T. *A Race So Different: Performance and Law in Asian America*. New York: New York University Press, 2013.

Chon-Smith, Chong. *East Meets Black: Asian and Black Masculinities in the Post-Civil Rights Era*. Jackson: University Press of Mississippi, 2011.

Clough, Patricia T., and Jean O. M. Halley. *The Affective Turn: Theorizing the Social*. Durham, NC: Duke University Press, 2008.

Clouse, Robert, director. *Enter the Dragon*. Warner Brothers, 1973.

Colbert, Soyica D. *Black Movements: Performance and Cultural Politics*. New Brunswick, NJ: Rutgers University Press, 2017.

Conquergood, Dwight. "Performing as a Moral Act: 1 Ethical Dimensions of the Ethnography of Performance." *Literature in Performance* 5.2 (1985): 1–13.

Conquergood, Dwight. "Performance Studies: Interventions and Radical Research." *TDR: The Drama Review* 46.2 (2002): 145–56.

Cresswell, Tim. "'You Cannot Shake That Shimmie Here'": Producing Mobility on the Dance Floor." *Cultural Geographies* 13.1 (2006): 55–77.

Cronson, Mary S, Valerie Gladstone, Fred W. Ho, Christal Brown, Yu-chen Hung, Aya Shibahara, Whitney George, Marcus Braggs, Dante Brown, Edwardo Brito, Roderick Callawa, Toni R. Johnson, Gilbert Reyes, Ricarrdo Valentine, Earl McIntyre, Art Hirahara, Tatum Greenblatt, Masaru Koga, Winston Byrd, Bhinda Keidel, Salim Washington, Marty Wehner, David Taylor, and Darius Jones. *Fred Ho, the Sweet Science Suite: Works & Process at the Guggenheim*, 2011.

Curtis, Eric. E, IV. "Islamizing the Black Body: Ritual and Power in Elijah Muhammad's Nation of Islam." *Religion and American Culture: A Journal of Interpretation* 12.2 (2002), 167–96.

Deleuz, Gilles. *Cinema: The Movement Image*. Minneapolis: University of Minnesota, 1986.

Dent, Thomas C., Richard Schechner, and Gilbert Moses. *The Free Southern Theater by the Free Southern Theater: A Documentary of the South's Radical Black Theater, with Journals, Letters, Poetry, Essays and a Play Written by Those Who Built It*. Indianapolis: The Bobbs-Merrill Company, 1969.

Deutsch, Nathaniel. "'The Asiatic Black Man:' An Afro American Orientalism?" *Journal of Asian American Studies* 3 (2001): 193–208.

Dominguez, Virginia. *White by Definition: Social Classification in Creole Louisiana*. New Brunswick: Rutgers University Press, 1993.

Du Bois, W. E. B. *The Souls of Black Folks*. New York: Bantam Classics, 1903.

Duncan, Ronald. *Way of the Winds System: Koga-Ryu Ninjitsu*. ESPY-TV. 1987. VHS.

———. Interview with George in Martial Arts World. *MartialArchiveTV*. 1989. https://www.youtube.com/watch?v=9UHZdJ3lUFc.

Dyer, Richard. *White: Essays on Race and Culture*. New York: Routledge, 1997.

Elam, Harry J. *Taking It to the Streets: The Social Protest Theater of Luis Valdez and Amiri Baraka*. Ann Arbor: University of Michigan Press, 2005.

Elam, Harry J., and Kennell A. Jackson. *Crossroads in Global Performance and Popular Culture*. Ann Arbor: University of Michigan Press, 2006.

Evans, Mark. *Movement Training for the Modern Actor*. London: Routledge, 2009.

Fanon, Frantz. *Black Skin White Masks*. New York: Grove Press, 1952.

Farrer, D. S., and John Whalen-Bridge. *Martial Arts as Embodied Knowledge: Asian Traditions in a Transnational World*. New York: State University of New York, 2011.

Fleetwood, Nicole R. *Troubling Vision: Performance, Visuality, and Blackness*. Chicago: University of Chicago Press, 2011.

Fleming, J. B. "Transforming Geographies of Black Time: How the Free Southern Theater Used the Plantation for Civil Rights Activism." *American Literature*. 91.3 (2019): 587–617

Floyd-Thomas, Juan M. "A Jihad of Words: The Evolution of African American Islam and Contemporary Hip-Hop." In *Noise and Spirit: The Religious and Spiritual Sensibilities of Rap Music*. Edited by Anthony B. Pinn, (49–70). NYU Press, 2003.

Forbes, Flores A. *Will You Die with Me?: My Life and the Black Panther Party*. New York: Atria Books, 2006.

Foster, Susan L. "Choreographies of Protest." *Theatre Journal* 55.3 (2004): 395–412.

Foster, Susan Leigh. *Choreographing Empathy: Kinesthesia in Performance*. London: Routledge, 2011.

Foucault, Michel. *Discipline & Punish: The Birth of the Prison*. New York: Vintage Books, 1977.

Frank, Adam. *Taijiquan and the Search for the Little Old Chinese Man: Understanding Identity Through Martial Arts*. New York: Palgrave, 2006.

Fujino, Diane C. *Heartbeat of Struggle: The Revolutionary Life of Yuri Kochiyama*. Minneapolis: University of Minnesota Press, 2005.

Fujino, Diane. "The Black Liberation Movement and Japanese American Activism: The Radical Activism of Richard Aoki and Yuri Kochiyama." In *Afro Asia: Revolutionary Political & Cultural Connections between African Americans & Asian Americans*, edited by Fred Ho and Bill V. Mullen, 165–97. Durham, NC, and London: Duke University Press, 2008.

Gallagher, Shaun. *How the Body Shapes the Mind*. Oxford: Oxford University Press, 2006.

Gast, Leon, dir. *When We Were Kings*. Polygram Filmed Entertainment. 1996. DVD.

Gates, Henry Louis. *The Signifying Monkey: A Theory of African-American Literary Criticism*. Oxford: Oxford University Press, 1989.

Goffman, Erving. *The Presentation of Self in Everyday Life*. New York: Anchor Books, 1959.

Gudde, Erwin Gustav. *California Place Names, a Geographical Dictionary*. Berkeley: University of California Press, 1949.

Hall, Stuart. "What Is This 'Black' in Black Popular Culture?" *Social Justice* 20.1/2 (51–52) (1993): 104–14.

Harris, Owen, dir. "Striking Vipers," *Black Mirror*. Netflix, series 5, episode 1, June 15, 2019.

Heath, R. Scott, "True Heads: Historicizing the Hip-Hop 'Nation' in Context." *Callaloo* 29.3 (2006): 846–66.

Hewitt, Kim. "Martial Arts Is Nothing if Not Cool: Speculations on the Intersections Between Martial Arts and African American Expressive Culture." In *Afro Asia: Revolutionary Political & Cultural Connections between African Americans & Asian Americans*, edited by Fred Ho and Bill V. Mullen, 265–84. Durham, NC, and London: Duke University Press, 2008.

Hilliard, David. *The Black Panther Party: Service to the People Programs.* Albuquerque: University of New Mexico Press, 2008.

Ho, Fred. "Kickin' the White Man's Ass: Black Power, Aesthetics, and the Asian Martial Arts." In *AfroAsian Encounters: Culture, History, Politics,* edited by Heike Raphael-Hernandez and Shannon Steen, chapter 16, 295–312, New York: New York University Press, 2006.

———. *Wicked Theory, Naked Practice: A Fred Ho Reader.* Minneapolis: University of Minnesota Press, 2009.

Ho, Fred, and Bill V. Mullen. *Afro Asia: Revolutionary Political & Cultural Connections Between African Americans & Asian Americans.* Durham, NC, and London: Duke University Press, 2008.

———. *Deadly She-Wolf Assassin at Armageddon.* Drexel University Press, 2008. DVD.

———. *Diary of a Radical Cancer Warrior: Fighting Cancer and Capitalism at the Cellular Level.* New York: Skyhorse Publishing, 2012.

———. Interview with Martial Arts World Staff. *MartialArchiveTV.* 1997. http://www.youtube.com/watch?v=TQ_jAxY69uc.

———. Interview with Valerie Gladstone. New York, November 13, 2011.

———. *Voice of the Dragon: Once Upon a Time in Chinese America.* Union, NJ: Kean University, 2004. DVD.

Hoffman, Jim. "Reading, Writing, and Fair Fighting in the Oakland Ghetto." *Black Belt,* August 1975, 40–41. https://books.google.com/books?id=X9gDAAAAMBAJ&ppis=_c&lpg=PA41&dq=steve%20mccutchen&pg=PA41#v=onepage&q=steve%20mccutchen&f=false.

Homer. *The Odyssey.* Trans. by Richard Lattimore. New York: Harper Collins, 1965.

Hunter, Kamau, dir. *Urban Dragons: Black and Latino Masters of Chinese Martial Arts.* 2012. DVD.

Johnson, E. P. *Appropriating Blackness: Performance and the Politics of Authenticity.* Durham NC: Duke University Press, 2003.

Jordan, June. "Report from the Bahamas, 1982." *Meridians* 3.2 (2003).

Liu, Jialiang. *The 36th Chamber of Shaolin.* London : Momentum Pictures, 2009.

Kanō, Jigorō. *Kodokan Judo.* Tokyo: Kodansha International, 1994.

Kato, M. T. *From Kung Fu to Hip Hop: Globalization, Revolution, and Popular Culture.* Ithaca, NY: State University of New York Press, 2007.

Kaufman, Michael T. "Florendo M. Visitacion, 88, Martial Artist Master, Is Dead." *New York Times,* January 10, 1999.

Kelley, Robin. *Freedom Dreams: The Black Radical Imagination.* New York: Beacon Press, 2008.

Kelley, Robin, and Betsy Esch. "Black Like Mao: Red China and Black Revolution." In *Afro Asia: Revolutionary Political & Cultural Connections between African Americans & Asian Americans,* edited by Fred Ho and Bill V. Mullen, 164–65. Durham, NC, and London: Duke University Press, 2008.

Kim, Claire Jean. "The Racial Triangulation of Asian Americans." *Politics and Society* 27.1 (1999): 105–38.

King, Joyce. "Critical and Qualitative Research in Teacher Education: A Blues Epistemology for Cultural Well-Being and a Reason for Knowing." In *Third Handbook of Research on Teacher Education,* edited by M. Chochran-Smith, 1094–1136. New York: Routledge, 2008.

Kurashige, Scott. *The Shifting Grounds of Race: Black and Japanese Americans in the Making of Multiethnic Los Angeles.* Princeton, NJ: Princeton University Press, 2010.

Kurwa, Nishat, "The Black Panthers House Funk Band." Studio 360, WNYC. January 31, 2014

Lee, Bruce. *Tao of Jeet Kune Do*. Valencia, CA: Black Belt Books, 2014.

Lee, Yimm. *Wing Chun Kung-Fu*. Los Angeles, CA: Ohara Publications, 1972.

Liebling, A. J. *The Sweet Science*. New York: North Point Press, 1954.

Lipsitz, George. *The Possessive Investment in Whiteness: How White People Profit from Identity Politics*. Philadelphia: Temple, 1998.

Lo, Jacqueline, and Helen Gilbert. "Toward a Topography of Cross-Cultural Theatre Praxis." *TDR: The Drama Review* 46.3 (2002): 31–53.

Locke, John, and Robert Filmer. *Two Treaties on Civil Government*. London: E. P. Dutton and Co., 1884.

Maeda, Daryl. "Black Panther, Red Guards, and Chinamen: Constructing Asian American Identity through Performing Blackness, 1969–1972." *American Quarterly* 57.4 (2005): 1079–103.

Manning, Mark, dir. "The Odyssey Project." 2012. Film. https://www.vimeo.com/59348805.

Margraff, Ruth, and Fred Ho. "Deadly She-Wolf Assassin at Armageddon." *PAJ: A Journal of Performance and Art* 29.2 (2007): 94–107.

Mauss, Marcel. "Techniques of the Body." *Economy and Society*, 2:1, 70–88 (1973).

McAllister-Viel, Tara. "(Re)considering the Role of Breath in Training Actors' Voices: Insights from Dahnjeon Breathing and the Phenomenon of Breath." *Theatre Topics* 19.2 (2009): 165–80.

McConachie, Bruce A. *Performance and Cognition: Theatre Studies and the Cognitive Turn*. London: Routledge, 2010.

McCutchen, Steve. *Instructor's Manual*. 7 Shadows Martial Arts Association, 1999.

McCutchen, Steve D. *We Were Free for a While: Back-to-Back in the Black Panther Party*. Baltimore: Publish America, 2008.

Merleau-Ponty, Maurice. *Phenomenology of Perception*. New York: Routledge, 1962.

Mishima, Yukio, Yukio Mishima, and Yoshiko Tsuruoka. *Patriotism*. Irvington: NY, 2008.

Mohler, Courtney Elkin. "How to Turn 'a bunch of gang-bangin' criminals into big kids having fun'": Empowering Incarcerated and At-Risk Youth through Ensemble Theatre." *Theatre Topics* 22.1 (2012): 89–102.

Moses, Gilbert, John O'Neal, Denise Nicholas, Murray Levy, and Richard Schechner. "Dialogue: The Free Southern Theatre." *Tulane Drama Review* 9.4 (1966): 63–76.

Moten, Fred. *In the Break: The Aesthetics of the Black Radical Tradition*. Minneapolis: University of Minnesota Press, 2003.

Moynihan, Daniel P. *The Negro Family: The Case for National Action*. Cambridge, MA: MIT Press, 1967.

Muhammad, Dora. "The Legacy Continues in the Movement." *Final Call*, March 17, 2005.

Muhammad, Elijah. *Message to the Black Man in America*. Phoenix: Secretarius MEMPS Ministries, 1965.

Muhammad, Steve, and Donnie Williams. *BKF Kenpo: History and Advanced Strategic Principles*. Burbank, CA: Unique Publications, 2002.

———. Interview with Pedro Bennett, December 7, 2017. https://www.youtube.com/watch?v=VwjSNuham8k.

Mullen, Bill V. *Afro-Orientalism*. Minnesota: University of Minnesota Press, 2004.

———. *W. E. B. Du Bois on Asia: Crossing the World Color Line*. Edited by Cathryn Watson. Jackson: University of Mississippi Press, 2005.

Murillo, John. *Impossible Stories: On the Space and Time of Black Destructive Creation*. Columbus: The Ohio State University Press, 2021.

Nagatomo, Shigenori. *Attunement through the Body.* Albany: State University of New York Press. 1983.

Nathan, John. *Mishima: A Biography.* New York: Da Capo Press, 1974.

Newton, Huey P, David Hilliard, Donald Weise, and Elaine Brown. *The Huey P. Newton Reader.* New York : Seven Stories Press, 2019.

Newton, Huey P., and J. H. Blake. *Revolutionary Suicide.* New York: Writers and Readers, 1995.

Newton, Huey P, and Toni Morrison. *To Die for the People: The Writings of Huey P. Newton.* San Francisco, Calif: City Lights, 2009.

Noland, Carrie. *Agency and Embodiment: Performing Gestures/Producing Culture.* Cambridge, MA: Harvard University Press, 2009.

Novotny, Lawrence. *Blaxploitation Films of the 1970s: Blackness and Genre.* New York: Routledge, 2012.

Oakland Community School Segment. *Rebop.* Boston: WGBH, 1978.

Omi, Michael, and Howard Winant. *Racial Formation in the United States: From the 1960s to the 1990s.* New York: Routledge, 1994.

Ongiri, Amy A. "'He Wanted to Be Just Like Bruce Lee': African Americans, Kung Fu Theater and Cultural Exchange at the Margins." *Journal of Asian American Studies* 5.1 (2002): 31–40.

———. *Spectacular Blackness: The Cultural Politics of the Black Power Movement and the Search for a Black Aesthetic.* Charlottesville: University of Virginia Press, 2010.

Peterson, William. "Success Story: Japanese-American Style." *New York Times Magazine,* January 9, 1966, 22.

Polly, Matthew. *Bruce Lee: A Life,* London : Simon & Schuster, 2018.

Prashad, Vijay, "Bandung is Dead: Passages in Afro Asian Epistemology." In *AfroAsian Encounters: Culture, History, Politics,* edited by Heike Raphael-Hernandez and Shannon Steen, forward, xi–xxiii, New York: New York University Press, 2006.

Prashad, Vijay. *Everybody Was Kung Fu Fighting: Afro-Asian Connections and the Myth of Cultural Purity.* Boston: Beacon Press, 2007.

Price, Zachary. "The Odyssey Project: A Martial Arts Journey toward Recovery and Liberation." *Theatre Topics* 24.1 (2014): 39–50.

———. "Remembering Fred Ho: The Legacy of Afro Asian Futurism," *Drama Review* 60.2 (2016): 48–67.

Raphael-Hernandez, Heike, and Shannon Steen. *AfroAsian Encounters: Culture, History, Politics.* New York: New York University Press, 2006.

Ratti, Oscar and Adele Westbrook. *Secrets of the Samurai: The Martial Arts of Feudal Japan.* New York: Tuttle, 1973.

Raya, Richard S. "Might for Right: Martial Arts as a Way to Understand the Black Panthers." *Tapestries: Interwoven Voices of Local and Global Identities* 4.1 (2015). https://digitalcommons.macalester.edu/tapestries/vol4/iss1/7.

Ressner, Jeffrey. "'The Last Dragon': THR's 1985 Review," *Hollywood Reporter,* March 22, 1985.

Rios, Victor. *Punished: Policing the Lives of Black and Latino Boys.* New York: New York University, 2011.

Roach, Joseph. *Cities of the Dead: Circum-Atlantic Performance.* New York: Columbia University Press, 1996.

Roberts, Tamara. *Resounding Afro Asia: Interracial Music and the Politics of Collaboration.* Oxford: Oxford University, 2016.

Roberts, Tamara, and Roger Buckley. *Yellow Power Yellow Soul: The Revolutionary Music, Artistry, and Political Struggle of Fred Ho.* Champagne: University of Illinois, 2013.

Robinson, Cedric. *Black Marxism: The Making of the Black Radical Tradition.* Chapel Hill: University of North Carolina Press, 1983.

Robinson, Cedric J. *Forgeries of Memory and Meaning: Blacks and the Regimes of Race in American Theatre and Film Before World War II.* Chapel Hill: University of North Carolina Press. 2012.

Rodney, Walter. *The Groundings with My Brothers.* London: Bogle, 1975.

Rose, Tricia. *Black Noise: Rap Music and Black Culture in Contemporary America.* Hanover, NH: Wesleyan University, 1994.

RZA. *Birth of a Prince.* Sanctuary Records, 2003.

RZA, and Chris Norris. *The Tao of Wu.* New York: Riverhead, 2009.

Sadick, Annette J. "Rap's Unruly Body: The Postmodern Performance of Black Male Identity on the American Stage." *TDR: The Drama Review* 47.4 (2003): 110–27.

Sanders, Steve, and Donnie Williams. *Championship Kenpo.* Valencia, CA: Black Belt Publications, 1983.

Schechner, Richard, and Victor W. Turner. *Between Theater and Anthropology.* Philadelphia: University of Pennsylvania Press, 1985.

———. *Performance Theory.* New York: Routledge, 1988.

Schultz, Michael, Berry Gordy, Rupert Hitzig, Louis Venosta, Taimak, Julius Carry, Christopher Murney, Leo O'Brien, Faith Prince, and Vanity. *The Last Dragon / [videorecording (dvd)].* Culver City, Calif: Sony Pictures Home Entertainment, 2005.

Shimazu, Naoko. "'Diplomacy as Theatre': Recasting the Bandung Conference of 1955 as Cultural History." Working paper, No. 164. Singapore: Asia Research Institute, National University of Singapore, 2011.

Steen, Shannon. *Racial Geometries of the Black Atlantic, Asian Pacific and American Theatre.* New York: Palgrave MacMillan, 2010.

Stewart, Jeffrey C. "Black Orientalism and the Invisible Man of the Harlem Renaissance." *Letteratura D' America Trimestrale* 22.93–94 (2002): 37–54.

Supreme Commander for the Allied Powers. *Political Reorientation of Japan: September 1945 to September 1948.* Vol. 1. Washington, DC: US Government Printing Office, 1949.

Tasker, Yvonne. *Spectacular Bodies: Gender, Genre, and the Action Cinema.* London: Routledge, 1996.

Taylor, Diana. *The Archive and the Repertoire: Performing Cultural Memory in the Americas.* Durham, NC, and London: Duke Univeristy Press, 2003.

Tse-Tung, Mao. *On Practice.* New York: International Publishers, July 1937.

Turner, Victor. *Dramas, Fields, and Metaphors: Symbolic Action in Human Society.* Ithaca, NY: Cornell University, 1974.

United States Congress. Chinese Exclusion Act of 1882 and the Immigration of Act 1924.

Van Clief, Ron. *The Black Heroes of the Martial Arts.* Brooklyn, New York: A&B Distributors, 1996.

Van Clief, Ron, and Sparky Parks. *The Hanged Man.* New York: CreateSpace Independent Publishing Platform, 2012.

Vasquez, Delio. "Intercommunalism: The Late Theorizations of Huey P. Newton, 'Chief Theoretician' of the Black Panther Party." *Viewpoint Magazine,* June 11, 2018. https://viewpointmag.com/2018/06/11/intercommunalism-the-late-theorizations-of-huey-p-newton-chief-theoretician-of-the-black-panther-party/.

Vincent, Ricky. *Party Music: The Inside Story of the Black Panthers' Band and How Black Power Transformed Soul Music.* Chicago: Lawrence Hill Books, 2013.

Walcott, Derek. *The Odyssey: A Stage Version.* New York: The Noonday Press/Farrar Straus Giroux, 1995.

Walker, David, F. *Macked, Hammered, Slaughtered, Shafted: A Documentary,* (1996). https://davidfwalker.com/macked-hammered-slaughtered-shafted/.

Whaley, Deborah, Elizabeth. "Black Bodies/Yellow Masks: The Orientalist Aesthetic in Hip-Hop and Black Visual Culture." In *AfroAsian Encounters: Culture, History, Politics,* edited by Heike Raphael-Hernandez and Shannon Steen, chapter 10, 188–203, New York: New York University Press, 2006.

West, Cornel. *The Cornel West Reader.* New York: Basic Civitas Books, 2000.

Wilderson, Frank B. *Red, White, & Black: Cinema and the Structure of U. S. Antagonisms.* Durham, NC: Duke University Press, 2010.

Wilkins, Che Fanon. "Shaw Brother's Cinema in the Hip-Hop Imagination." In *China Forever: The Shaw Brothers and Diasporic Cinema,* edited by Poshek Fu, chapter 10, 224–45, *China Forever: The Shaw Brothers and Diasporic Cinema* Urbana: University of Illinois Press, 2008.

Wong, Casey. "The Pedagogy and Educaton of the Black Panther Party: Confronting the Reproduction of Social and Cultural Inequality." Masters of Arts Thesis, New York University, 2012.

Woods, Clyde. *Development Arrested: Race, Power and the Blues in the Mississippi Delta.* New York: Verso, 1998.

Xiang Hua, Chen. "Shaolin Temple Prodigal Son: Monk Shi Yanming's Return to Shaolin after His Defection." *Kung Fu Magazine,* August–September, 2000.

Yi, Joseph. *God and Karate on the Southside: Bridging Differences, Building American Communities.* Lanham, MD: Lexington Books, 2009.

Young, Harvey. *Embodying Black Experience: Stillness, Critical Memory, and the Black Body,* Ann Arbor: University of Michigan Press, 2010.

Zwart, Harald, Christopher Murphey, Robert M. Kamen, Jerry Weintraub, Long Cheng, Jaden Smith, Taraji P. Henson, and James Horner. *The Karate Kid.* Culver City, CA: Sony Pictures Home Entertainment, 2013.

INDEX

Abdul-Jabbar, Kareem, xii–xiii, 3, 76
adornment, 6–7, 46, 64
affect theory, 10
Afro Asian: Black masculinity and, 106–7; films, 17; futurism, 172–74; martial arts imaginary and, 79–82; performance, 15–18, 36, 76–77, 106, 123; semiotics, 109; as third vision, 32; "Tribe of Shabazz" and, 36–37
Afro Asian Music Ensemble, 141, 143, 159–60, 173
aikido, xii–xiv, xiv fig. 0.1, 3n3, 4, 31, 38–40, 43, 47, 69, 140, 177–80, 180n10, 182, 186–87, 187n35, 189–92
Aldridge, Byron, 80
Alexander, Jacqui, 19, 28, 74
Alexander, Michelle, 176
Ali, Muhammad, 76, 162–66, 169–70. See also *Sweet Science Suite: A Scientific Soul Session Honoring Muhammad Ali* (Ho)
American Taekwondo Association (ATA), 100
Aoki, Richard, 16n44
appropriation, 7–8, 16, 22–23, 27–28, 30–32, 42, 50, 59–60, 105, 112, 121, 124, 126–28, 138–40, 154–55, 188

Armstrong, Aaron, 153 fig. 4.3
Asian American Political Alliance, 16n44
Asian Americans: Afro Asia and, 16; Immigration and Nationality Act of 1965 and, 61; masculinity and, 8–10; "model minority" concept and, 9–10, 125, 140, 143–44; in *Voice of the Dragon*, 143–44; yellowfacing and, 22, 119–20, 124, 126–27, 151. *See also* Japanese Americans
ATA. *See* American Taekwondo Association (ATA)
atemi, 40
Aziz, Maryann, 66
Azumi (film), 156

Baker, Julius, 98
Baldwin, James, 177–78
Baltimore, Maryland, 78
BAM. *See* Black Arts Movement (BAM)
Bandung Conference, 15, 31, 142, 164
Bank, Aaron, 47
Baraka, Amiri, 132, 140
Barbara, Eugenio, 20, 30, 34, 186
Barson, Ben, 173

BART. *See* Black Arts Revolutionary Theater (BART)
Berry Gordy's *The Last Dragon* (film), 58–59
Berwick, Stephan, 27, 187–88
Big Daddy Kane, 131
binaries, racial, 9–10, 17, 32, 156, 159
Birth of a Prince (Wu-Tang Clan), 133
BKF. *See* Black Karate Federation (BKF)
Black, as term, 1n1
Black Arts Movement (BAM), 66, 140
Black Arts Revolutionary Theater (BART), 66
Black Belt (magazine), 1, 3–4, 71, 92
Black body(ies): in "Chi Kung" video, 136; as dangerous, 88; as enforcer, 52; in *Enter the Dragon*, 113; Islamization of, 37; white fury directed at, 64–65
Black Christianity, 37
Black Dragon, The (film), 58
Black expressive culture, 29–30, 141
blackfacing, 22, 119–20, 124
Black Karate Federation (BKF), 29, 34–35, 59–60, 62–66, 63 fig. 1.2, 64 fig. 1.3, 64 fig. 1.4, 69–70, 110 fig. 3.1, 111
Black Kung-Fu Experience, The (film), 32–33
Black Lives Matter, 177
Black masculinity: in affirmation of racial regimes, 105; Afro Asian performance and, 106–7; "Black buck" trope and, 111; as dangerous, 107, 112–13; in *Enter the Dragon*, 112–13; in *Karate Kid*, 123; in *The Last Dragon*, 117–18; martial arts and, 27–28; racial kinesthesia and, 137; racial magnetism and, 8–10; racial order and, 107; racism and, 68; as unwanted, 88; villainy and, 57; wounded, 137; Wu-Tang Clan and, 128
Black Mirror (television series), 196–97
Black Muslim, 37–39. *See also* Nation of Islam (NOI)
Black nationalism, 64 fig. 1.2, 68, 68n79, 74, 109, 141, 163
Blackness: Afro Asian performance and, 17; in *Deadly She-Wolf Assassin at Armageddon*, 160; in *Enter the Dragon*, 111–12; in *The Karate Kid*, 126; in *The Last Dragon*, 120; "model minority" concept and, 144; modernity and, 73n4; as Other, 184;

tournament fighting and, 65; in Van Clief films, 58
Black Panther Intercommunal News Service, 76
Black Panther Party for Self-Defense, 12, 16; Afro Asian cultural collaborations and, 73; Aoki and, 16n44; communal kinesthesia and, 76–77, 87; community and, 77; emergence of, 73; local politics and, 82–95; masculinity and, 173; McCutchen and, 78; philosophy of, 74–75, 86–87; Political Education classes of, 75n12
Black Power, xiv, 4, 29, 166, 168–69
Black Revolutionary Theater, 140
Black soldiers, 49–50, 171
Black visibility, 123
blaxploitation, 54, 57, 108, 114–16
Braggs, Marcus, 164n43
breakdancing, 67, 188
breathing, kung-fu, 138–40
Brecht, Bertolt, 30
Brito, Edwardo, 164n43
Brook, Peter, 30
Brown, Christal, 24, 102, 165, 170–71
Brown, Dante, 164n43, 170–71
Brown, Dennis, 59
Brown, Elaine, 74, 75n13, 77
Brown Berets, 142
Brown v. Board of Education, 60–61
Buddhism, 129–31
budo, 11–14, 11n26
Burton, LaVar, 83, 83n29
Busta Rhymes, 131
Butler, Judith, 6

Calhoun, William, 76
calisthenics, 41
Callaway, Roderick, 164n43, 169 fig. 4.7
Calmore, John O., xii, 88
capitalism, 9, 18, 28, 32, 74n9, 107, 128–29, 132, 142n11, 143–44, 163, 173–74
Capri, Ahna, 111
Carlos, John, 169
Carmichael, Stokely, 166n45, 170

Carradine, David, 108
Carroll, Tom "Lapuppet," 51n48
Carter, Bunchy, 72n3
Certeau, Michel de, 34
Cesar, Adolph, 55–56
Chambers Brothers, 51
Chan, Jackie, 122
"Chi Kung" (Wu-Tang Clan), 133–36
Children's House, 85
Chin, Bob, 52
China, 74, 74n9, 75, 75n13, 148
Chinese Connection, The (film), 120
Chinese Exclusion Acts, 9
Choi Hong Hi, 81–82, 87
Chon-Smith, Chong, 9
Chou En Lai, 74, 75n13
Christianity, 37, 129–30
Civil Rights movement, 4, 9, 76, 168
Clay, Cassius. *See* Ali, Muhammad
Cleaver, Cathleen, 75n13
Cleaver, Eldridge, 75n13
Cleveland, Ohio, xi
COINTELPRO, 49, 77, 85
colonialism, 18, 28–29, 31–32, 49–50, 74, 153, 165, 173, 184
Coltrane, John, 66
Commando (film), 114
communal kinesthesia, 21, 75–77, 87–89, 94
community, 45–46, 56–57, 77, 95
Conquergood, Dwight, 20, 30, 141, 181
Cronson, Mary Sharp, 164
crossbordering, 28–30, 36–38, 50, 67–68, 74
Curtis, Eric E., 37

dance, 105–6
Davis, Miles, 66
Deadly She-Wolf Assassin at Armageddon (Ho), 143, 150–62, 153 fig. 4.3, 153 fig. 4.4
decolonization, 28–29, 74–75, 164
desegregation, 61
Digable Planets, 131
Diggs, Latasha, 117

Diggs, Robert F. *See* RZA
Diggs, Soyica, 4
discipline, 185–86
documentary film, 32–33, 39n27, 55
Dom, The (discotheque), 51–52
Douglas, Emory, 75n13
Du Bois, W. E. B., 15–16
Duncan, Gregory, 12
Duncan, Ronald, 1 fig. 0.2, 1–5, 7–10, 12–14, 27–28, 34, 55, 118, 121

Earth, Wind, and Fire, 51
Eco-Music Big Band, 173
ecosocialism, 172–73
Electric Circus, 51–52
Ellison, Ralph, xii
Enter the Dragon (film), 11n24, 22, 57; Black masculinity and, 106, 112–13; Blackness in, 111–12; Bruce Lee and, 107; Kelly in, 107–15, 110 fig. 3.1, 113 fig. 3.2; performance in, 94
Enter the Wu-Tang (36 Chambers) (Wu-Tang Clan), 105, 127–28, 131
Eurocentrism, 19, 31–32, 36, 105, 137–38, 181
"Exploding Plastic Inevitable" (Warhol), 51

Fanon, Frantz, 73–74
Farrer, D. S., 188
Federal Bureau of Investigation (FBI), 16n44, 33, 38, 49, 77, 85
Figueroa, José, 144
Fists of Fury (film), 119
Five Deadly Venoms (film), 134
Five-Percent Nation, 128, 128n32, 130–31
FOI. *See* Fruit of Islam (FOI)
Forbes, Flores, 103
Foreman, George, 163–64
Foster, Susan Leigh, 6
Foucault, Michel, 185–86
Free Southern Theatre, 31
freestyling, 131
Fruit of Islam (FOI), 33
Fujino, Diane, 16

futurism, 172–74

Gallagher, Shaun, 185
Game of Death (film), xii–xiii
Gates, Henry Lewis, 14
George, Whitney, 165
Gilbert, Helen, 30
Gladstone, Victoria, 162, 170
globalization, 15–16
Global South, 74
Goju Ryu system, 29, 33, 47–59, 69
Gordy, Berry, Jr., 115n18
graffiti, 188
Gramsci, Antonio, 10
Gray, Christopher, xii–xv, *xiv* fig. 0.1, 4
Great Migration, 4, 137
Green, "Bruce" Leroy, 115
Green Monster Big Band, 143, 164–65
Grotwoski, Jerzy, 30
grounding, 19, 28–29, 38–41, 44–45, 50, 74
Grove Street College, 78–79
Guariello, Taimak, 115–22, 132
gunpowder, 149–50

Hall, Stuart, 5, 130
Hamilton, Fred, 51n48
Harlem, 39–40
Havens, Richie, 54
Hawaii, 8–9
Hell's Angels, 52
Hendrix, Jimi, 51, 53–54
Here Be Dragons (Baldwin), 178
heroes, 105, 113–14, 153
Hewitt, Jim, 29–30, 41
Hewitt, Masai, 75n13
hierarchy, racial, 8–9, 14, 61, 150
Hilliard, David, 85
Hines, Gregory, 54
hip-hop, 22, 67, 105, 128, 136, 179–80, 188, 193. See also Wu-Tang Clan
Ho, Fred, 16, 18, 23–24, 137, 139–41, 172–73, 178. See also *Deadly She-Wolf Assassin at Armageddon* (Ho); *Sweet Science Suite: A Scientific Soul Session Honoring Muhammad Ali* (Ho); *Voice of the Dragon: Once Upon a Time in Chinese America* (Ho)
Hoffman, Jim, 71, 79, 92
Homer, 175, 177, 181, 190–91
Huggins, Ericka, 72, 77, 84–85
Huggins, John, 72n3

identity: Black Muslin, 37–38; consciousness and, 53–54; cultural, 30, 37, 82; formation, 26, 28, 138, 181, 188; gendered, 11, 177; group, 41; marginalization and, 5; masculinity and, 52, 121; movement practices and, 5; nationalist, 32; negotiation of, 140; performance and, 25; racial, 8, 11, 151; slavery and, 36
Immigration Act of 1965, 61, 61n67
imperialism, 28, 31–32, 50, 77, 173
improvisation, 66, 94
incarceration, 4, 9, 18, 24, 45, 172n56, 175–82, 193, 195
Incontrera, Marie, 173
Inosanto, Dan, 61
Intercommunal Youth Institute, 84–85, 85n33, 86 fig. 2.3
intersectionality, xii, 10n24, 25, 52, 57, 114
Invasion USA (film), 114
Invisible Man, The (Ellison), xii
Ip Man, 93–94
Islam. See Black Muslim; Nation of Islam (NOI)

Jackson, Phyllis, 102
Jackson, Samuel L., 54
Japan: colonialism of, 32, 50, 81; films from, 13, 156; imperialism and, 31–32; industrialism in, 151; nationalism in, 31–32, 50, 150, 159; ninjas in feudal, 12, 14, 25; patriarchy in, 156
Japanese Americans: Black liberation movements and racial consciousness among, 16; as gatekeepers, 3; internment of, 9, 16n44; masculinity of, 10. See also Asian Americans
jazz, 18–19, 23, 52, 66, 141. See also Ho, Fred
jeet gak kune, 90

jeet kune do, 3, 61n70, 73, 76–77, 87–90, 93–94, 139, 147
Johnson, E. Patrick, 140
Johnson, Toni Renee, 166, 167 fig. 4.5, 167 fig. 4.6
Jones, Rhodessa, 181
Jones, Russell. *See* Ol' Dirty Bastard
juche, 21, 74
judo, 2, 31, 35, 38–40, 42–44, 91, 94–95, 179
jujitsu, 29, 31, 33, 35–36, 39–40, 43, 47, 55, 91, 122, 140
justice: incarceration and, 24; restorative, 24, 177, 179–80, 179n8, 195; social, 168, 181; socioeconomic, 144

kappo, 179–80
Karate Kid (1984 film), 124, 124n27, 128
Karate Kid (2010 film), 106, 122–27
Karenga, Maulana, 68n79
Kato, M. T., 77, 188
Kawahara, Sonoko, 151–52, 155–57
Kelley, Robin D. G., 31–32
Kelly, Jim, 107–15, 110 fig. 3.1, 113 fig. 3.2
Kill Bill Volume 1 (film), 133
Kim, Claire Jean, 10
Kim Chon Youn, 89
Kim Il Sun, 74, 195
kinesiology, 5–6
kinesthesia, 6; categories of, 18–19; communal, 21, 75–77, 87–89, 94; defined, 7; as knowledge production, 42–43; mediated, 21–22, 106–7, 195–96; restorative, 24–26, 177, 179–80, 190, 195; sonic, 23–24, 138, 144, 150, 173–74, 195; transcultural, 19–20, 28, 30, 44, 195; virtual, 194–97. *See also* racial kinesthesia
kinesthetic response, 8–11
kinesthetics, 6
Kinetic 9, 135
King, Joyce, 181
King, Rodney, xii
Kingsley, Mira, 144
Klar, Jim, xiv fig. 0.1
Kochiyama, Yuri, 16
Kollar, Carl, 101 fig. 2.6

Korea, 74, 74n9, 75, 75n13, 80–82
Kung Fu (television series), 108
Kurashige, Scott, 9
Kurosawa, Akira, 69
kuzushi, 40
Kyokoshin Karate, 69

Laney College, 78–79
Last Dragon, The (film), 22, 106, 115–22, 128, 133
Last Samurai, The (film), 153
Leary, Timothy, 54
Lee, Bruce, xii–xiii, 3, 11n24, 54; in *The Chinese Connection*, 120; Ip Man and, 93–94; on jeet kune do, 89; Long Beach International Karate Championship and, 64–65; masculinity of, 76–77; as non-white, 107; Oakland Community School and, 72; philosophical approach of, 88–89; Van Clief and, 57
Lee, Malachi, 51n48
Lee, Spike, 116, 164
Letty, Brandon, 102
Lo, Jacqueline, 30
Locke, John, 8
Lone Wolf and Cub (manga and film), 150–51
Long Beach International Karate Championship, 64–65
Los Prietos Boys Camp (LPBC), 24–25, 177, 181–85, 188–93
LPBC. *See* Los Prietos Boys Camp (LPBC)
LSD, 53–54
lynching, 5n6, 107, 127, 144

Madame Butterfly (Puccini), 151, 151n28
Maeda, Bill, 16
Malcolm X, 33, 36–39, 45–46, 74, 140
Man with the Iron Fists, The (film), 133, 133n41
Mao Tse-Tung, 74, 86, 195
marginalization, 5, 45, 67–68, 75, 79, 89, 136, 140, 176–77, 179, 181, 188, 194
Margraff, Ruth, 144, 154
martial arts: Black expressive culture and, 29–30; Black masculinity and, 27–28; as contested cultural terrain, 10; hip-hop

imagination and, 105–6; imaginary, Afro Asian connections and, 79–82; neocolonialism and, 18; performance and, 4, 15–18; political aspect of, 12–13; rise of, in America, 11–12; transculturalism and, 31–32

masculinity: Asian, 8–10, 153–56; Black Panther Party and, 173; of Bruce Lee, 76–77; Japanese American, 10; Korean, 81–82; performance and, 10; racial identity and, 8; racial magnetism and, 9–10; repatriation of white, in film, 113–14; security and, 52; white, 8, 52, 113, 152. *See also* Black masculinity; patriarchy

Mauss, Marcel, 7

McCutchen, Steve, 72 fig. 2.1, 75n12, 77–81, 78n18, 81 fig. 2.2, 85, 89–91, 93 fig. 2.4, 95–103, 101 fig. 2.6, 195

mediated kinesthesia, 21–22, 106–7, 195–96

meditation, 37–38, 38 fig. 1.1, 49, 53, 132, 180

Mei Lanfang, 17

Merritt College, 78–79

Middle Passage, 14

military, 49–50, 171

Ming, Shi Yan, 22, 129, 132

Mishima, Yukio, 153–54

Missing in Action (film), 114

Mixed Martial Arts (MMA), 10n24, 64

MMA. *See* Mixed Martial Arts (MMA)

Mobb Deep, 131

"model minority" concept, 9–10, 125, 140, 143–44

Monk, Thelonius, 66

Monroe, Earl, 51n48

Moorehead, Fred, 80, 83–86, 102

Morgan, Michael, 171, 177–78, 182, 185, 188–90

Moses Powell Harlem Dojo, 39–42, 39n27, 42–45

Mosque Number Seven, 46

Muhammad, Elijah, 33, 36, 130

Muhammad, Musa. *See* Powell, Moses

Muhammad, Steve, 29, 34–35, 59–64, 67–69, 68n79, 109, 195

Mullen, Bill, 15–16

Murphy, Eddie, 54

music videos, 116

nationalism, 31–32, 50, 64 fig. 1.2, 68, 68n79, 74, 109, 141, 150, 159, 163

Nation of Gods and Earths, 128

Nation of Islam (NOI), 11–12, 33–34, 36–37, 39, 46, 49, 130, 168, 171, 172 fig. 4.8

Negro Ensemble Company, 54–55

"Negro problem," 79

neocolonialism, 18. *See also* colonialism

New Negro, 32, 66

Newton, Huey P., 73–75, 75n13, 76, 85, 88, 102, 168

ninjas, 12, 14, 25

ninjutsu, 1–4, 7–8, 12–14, 34, 55, 115, 118, 121

Nisei Goju Ryu dojo, 51–53, 56

NOI. *See* Nation of Islam (NOI)

Nokem, Derek, 91–92

Noland, Carrie, 7

Norris, Chuck, 77, 114

Oakland Community Learning Center (OCLC), 71–77, 79, 82–85, 91–92, 93 fig. 2.4, 95–103, 195

Oakland Community School (OCS), 71–77, 79–80, 81 fig. 2.2, 82–85, 93 fig. 2.4, 195

OCLC. *See* Oakland Community Learning Center (OCLC)

OCS. *See* Oakland Community School (OCS)

Odyssey, The (Homer), 175, 177, 181, 190–93

Odyssey Project, 18, 175n1, 176 fig. 5.1, 177–81, 185–89, 191–93

Okinawa, 49–50

Ol' Dirty Bastard, 105

Omi, Michael, 8

Once Upon a Time in China (film and television), 143

O'Neal, John, 31

Ongiri, Amy Abugo, 75–76

orientalism, 27, 109, 116, 124–26, 151n28

Oriental World of Self-Defense, 47

ornamentation, 6–7, 46, 64

Owens, Sifu Bill, 98

Oyama, Mas, 68

Parker, Ed, 35, 59–61, 61n68, 67

Parks, Sparky, 48n38
Pathfinders, 60, 60n65
patriarchy, 24, 42, 143, 152–54, 156, 159–60, 173. *See also* masculinity
Patriotism (Mishima), 150–51, 154, 159
performance: Afro Asian, 15–18, 36, 76–77, 106, 123; Black masculinity and, 106–7; disciplines, 186–87; in *Enter the Dragon*, 94; martial arts and, 4, 15–18; masculinity and, 10; Nation of Islam and, 36–37; ornamentation and, 6–7; in racial kinesthesia, 5, 11, 14; repetition and, 11; as restored behavior, 177
personhood, 5
Peterson, William, 9
Poor Righteous Teachers, 131
postmodernism, 31, 51, 140
Powell, Moses, 29, 33–34, 33n16, 35–47, 38 fig. 1.1, 55, 195
Prashad, Vijay, 15–16, 107, 142
Presley, Elvis, 59–60
prieto, 184
prison, 4, 9, 18, 24, 45, 172n56, 175–82, 193, 195
Professor Griff, 131
Professor Vee. *See* Visitacion, Florendo M.
proprioception, 6
Pryor, Richard, 54
Public Enemy, 131
Puccini, Giacomo, 151

qi, 125–26, 134, 138–39

racial binaries, 9–10, 17, 32, 156, 159
racial formation, 8–11
racial hierarchy, 8–9, 14, 61, 150
racial identity, 8, 11, 151
racial kinesthesia, 70, 194–96; Black masculinity and, 137; boxing and, 164; of Bruce Lee, 77, 108; in construction of bodies and communities, 56–57; defined, 5, 137; kinesthesia in, 7; in *The Last Dragon*, 119–20; ornamentation in, 6–7; performance in, 5, 11, 14; racial identity and, 11. *See also* kinesthesia
racial magnetism, 9–10
racial triangulation, 10, 15, 107, 113, 121, 144

racial uplift, 37
racism, xii, 4, 137, 165, 169–70; anti-Asian, 144; Asian Americans and, 144; Black Karate Federation and, 66; Black masculinity and, 68, 105; gendered, 9; Japanese masculinity and, 10; martial arts and, 18, 34–35; in military, 49–50; structural, 11
Radical Action Movement, 168
Rakim, 131
Rambo: First Blood (film), 114
Raphael-Hernandez, Heike, 17
Raya, Richard, 87
Rebop (documentary), 82–84, 83n29, 91
Red Guards, 16, 142
Reed, Lou, 51
Ressner, Jeffrey, 116
restorative justice, 24, 177, 179–80, 179n8, 195
restorative kinesthesia, 24–26, 177, 179–80, 190, 195
Reyes, Gilbert, 164n43
Rhee, Syngman, 82n28
Rios, Victor, 184
Roach, Joseph, 13
Roach, Max, 66
Roberts, T. Carlis, 15, 17
Robeson, Paul, 17
Rocky (film), 113–14
Rodney, Walter, 19, 28, 45, 74
Rolling Stones, 51
Roman, Elsie, 56
Romeo Must Die (film), 17
Ruiz, Frank, 51n48, 52–53, 55
"Rumble in the Jungle," 163–64
Rush Hour (film), 17, 142
Rush Hour 2 (film), 17
RZA, 18, 22, 104, 104n2, 105–7, 116, 118, 128–34, 133n41

Sanchez, Sonia, 140
Sanders, Steve. *See* Muhammad, Steve
San Nukas (film), 39, 39n27
Santana, 51
Sanuces Ryu Jujitsu, 29, 33–47
Saxon, John, 109

Schechner, Richard, 11, 30–31, 177
Schultz, Michael, 115–18
Schwarzenegger, Arnold, 114
Scientific Soul Sessions (SSS), 172–73
Seale, Bobby, 78, 85, 102
self-reliance, 74
Seven Samurai (film), 69
Shaker Heights, Ohio, xi–xii
Shaolin and Wu Tang (film), 22, 105, 127–28
Shaolin Temple, 22, 108, 127, 129, 131, 148
Shaw Brothers, 48, 105
Sheenway Community Center, 69, 69n82
Shepp, Archie, 66
Shimazu, Naoko, 15
Shoatz, Russell "Maroon," 172–73
Shogun, 153
shorenji-kenpo, 50
Short, William, 67–69, 68n79
shuriken, 1–2
signifyin'(g), 14, 47, 124
Simba Wachanga, 68n79
Simms, David, 102–3
slavery, 14, 30, 36, 106, 112, 175–76, 179n8, 184
Sly and the Family Stone, 51
Smith, Jaden, 122–27, 124n27
Smith, Tommie, 169
Smith, Will, 127
soldiers, Black, 49–50, 171
sonic kinesthesia, 23–24, 138, 144, 150, 173–74, 195
Spectacular Blackness (Ongiri), 75–76
SSS. *See* Scientific Soul Sessions (SSS)
Stallone, Sylvester, 114
Steen, Shannon, 17, 151
stunt work, 54
subjectivity, 8, 19, 28, 32, 59, 75, 77, 83, 173, 180, 185, 193
Sullivan, Chuck, 61
Super Weapon, The (training documentary), 55–56
surrealism, 31–32

Sweet Science Suite: A Scientific Soul Session Honoring Muhammad Ali (Ho), 162–71, 167 fig. 4.5, 167 fig. 4.6, 169 fig. 4.7, 172 fig. 4.8

taekwondo, 11, 21, 62, 73–74, 77, 79–84, 82n28, 86–98, 100, 103
Taganashi, Ron, 51n48, 54
Tao of Wu, The (RZA), 128
Tarantino, Quentin, 133
Tasker, Yvonne, 113
Taylor, Diana, 16, 47
Third World Liberation movement, 9, 142
36th Chamber of Shaolin, The (film), 105
tournaments, 64–66, 91–94, 98–99, 102–3
Townsend, Robert, 116
transcultural kinesthesia, 19–20, 28, 30, 44, 195
triangulation, racial, 10, 15, 107, 113, 121, 144
"Tribe of Shabazz," 36
tricksterism, 14

Ueshiba Morihei, 3n3, 68
ukemi, xiv fig. 0.1, 42–44, 47, 187n37
Underground Railroad, 4
Unusual Suspects, 180–81
uplift, 37
Urban, Peter, 51n48
Urban Dragons: Black and Latino Masters of Chinese Martial Arts (documentary), 187–88
US Organization, 68n79
Uyehara, Mitoshi, 3, 3n3, 5, 7–10, 14, 27–28, 34

Valentine, Ricarrdo, 164n43, 168
Van Clief, Ron, 29, 33–35, 47–59, 48n38, 69, 105, 116–18, 132, 195
Vee Jujitsu, 36
Velvet Underground, 51
Vietnam War, 19, 29, 32, 49, 60, 60n65, 78, 113, 170
villains, 57
virtual kinesthesia, 194–97

Visitacion, Florendo M., 35–36, 38 fig. 1.1, 38–39
Voice of the Dragon: Once Upon a Time in Chinese America (Ho), 143–50, 146 fig. 4.1, 148 fig. 4.2

Wakayama, Tomisaburo, 150
Warhol, Andy, 51–52
Watson, Owen, 51n48
Way of the Dragon (film), 77
Whalen-Bridge, John, 188
When We Were Kings (documentary), 164
White, Norman, 98, 103
white hegemony, 28, 32
white heroism, 105, 113–14, 153
white masculinity, 8, 52, 113, 152
whiteness, 109, 123, 143, 184
white supremacy, 70, 73, 74n9, 137, 143–44, 152, 194
Wilderson, Frank, 73
Wilkins, Fanon Che, 105
Williams, Donnie, 29, 34, 59–60, 62, 111
Williams, Robert F., 168
Wilson, Lionel, 77, 102
Wilson, Robert, 30
Winant, Howard, 8
Wong, Anna May, 17
World's Fair, 47
World War II, 9, 16n44, 27, 49
Wu-Tang Clan, 22, 104–5, 116, 127–36
Wu-Tang Forever (Wu-Tang Clan), 132
Wu-Tang Manual, The (RZA), 128, 132

Xian Nan Yang (film), 58

Yamaguchi, Gogen, 68
Yangtze Films, 57–58
Yee, Ken, 89–90
yellowfacing, 22, 119–20, 124, 126–27, 151
Youn, Ken, 78–80, 87, 89–90
Young, Harvey, 5n6
Young Lords, 142
Yu, Byong, 62, 100–102

Zaire, 163–64
Zarrilli, Phillip, 186
Zhou En Lai. *See* Chou En Lai

BLACK PERFORMANCE AND CULTURAL CRITICISM
Valerie Lee and E. Patrick Johnson, Series Editors

The Black Performance and Cultural Criticism series includes monographs that draw on interdisciplinary methods to analyze, critique, and theorize black cultural production. Books in the series take as their object of intellectual inquiry the performances produced on the stage and on the page, stretching the boundaries of both black performance and literary criticism.

Black Dragon: Afro Asian Performance and the Martial Arts Imagination
ZACHARY F. PRICE

Staging Black Fugitivity
STACIE SELMON MCCORMICK

Contemporary Black Women Filmmakers and the Art of Resistance
CHRISTINA N. BAKER

Reimagining the Middle Passage: Black Resistance in Literature, Television, and Song
TARA T. GREEN

Conjuring Freedom: Music and Masculinity in the Civil War's "Gospel Army"
JOHARI JABIR

Mama's Gun: Black Maternal Figures and the Politics of Transgression
MARLO D. DAVID

Theatrical Jazz: Performance, Àṣẹ, and the Power of the Present Moment
OMI OSUN JONI L. JONES

When the Devil Knocks: The Congo Tradition and the Politics of Blackness in Twentieth-Century Panama
RENÉE ALEXANDER CRAFT

The Queer Limit of Black Memory: Black Lesbian Literature and Irresolution
MATT RICHARDSON

Fathers, Preachers, Rebels, Men: Black Masculinity in U. S. History and Literature, 1820–1945
EDITED BY TIMOTHY R. BUCKNER AND PETER CASTER

Secrecy, Magic, and the One-Act Plays of Harlem Renaissance Women Writers
TAYLOR HAGOOD

Beyond Lift Every Voice and Sing: The Culture of Uplift, Identity, and Politics in Black Musical Theater
PAULA MARIE SENIORS

Prisons, Race, and Masculinity in Twentieth-Century U. S. Literature and Film
PETER CASTER

Mutha' Is Half a Word: Intersections of Folklore, Vernacular, Myth, and Queerness in Black Female Culture
L. H. STALLINGS

www.ingramcontent.com/pod-product-compliance
Lightning Source LLC
Chambersburg PA
CBHW020946230426
43666CB00005B/188